My Overdue Book
Too many stories not to tell.

by

Peter Bright

PREFACE

I have to start somewhere, so here I go.

It all began, that is, I began, some time in early June, 1946. Nine months later I popped out on April 7, 1947, (the same day that Henry Ford died). Apparently I was one of two from that pregnancy. My mother told me repeatedly, as I grew up, that I was living for two. Early in her first term she suffered a miscarriage during a routine visit with her Gynecologist, Doctor Stan Garber. He told her, "I'm sorry Martha, but, you've lost your baby".

Unhappy, she went home and rested for a few weeks. Still feeling pregnant, she called Garber's office and made an appointment. Turned out she was right. So, some sixty-six years later, here I am, still roaming the Earth like some human dinosaur, and apparently still "living for two".

I say two, because, as I look back over my tawdry collection of years, I've had twice the number of life experiences a normal person should have. I'm sure knowledgeable friends would say that "normal" in no way describes me.

Like anyone who has managed to make it this far down the road of life, I have made my share of mistakes. Some were by design. For those I apologize. Others, well, we all wind up at the wrong end of the shooting gallery of life from time to time…it's an opportunity for growing, if we choose to make it so. If not, then we get to continue to slip and slide over the same area until we "get it".

I have been promising myself that I would sit down and pound out this volume for some time. That it is now in your hands is, for me, quite an accomplishment. Up to this time I have not been willing to reveal many of the experiences contained herein. But, potential lawsuits aside, pieces of my life have been more than ordinary and they are worth sharing printed on parchment, if for no other reason than to provide kindling for your next bonfire. That decision is yours and yours alone.

Peter

Chapter One / And so I Begin

I was born into a musical house. Mom was a classically trained pianist. She could get all over the eighty-eight keys reading verbatim the notes left us by the masters. Recognizing her talent, her father bought a beautiful Steinway before she was five. Lessons followed and she took to them with enthusiasm. She went a step further. Her ear was so keen that she could play anything by ear, an attribute that kept current tunes' melodically bouncing off our household walls all of her life.

Dad's music appreciation, like mothers, was broad. 78 RPM records were still the only kind available in the late forties and my father had an impressive collection of classical and jazz. He loved Rachmaninoff, Fritz Kreisler, Duke Ellington and Fats Waller, among others. I liked them too, in fact, more so than the little yellow kiddy discs popular with the "under five" set at the time. After hearing them once, or twice, those discs intended for young fry bored me. When I was two and a half, my father gave in and taught me how to handle his collection properly so I could play them without breaking or scratching the brittle discs. *This ability would come in handy in my late teens when I became a radio DJ.*

Though I had not yet learned to read, I quickly connected the artwork on the album covers with the selections I wanted to hear. Rachmaninoff, Tchaikovsky, Grieg, Gershwin, and many others were regulars on my play list. Since 78's only played nine to twelve minutes a side, many disc changes were required. I got quite adept at changing and replacing them back in their album folders in numerical order. Why so careful? Simple, you take care of things you love…and I love great music. I took to it like a duck to water. If that makes me a quack, then so be it.

I was fascinated by radio and television, (my dad bought our first TV set in 1949 before I was two). I found myself listening to radio at all hours of the night and day. Dialing from station to station, especially at night when the AM signals would skip across the countryside enabling me to hear New York, Chicago, Fort Wayne and Detroit direct. My parents would shut me down at 3am, if they awoke and found my listening prowess in progress. At that age sometimes they discovered a sleeping boy in front of the wireless, but more often there I'd be fixated on the next information emanating from the speaker.

Creative juices flow in many directions. Much like water winding its way until it finds the sea. Mine have always oozed out condensing into word, sight and sound.

All through my days at Withrow High School, I was forever expressing for public consumption. I spent three years writing on the yearbook; got periodic articles published on the school newspaper, acted in and wrote many items for the stage and announced the bands halftime presentations during football games. It was a rewarding and growing time for my creativity.

Aside from my productions at school, I began experimenting with 8 millimeter film around the time I was fifteen. Neighbor and friend Bob Ruff and I picked up his parents aged 8MM camera one day, started farting around with it and never stopped. I saved my grass cutting dollars and bought a Bell & Howell 8MM camera that would shoot single frames. Not long after that I bought an affordable 8MM Editor which enabled me to cut and splice storylines into "features". Our creative juices culminated in shooting "THE SLUM", an epic that took three months to shoot. Once edited, it ran for maybe four minutes and featured the antics of two whacked adolescents and their peripheral of friends. That epic and my other celluloid efforts still exist. Someday I need to convert them to a digital format.

I learned a lot about motion photography during my 8MM days. All of it came into play professionally some nine years later when I began wearing early handheld video cameras for first, live television sports, and later, taped production shows of various genres. I will forever pick up a video camera to capture moments of life for personal or professional reasons. The videos of my family, especially my Bright Kids as youngsters, are treasures beyond measure.

In the spring of my senior year at Withrow, I submitted for an award from the Ohio Association of Broadcasters as the Cincinnati nominee for local NBC affiliate, WLWT. I wound up representing TV-5, but missed getting the state award. I got face time on Channel Five News and because of that I hit WLWT up for a job a month later. They hired me for summer vacation relief on the studio crew.

At the time WLWT was the creative hub of a four city regional broadcast network dating back several decades featuring two daily, live, ninety minute entertainment shows each lead by a very popular host, (Ruth Lyons and Paul Dixon). Both shows featured a house band, popular singers on staff, and a studio audience of two hundred. Frequently national celebrities would stop by to promote their concerts, or whatever, when they were in the area. Audience members would hold on to their dated tickets for several years in order to attend a broadcast.

On the weekends a nationally syndicated country-western music show, MIDWESTERN HAYRIDE was rehearsed and taped in front of a live audience. WLWT covered live, broadcasts of Cincinnati Reds baseball and, of course there were nightly newscasts to get on air. For me, it afforded opportunities to learn volumes about live and tape television production on the job. For this kid, it was like working in a candy store. I could not get enough.

The year was 1966 and all this production was in color. WLWT had been producing locally in color for ten years, which was unheard of outside New York, Los Angeles, or Chicago. Due to the four WLW stations, (Cincinnati, Dayton, Columbus and Indianapolis), daily color productions, RCA and other color television manufacturers recorded their highest sales of color TVs around these stations from the late 1950's into the middle of the 1960's.

As my summer studio job at WLWT was winding down, I had been negotiating my way around the halls connecting for yet another opportunity. It came in the form of driving WLWT executives and personalities around to meetings and events. Wearing suit and tie, and looking older than my nineteen years, I got friendly with many of the executives and learned much about their thinking behind the deals that were in the making. Further, I got a quick grasp on how to keep my mouth shut about the details. WLWT was owned by AVCO Broadcasting. This was the home office for the broadcast conglomerate which had radio and television stations in Ohio, Texas, California, Indiana and Washington D.C.

Lyndon Johnson was President. His wife, Lady Bird was in the broadcasting business with key holdings in Texas. AVCO owned WOAI, a big fifty thousand watt, clear channel radio station in San Antonio. It was a thorn in Lady Bird's side because WOAIs signal covered most of Texas and she *wanted* that license. The Avco boys had no intention of selling it, but, funniest thing, found AVCO regularly under intense scrutiny by the Federal Communications Commission. I got to hear and converse with them about that and other power struggles during my driving days late in the summer of 1966. It was a valuable education and insight into the American broadcast, political and financial power structure.

7

My driving AVCO executives ended as I began daytime college courses at The University of Cincinnati. I would continue to work nights and weekends at WLWT answering the phone and being the receptionist. That meant dealing with all the incoming calls from the public and their reactions to what they had just seen on TV-5, or had heard on WLW radio, (the largest radio outlet in the tri-state of Ohio, Indiana and Kentucky at the time). It afforded me an opportunity to experience a very important side of the business; hearing from and dealing directly with the public.

One Friday night after the eleven o'clock news, some friends in the news department invited me to come by a late night "bring your own" gathering at news reporter Gene Randall's apartment, (yes, THAT Gene Randall, who wound up on NBC and CNN).

Not much later I'm wandering around Randall's place. I walk into the kitchen, turn a corner and find myself locked in eye to eye contact with a very pretty, tall young lady leaning up against the refrigerator, a teasing smile on her face directed right at me. Without hesitation, holding eye contact, I walked right up and said, "Hi, and who are you?" "Barbara", says she, "and who are you?" We made funny small talk for a few minutes and then I moved right on to getting her phone number to set up a first date. That began an escalating romance for the next five months.

Schott was her last name. She said her dad was a policeman and her mom was a nurse. Cincinnati had a lot of Schotts living across the city's seven hills in various walks of life and I made no connection in my little P-brain about her dad until I picked up the Cincinnati Post & Times Star one night about six weeks into our dating. There in black and white on the printed page the announcement that Colonel Jacob W. Schott was chosen to become Cincinnati's next Police Chief. I read on, "Jake's a family man", under which was a picture of the Colonel, wife Dollie, and their three grown children, Jake, Michael and Barbara. My mind was

8

racing, asking; why didn't I know that? I was so into being with and dating Barb that I'd never connected the dots.

Ain't human nature great? I'd never seen her dad around their house in uniform. He was always friendly with me and put on no airs suggesting he was a man of "position". There was always a plain, unmarked city Ford in the driveway. It wasn't even painted the blue that Cincinnati PD cars had. It seemed logical to me that at his age and intelligence he would be in some position of authority therefore the car was not a surprise.

Barbara was my dating life. I loved her and every moment we were together. Doctor Zhivago came out and of course we went to see it. All that cinematic love and emotion just aided the love that was growing between us. Winters are cold in Cincinnati and we ended many a date night cuddled together in front of her parent's fireplace.

Having spent the last three plus years flourishing in high school, I was quite surprised to find myself not really into college life at all. In fact I could hardly wait to get into my ten year old Ford every day and drive to WLWT to answer the phones and manage the reception desk at that very large and active broadcast station. As a result, my fall quarter at UC was a scholastic disaster.

My burning desire was to get on air at a radio station. I knew that I would have to leave WLWT and find a small station in order to gain on air experience. I was in the radio-television department at UC and therefore was privy to any radio job openings in greater Cincinnati.

The third day in January, 1967 I heard of an opening at WPFB, an AM and FM radio station in Middletown, some 35 miles north of Cincinnati. I immediately called and got an interview the next day.

Dressed in my best suit and tie, I jumped into my 56 Ford, got on Interstate 75 and headed north. It was a cold and gray day as I began my drive. Speeding along at sixty-five miles an hour, I was attempting to tune in WPFBs signal when the hood of my decade old Ford raised up, bent backward towards the windshield blocking my entire front view. Scared shitless, heart pumping; I ducked my head down to the maybe inch high opening at the bottom of the windshield where I could see the road and cars ahead of me.

I was in the far left lane of three and knew getting over to the right, off the road as soon as possible was imperative. I hit my right turn signal. Holding the steering wheel as straight as possible I glanced to my right, then out the forward inch opening and then a dangerous head turn to the rear. Sensing an opening in the lane to my right and not sure at all, I moved over one lane. Repeating those actions I dared again, got in the far right lane and then peeked forward looking for a place to pull off to the side of the freeway. Bumpity-bumping on the berm, I knew I was clear of the lane and slammed on my brakes, sliding to a dust clouded stop. The cloud was immediately cleared by an eighteen wheel semi as it roared by me to my left. I was off the road and alive…whew!

I got out, pulled the hood down, hooked it, drove away, nearly speeding to the interview and got the job. (Later I had my suit pants dry cleaned, if you know what I mean).

Chapter Two / My Radio life Begins

My WPFB job had many layers to it. My on air hours were 7am to 4pm, Saturdays and Sundays and to be on call for filling in during the week. I was very happy as this would allow time to go to classes, Saturday nights would be completely open to be with Barbara; while I began my on air broadcast career. In my nineteen year old life, this was a win-win.

WPFB was a throw back to older radio. The call letters were the initials of the man who started, built and owned it, one Paul F. Braden. The station and I were the same age.

Middletown was the home of ARMCO Steel. They were the city's biggest employer with many industries around it in supporting roles. The local High School was a repetitive state champion in both football and basketball.

Braden had been very smart about how to go to business with WPFB. The old adage in radio; "To succeed, play to your audience", was never exhibited better. Braden had very active news and sports departments that covered Middletown news and sports from top to bottom.

Middletown's High School teams were known as the Middletown Middies. All their football and basketball games were broadcast live, no matter where they originated from. With both teams being successful, it was easy to get local businesses to sponsor the games.

Nearby Miami University of Ohio football and basketball teams were broadcast by WPFB too. The broadcasts kept the on air team of Warren Johnson and Dan Humphries on the run all over the Ohio Valley from September to May every year.

FM radio had not yet come into its own commercially, but broadcasters, like Paul Braden, understood the potential for high fidelity, static free FM broadcasting. Additionally Braden, was technically astute and was using what is known in FM broadcasting as sub carrier signals that could carry background music that would be sold to subscribers that owned department stores and other commercial businesses. This sub carrier background music did not interfere with the main FM signal, but permitted multiple revenue sources from one tower, one antenna and one transmitter. In short it was a cash cow.

Braden put up similar situations at several locations around Ohio, Indiana and Florida. After many years of providing recorded music for this sub carrier market, he got caught by broadcast music rights attorneys for not paying for the rights to play all the recorded music he had used. Reportedly he paid a seven figure fine in the early 1970's for the unpaid music rights and had to immediately cease that part of his enterprise.

So here I was on WPFB doing all kinds of broadcasts. The easiest was doing commercials for the Cincinnati Reds Baseball games. It was an ad-hoc "network", if you will. Cincinnati station, WCKY originated the broadcasts. WPFB got the game on a broadcast quality line provided by the phone company that tapped right off WCKYs output to their transmitter. I had to cover all WCKY material and commercials with our own based on a well designed format.

Now here was the fun kicker for me. There were twenty other lesser stations within forty miles of us who would pick up our broadcast off the air and do their own local cutouts the same as I did with WCKY. Sitting in the studio during a rain delay one afternoon, mischief overtook me and I opened my microphone and began yelling the same sort of things you hear when you're at a ball game. Keeping the level low so it sounded like it was happening at the ball park, I started by yelling, "Ice Cold Beer…..get your ice cold Hudee, ". The more time there was to fill, the more I would do. I'd take big paper cups, place them on the studio floor and stomp on them to make the same big noise spectators would make doing it at the game. If the Reds were playing at Crosley Field in Cincinnati, I'd call out local beers from Pittsburgh, or any other city. If they were playing out of town, I'd "sell" Cincinnati brews…it gave me a chuckle and kept me awake. Despite the many times I did that over the summer of 1967, I never got a phone call from a listener, or, got caught by station management.

My favorite moment during a rain delay came one Saturday in May. The Reds had Jim McIntire doing play-by-play, a good sounding fun guy who knew the game and had been around professional baseball broadcasting for a while. New that year in the broadcast booth as his sidekick was veteran Reds catcher, Joe Nuxhall. "Nux", as he was known in professional baseball circles, had a wealth of stories on the players, teams, and team owners from all his years of playing the game.

OK, middle of the fourth inning at Crosley Field on this particular May Saturday. The heavens open up with a downpour of the wet stuff. Nuxhall is whipping out one great story after another. McIntire had only to listen, laugh and react as Joe moved from one tale to another. I had even stopped with all my "ball park noise" so I could enjoy these great tidbits on baseball legends spewing forth from The Old Lefthander. Sitting way back in my chair with my feet up, I was getting way too comfortable in a radio studio. Nux tells another story and on finishing it, he pauses for a count of three and then he says, to no one in particular, "you know this is fun sitting up here bull shitting like this"…I hear McIntire gasping and laughing as he throws a commercial cue. I'm choking I'm laughing equally hard as I dive from my reclined position towards the audio

13

board to do a commercial. I managed to kill the WCKY commercial before I aired it, but I had a live commercial to read and I'm still convulsed. I managed to get the next commercial spot on air and rejoined the boys at Crosley Field who picked up like nothing had happened.

That just did not occur on radio in those days. Four letter words were absolutely not allowed…ever. It was beaten into every hopeful broadcaster long before any of us ever got near a live microphone. Stations could be hit with heavy fines, or loose their broadcast licenses for that. It was certainly a great way to get fired. For my part, I loved what he said and my already high opinion of Joe Nuxhall went even higher. He did the Reds radio broadcasts for many years and would always end his post game show with, "this is the old lefthander rounding Third and heading for Home. Good night everybody".

WPFB-AM had a twice daily radio personality named Moon Mullins. (There was another Moon Mullins at the time who was known nationally, so just to be clear this colorful guy was not that one). Monday through Saturday mornings from 5-7 he spun his very funny verbal BS and one Blue Grass Hill Wacker tune after another. On weekday afternoons from 4-6 he did the same thing, but for them, he was always showered, shaved with clean clothes. Those morning shows were accomplished through an alcohol induced haze, and or the on-going end of an all night drunk. Most of his sponsors were establishments with owners who were his friends that knew that Moon's live chit-chat approach would bring customers in by the hundreds every week. One example; Triangle Fish'in Lake, where, as Moon put it, "they got them female fish'in worms".

Area wide he was a very popular hillbilly-bluegrass singer-musician with his own group that played at least three nights a week around his radio show listening area. The blue collar factory workers from Dayton to Cincinnati were avid listeners, which is

14

why he was on air when they drove into work and when they drove home.

Saturday mornings I would have a fifteen minute, live newscast originating from the same studio where Moon had just been. Frequently, I would literally have to step over passed out men on the floor of the studio as I made my way in. One morning I was delayed getting in because one of the passed out bodies was leaned up against the door.

Most Saturday mornings the air in the studio reeked of old beer, pizza, subway sandwiches, rotten farts, and sometimes puke in the trash can. There would be empty beer cans, soda bottles, smashed pizza boxes and other assorted trash strewn about as, in Moon's words, he and his in-studio "buddies" had been out "roar'in" all night.

Another part of my weekends at WPFB required that I call on area police, sheriff and highway patrol stations to collect any news worthy tidbits. The reasons were two fold, first to get the stories to report and secondly to establish myself with the on duty dispatchers and commanders so that if and when something really important occurred, I would be able to get direct, first hand information from them. This traveling around I would do for several hours in the afternoon between broadcasts, if I didn't have a Reds baseball game to cover.

Among the other on air duties were disc jockey hours when I would play records and practice my radio personality skills. Some were good, some were bad and some were down right awful.

Sundays were a trip as the mornings were all religious. Some were on tape, some were live remotes and others were live in our large studio, which featured a Hammond Organ and a grand piano. Funniest thing was that neither of those instruments was used for these broadcasts. The studio could comfortably accommodate up to fifteen people. These Holy Roller religious hours averaged twenty-five people crammed into that space, with a wailing preacher leading the group and someone with a tambourine. These hours were paid for in cash to the Master Control engineer, before getting on air. The engineer would then have to mix the audio for the hour. He had no other choice but to actually listen to all of it. Once in a great while I would have to go in with the sweated up group and read a live commercial. By the time I got in there, they all would have worked up a good revival lather and I can tell you, that crowd was ripe.

My relationship with Barbara ended upon her return from a two month stint in Fort Lauderdale babysitting two young boys for friends of her parents. Unknown to me, she met someone there and returned to say that we were over. This came just after my 1-A Draft notification. Talk about feeling adrift at sea without an oar! My heart was lower than low.

It was early May, my favorite time of the year. I joined a swim club not far from my parent's house so I could at least have a place to go on those days when I wasn't working. I could get a tan, (we all did that a lot in those days), be around people my age, get some exercise and be open to whatever developed socially.

The summer of 1967 was one of tumult across our nation. We had hundreds of thousands of troops fighting the war in Vietnam. Race relations and civil rights were coming to a head from coast to coast. All the simmering issues boiled over in Cincinnati on Monday, June 12th.

The long trial ordeal of a Cincinnati black man accused in the deaths of half a dozen women had come to a legal conclusion in mid April ending with a guilty verdict and a death sentence by electrocution. The facts were suspicious and lacked physical evidence, thus the feelings in the black community had been growing and were on edge. Riots broke out June twelfth and on the

16

thirteenth, I had gotten clearance through WPFB to ride with the news team of then Cincinnati radio powerhouse, WSAI.

My intent was to write about and report the human side of my hometown being torn apart by bad feelings and horrific actions. I was twenty and really had no idea what I was getting myself into. Somewhere in the depths of my being, I knew there were stories to tell.

The actual rioting was taking place at night in Avondale and surrounding neighborhoods that had predominantly black residents. I met up with the WSAI news team at their studios in Price Hill, some miles away. They had just bought a brand new air conditioned Ford station wagon. Silly me thought, we'll drive around for a few hours monitoring the Police radio, drive to where the action is sitting in our air conditioned comfort. Gather some meaningful stories, radio them in and go home.

An hour before it got dark, we went to the Cincinnati Police forward command post which had been set up in a large Sears parking lot on the edge of the primary area of the previous night's riots. All three television stations were there as were all the radio outlets that had news departments plus the two Cincinnati newspapers and some national broadcast and print reporters who had come to town. We were one of the last teams to arrive and had to park away from the cluster of media and police. Walking across the large open area of the parking lot, I spot Chief Schott, who sees me and walks away from the group towards me. We meet alone in the middle and took a moment to catch up. I asked about Barb who had broken it off with me the previous month. We chatted about the mess with the riots and then went our separate ways. It turns out the rest of the reporter pool raised hell with him for talking with me alone. They thought he was giving me some news scoop exclusive. He didn't, the Colonel was not that kind of person.

Before too many hours went by after darkness set in, except for the windshield, all the glass in WSAI's pristine, new news wagon was broken out by rioters. Having WSAI painted all over the outside didn't help. Any news cruiser was a target that week, but in the case of WSAI, the target size was doubled. Being the number one Top 40 Rocker, the station's main audience was Cincinnati's white teens.

There were five of us in the news cruiser. We came to know each other quickly as the unfortunate civil unrest came to threaten our physical beings as hand propelled mini missiles made their way first through breaking windows and then directly to our skin and bones.

While preserving life and limb was an immediate personal concern, the bigger picture for me was the sickening feeling I had in my gut as I witnessed my city, and more, neighborhoods I knew, becoming battle grounds. Store fronts were being smashed out in wholesale numbers with store contents gaining legs and running away. Fires were breaking out everywhere. By one in the morning the acrid smell of smoke was common. The fire department was stretched beyond its capacity to respond to all the calls for help.

There were so many police and fire reports on the radio scanners in our news car that many times we were not sure which to cover. We took one call of a growing fire at an address on Madison Road in Madisonville. Up to that point in time, Madisonville had been off the active map. It was home to mostly middle class blacks and whites.

We arrived and found a lumber yard fully engulfed. There was one lonely Fire Department pumper truck with two young firemen scrambling to save anything. I had to do something. I couldn't remain a reporter. I said to the rest of the guys, "they need help." I jumped out of the news wagon and ran up to one of them and asked how I could help. He pointed to a hose lying on the ground.

He told me to hold on to the nozzle with both hands then said to aim it at the biggest amount of flames to my left. Once I had done that he yelled from thirty feet way "thank you…hold on" and with that I found out how hard it is to hold a fire hose and aim it in the right direction. I ruined everything I was wearing standing in an ever deepening ash blackened flow of expended fire water. After about half an hour the lumberyard fire was out. It had not spread to the adjacent buildings. Had it continued, most of the businesses in that block would have burned to the ground. I was filthy, exhausted and had an even higher respect for firefighters and what they do day and night.

On the third night around four in the morning, we heard a radio call for a multiple vehicle accident on the edge of where the worst of the rioting was taking place. We were close by and elected to go check it out. A white family of three had been hit by a truck and thrown out of their car. The truck had hit another car and hit a utility pole. As we drove up a black man and his wife were doing what they could to help the white couple and their badly injured child. Police and the Life squad, (the paramedic world had not yet started), had not arrived. We did what we could to help until they arrived.

After all the bad behavior I had witnessed over those June nights, it was personally comforting to see these two couples responding to each other as human beings in a time of need. That became my story for the night.

Here's a kicker to the June civil unrest in Cincinnati. Ohio Governor James Rhodes called out The Ohio National Guard to help restore law and order by the second or third night. There they were, in uniform, helmets on their heads, M-14 rifles at the ready standing in rows at strategic intersections and not one round of ammunition had been issued to any of them. They did have bayonet's that could have been attached to the front of their weapons, but if a gunfight were to have broken out, it would have been lethal to the Guardsmen. We in the Press knew this, but made no mention of it until long after civility had returned to the city.

Four hundred were arrested that week, one person died and sixty three were reported injured. In our mixed up twenty-first century world, those numbers seem small, but in 1967 Cincinnati, this was a big, and sad, deal.

1967 was not a good year for an American male over eighteen to be invited to sit out a semester from college. I got notified by the Draft Board that my status had changed from 2-S (student deferment) to 1-A, (eligible for military draft at anytime without warning). This lovely notice arrived before I got my quarterly grades from The University of Cincinnati. (*Yes, the head of the Draft Board had her tendons buried at all the schools in her district*).

I take responsibility for letting my accumulative grade point average fall below the threshold of 2-S. Yes, I had A's in several elective courses, but they did not carry enough weight in the area of academia to keep me in school.

I resolved to work at WPFB as much as possible. If the military didn't summon me, I would re-enter school that fall.

Talk about wearing a dark cloud over your twenty year old self. Other than getting as much work as I could out of WPFB, making any plans was not possible. I wasn't able to advance my career because the first question asked by any radio Program Director was, "what's your Draft status?" They were not about to put someone on the air who could be snatched away at anytime with little, or no warning.

That summer I got a lot of hours in at WPFB, especially with everybody taking vacation. Being very versatile, I became the station's chameleon, doing news, rock and roll, jazz, country western, commercials, general announcing and reporting live news events as they happened.

Chapter Three / Decisive Action

August hit and I decided to take action on my life. I went downtown and volunteered for the Draft. I talked with no one in advance of my long, thought over decision. I wanted the military to either take me or throw me back like an unwanted fish. I wasn't willing to continue in limbo and I did not want to return to college at that point. I ruled out enlisting for that would take more than two years out of my life. If I passed my physical and they wanted me, then they would get two years and no more.

In those days many guys my age were either burning their Draft Cards in protest of the Vietnam War, or were literally disappearing to Canada, Sweden, or other countries beyond Uncle Sam's immediate reach.

If they took me, I was willing to go and serve my country. Understand, at the time I was ignorant of the lie that got us into Vietnam. That lie being The Gulf of Tonkin Resolution. Had I known all the real truths, I may have had a different personal resolve, but, bottom line, I love my country, and there were many other possibilities for my military involvement other than being sent to Vietnam. I stepped forward and rolled the dice of life.

The vacation fill-ins at WPFB were coming to an end as the days of summer waned. Having volunteered for the Draft, the next step would be a physical, which, if passed meant you left that day for the military. I needed a break. I called my cousin Nan who lived in San Mateo, just south of San Francisco.

Nan is the daughter of my first cousin Lloyd. By age he is a full generation older than me. His father, John, was the oldest in my

*dad's family and an adult when my dad, Howard, the youngest was
born. Clear as mud, right?*

I spent the week of Labor Day, 1967 hanging out with Nan, her
three younger siblings, her folks and their many pussy cats. Nan
took me on excursions to San Francisco, which immediately
became my favorite city. So alive, beautiful, stimulating, ever
changing from Sun, to fog, rain, up hill, down hill, wonderful cable
cars clutched to the steep slopes and the smells in the breezes…
from those precious days forward, the city by the bay has always
brought a warm flow to my being.

I returned from San Francisco to find in the mail my "Order to
Report" for a physical at 07:30 Hours on 16 October 1967. "Arrive
prepared to ship out at the end of the day if you pass your
physical".

That was a head turn around following a beautiful week with Nan
in the shadows of The Golden Gate. In a fleeting micro-second my
heart sank and I got resolve all in one breath.

Like what it was, or not, there was now direction in my immediate
life.

It was a fast month between returning from San Mateo and that
Monday, October 16th when I had to report for my physical. I
worked right up to and including the night before. My parents were
not happy with me about my decision, but hid their upset feelings
from me. In retrospect I learned that my rash move was selfish to a
degree, and sadly, with a total disregard for my parents and their
love for me.

It was a gray October morning. My parents both went to drop me
off. There was idle chit chat between us for the fifteen minute
drive down Columbia Parkway. The Draft Board office was in a
multi-story building mere steps north of Fifth Street, adjacent to

The Federal Building in downtown Cincinnati. Dad pulled up to the curb. From the back seat I gave them each a kiss, and told them that if I flunked the physical, I'd give them a call and come home. Knowing of my good health, the possibility of them getting that phone call was, in two words, slim and none. I promised I would call if I could to let them know what was happening.

I stepped out on to the sidewalk, closed the door looked in at them and waved. When I turned towards the building front door I saw a crowd of people between me and the door. The closer I got the situation came into focus. There were antiwar demonstrators. Some were standing, some were sitting or squatting on the sidewalk. Handmade antiwar signs were scattered among them. The Press was there too. Alan White, reporter for WCPO-TV, Channel 9 was there with a sound on film news cameraman. (In those days video tape was only found in studio situations). While he did not know me, he recognized me from the summer riot news briefings and walked up to me asking if I was going in as a potential draftee. I said yes. He then asked if I was willing to make an on-camera comment about the demonstrators in front of me. I said I would. He turned to his cameraman and told him to roll film. On film he asked me my name and why I was there and then asked if I had any comment about the demonstrators in front of me. Without hesitation I said I respected them and their right to stand up for what they believed in, but my question was why. (*It would take the next two years, going to Vietnam, coming home and doing some reading for me to answer my own question*).

The process at the Draft Board took all day. There were maybe forty or so of us going through various demeaning steps. An example: you're in line, naked, with twenty other guys. You've put your wallet, watch and any other personal valuables in a white cotton bag which hangs around your neck on a string. A doctor comes down the line accompanied by an assistant with a clipboard. You're asked your name, age and social security number and then the doctor has you turn your head and cough while he holds your testicles in his gloved hand. He then moves on and repeats these steps until all of you have been "coughed". Next, the doctor moves to the center of the room and instructs the entire line of twenty to turn around, bend over, grab their buttocks checks pulling them apart and to stay that way until you're tapped on your back at which point you may stand up and turn around. They were looking for hemorrhoids, and trust me, they checked up close and personal. Hey, it has to be done, but when you come straight out of your happy home, it is, shall I say different?!

We were then allowed to get back in our clothes, were given a leader for our group and then were sent to some storefront dive down the street to get a late afternoon meal. We were to go together and return together. They made it very clear that if we did not return with the group, we would be treated as absent without leave for which we would be prosecuted, fined and imprisoned by the military.

When we got back they called out a few names, took them in a room told them they failed the physical and then released them to go home. Mine was NOT one of those names.

The rest of us were told that we would be going that night to begin our military training. Some would be sent to each of the branches of the armed services, but the majority of us would be sent to Fort Benning Georgia where we would commence our training in the US ARMY.

We were then told the severity of the step we were about to take which was the Oath to serve and defend the Constitution of The United States. We stood at attention with our right hands raised, repeated the Oath as it was given us in phrases, and then at the appropriate time took a step forward. We were officially members of the United States Armed Forces. We were no longer civilians. Our rights, as civilians no longer existed. We were now subject to military law and would remain so until we were formally notified in writing that our term of military service to the United States was over.

We were grouped with a leader who carried all of our newly made military files, and put on a chartered bus to Greater Cincinnati Airport. We were to fly to Atlanta and be bused to Fort Benning to commence Basic Training.

We were booked on a regularly scheduled Delta airlines flight to Atlanta. We were mixed in with normal passengers throughout the plane. It was a dinner flight, but we were ordered not to drink beer, wine or alcohol. It turns out that this plane was on its last commercial flight. The captain announced proudly that this DC-7 was to be retired after we landed in Atlanta and that from now on jet aircraft would be used. The DC-7 was a four engine, piston driven propeller aircraft. They were a good plane, entering service in the late fifties. But, this one would be memorable for a reason besides being my ride to the Army.

About half way through the flight, the entire cabin filled with smoke. To me it definitely smelled like burning engine oil. I looked out both sides towards the wings to see if I saw fire coming from any of the engines. There was none. The passengers were remarkably calm despite the amount of smoke. The captain came on the PA and explained that the one engine blew an oil seal, had been shutdown and that we would be able to complete the flight to Atlanta on the three remaining engines without a problem. The smoke lessened in time and we got there OK. I never really bought the Captain's story, but I lived to tell it.

Chapter Four / I'm in the Army now

Basic Training

I was at Fort Benning from mid October to mid December. I was naïve enough to think that I would be able to get into the area of the Army's Radio-TV media department without giving up more years of my life. Surely they would want someone with my experience. Ha, ha, ha. To be fair, had I been willing to sign up for three, or more years, I would have been in a better place to get that assignment, but there were/are no guarantees in the Army. Lets put it this way, the odds were that I would have found myself in the Army for four years no where near a microphone or broadcast transmitter.

I won't bore you with all the fun I had during basic training. Like all the others with me, I was just damn glad I survived it, didn't have to repeat it, (some did), and got to go home for the holidays.

The Army gave me a voucher for airfare home and to report after the holidays to my next duty station. My dad made the ride home for the holidays even more pleasant by upping my seat to First Class. That was a major change in service then unlike today, where maybe on an in country flight your seat will be a bit larger and whatever is served is free.

When I knew for certain what dates I'd be home, I called Stan Reed, the Program Director at WPFB to set up days to work. I was on air sixteen of the seventeen days I was home.

Decembers in Cincinnati are cold and December, 1967 was no exception. I bring this up because in Basic Training you have one hair length…none. I got off the plane with essentially a chrome dome. I had never been one to wear a hat, suddenly it be came a necessity to do so. My many hours at WPFB, did allow for family time and some hours with friends.

I was still hurting from Barbara's ending of our relationship seven months earlier. I had no interest in looking for a girl friend with all those feelings still burning inside. I didn't want to be in the Army panging away anymore than I already was. Besides in my brief two months in the Army I watched several guys go through major meltdowns when they got "Dear John" letters.

There were many lonely days, but I was not willing to put myself out there in the world of relationships at that time in my life. I had a pretty good idea, unless lightening struck, that I was Vietnam bound.

There was nothing remarkable about New Years Eve, if there were I would have remembered it all these years later. I went to bed early because I had to catch the 9am Delta jet to Atlanta, change planes, fly to New Orleans, change planes and fly into Fort Polk, Louisiana, where I was due to begin Advanced Infantry Training.

Advanced Infantry Training

1968 began on a Monday. I had on my Army dress uniform, which was required to get military airfare and priority treatment. Additionally I traveled with a duffle bag full of all my fatigue work uniforms, boots, underwear, socks, and separate from that a small bag that had immediate toiletries, small personal items and my Army 201 File, my complete Army records and orders up to that point which I was to turn in when I reached Fort Polk.

At Greater Cincinnati Airport I said good bye to my folks, grabbed my duffle bag, threw it over my shoulder and grabbed my smaller bag, (known in the service as an AWOL Bag because that was what guys going Absent Without Leave would usually take to make a fast exit), in my other hand and walked in towards the ticket counter.

The Delta agent asked for my ticket, looked at it, said the flight was on time and did I have any bags to check. I said I did. The next thing I did was probably the dumbest thing I could have done, but in the long run, it just may have saved my life. I put both bags up to be checked. She tagged them, stapled the claim checks on my ticket, threw the bags on the conveyer belt, handed me back my ticket showing me that she had checked my bags all the way to Fort Polk, told me my gate number and wished me good luck. I thanked her, put my ticket in my inside jacket pocket and walked away.

Several hours later I was in Atlanta's airport standing at the gate for my flight to New Orleans. Many for that flight were also standing around but nothing was happening behind the Agent's counter. Looking out towards the runways, it was cloudy with some fog, but everything in sight was easy to distinguish. After a few minutes an agent announced that our flight was delayed due to fog, not in Atlanta, but in New Orleans. We were told as soon as it burned off in New Orleans; we would board our plane and be on our way. That was around one in the afternoon. I walked to a nearby Coke machine, got one and went back to sit in the waiting area. There were several more announcements telling us that New Orleans was still fog bound.

By around four o'clock, it was looking foggier outside our windows. At five, they announced that our flight was cancelled and that they had arranged for hotel rooms for all ticketed passengers for that night. I figured I would reclaim my bags, go to the hotel, get a bite to eat, watch a little TV, get some sleep and come back the next day and travel on.

My bags, I was told, were not retrievable, but Delta would give me money for supper and breakfast and provide a room at the airport hotel.

I had no choice so I went along with it. I bought a cheap Gillette razor and went to the hotel, checked in, walked next door for some crappy food, walked back to the hotel watched a little TV and went to bed.

Tuesday, January 2nd I woke up to find fog so dense out my hotel window that I couldn't see the street out front. Damn. I took a shower, shaved, got dressed and decided to get back to the airport. I could scrounge some breakfast there once I had talked with someone with Delta Airlines.

I got out of the hotel van and as I walked into the terminal I noticed I heard not one aircraft engine on the ground, or in the air. It was eerily void of any sound of aircraft.

Inside the terminal, it was wall to wall passengers going nowhere. Some were sitting on their luggage. It appeared they had been sitting on their bags for hours; others were in line at the ticket counters looking towards the agents who were busy talking to the passengers at the counter who were either shaking their heads, or in a few cases swearing out the sides of their mouths.

I obediently got in line to speak with an agent. After some time I eventually got to the counter. I was told that I was now a stand by passenger, therefore I would no longer be eligible for hotel or food vouchers, but that Delta would do everything they could to get me on my way when the weather would permit. Atlanta was closed due to fog and New Orleans remained as such. I was told that if they could get me out of Atlanta, they might send me to Houston where I could get a flight into Fort Polk.

Fort Polk had a very small airport which was served by one commercial airline, Trans Texas, which flew older two engine prop aircraft. I would find out later that Trans Texas was owned by our then First Lady, Lady Bird Johnson. Interesting how that worked out, eh?

I was now on a waiting list, a very long and growing waiting list. All through ATL, (the designation for Atlanta's airport), everywhere you looked people were killing time anywhere, and anyway they could. ATL has been Delta's main Hub for years and it is a major point for changing planes to then continue on to another city. All of us got in to ATL, but now we couldn't get out. There were lines everywhere. If you needed to pee, get in line, if you were hungry, get in line. Business men in suit and tie were beginning to appear disheveled, unshaven. Families trying to get home from the holidays were all over the place with haggard parents trying to entertain and pacify their young charges, who were understandably completely out-of-their-minds. Military travelers like me were peppered throughout. The term zombie comes to mind as I remember the eyes of many as I walked around attempting to keep my own sanity.

I kept checking on the possibility of going anywhere. My efforts were fruitless as all the many lists of flights had one word up and down; CANCELLED.

There were literally tens of thousands of us stuck inside ATL. Things were beginning to run out. The Coke machines were empty, the various eateries had less and less on their menus. Trash cans throughout ATL were over flowing with paper cups, napkins and food wrappers. Darkness came with no break in sight.

Fatigue and irritability were on the rise. Hard working Delta and building service personnel became unfortunate targets for release of built up frustration among the going nowhere fast passengers-in-waiting.

Standing in a corner looking over the scene before me, the fertile, creative observer part of me likened the experience one might find in a Rod Serling TWILIGHT ZONE. "A major airport, anywhere, USA, thousands of passengers, between planes for days, no one is leaving, or arriving, for they're in the airport to nowhere somewhere in The Twilight Zone." For that moment I had a large internal chuckle, and then I reminded myself, it's real and I'm part of it. Shit.

People were staking claim to areas on the comfortable granite floor for sleeping. Every chair had long since been taken. For me to get a chair was short lived because the minute I went to use the bathroom, fifteen people would scramble over each other to get it.

I'd kept the cheapo Gillette wrapped in a paper towel in my suit coat pocket. It was important to maintain a clean military appearance especially for when I finally got to my training unit at Fort Polk.

Trying to sleep on granite among thousands of newly acquired roommates was easy once I reached the point that my fatigue over

32

powered me and I passed out. Waking was worse than trying to get to sleep. I was sore, stiff and completely disoriented. I've always been an early riser and Wednesday, January the third nineteen sixty-eight was no exception.

The terminal floor was littered with humans slumbering among each other surrounded by luggage, brief cases and building piles of trash.

I slowly rose to my feet, picked my service cap off the floor and sorely limped my way towards the Men's Room. Having taken care of Nature's business, I stripped out of my suit coat, shirt, tie and did the best I could to wash my face and shave. I felt somewhat better as I left the bathroom…a little cleaner at least. The early bird gets the worm and that meant me being one of the first in line for some breakfast and coffee.

I eventually got a flight to New Orleans. Due to fog induced airline problems, the Army had chartered some buses from New Orleans Airport to Fort Polk. I got there with no idea of where my luggage was.

Arriving without my gear and the lack of my Army Records 201 File, I spent several more days in my dress uniform.

After breakfast in Headquarters Mess Hall, I found my self at attention in the office of a Sergeant Major who was drilling me on the where-a-bouts of my 201 File. I told him how I had checked my bags to Fort Polk airport in Cincinnati and showed him the stubs on my ticket. He told me I better hope that 201 File comes through, or I would have to completely build it from scratch around my Advanced Infantry Training. He said that it would take months and during that time the Army would not be able to pay me. I'd be eventually paid, but not until my file was complete.

My bags never did get to me at Fort Polk. I was issued a complete duffel bag full of fatigue uniforms, underwear, field jacket, gloves, hats, socks and two pairs of boots.

Not too many weeks into training, I got hit with pneumonia. My temperature went way up and I went on sick call. The medics had me hospitalized, which was immediate when body temp went above one hundred. I couldn't lie down, because when I did, I would choke uncontrollably on all the congestion in my lungs. The minute my temp went below one hundred, they sent me back to training.

The congestion in my lungs had not lessoned. I had to sleep with my head elevated to avoid choking. The choking was frequent with volumes of congestion coming up. In the barracks, it was very disturbing to the other men who needed the few hours of sleep we were allowed. During the days in training, if I moved too much, again the convulsing and the volumes of congestion to follow. Second trip to the hospital my temperature went way up and added to my fun I found I could not make a sound. Literally, I had no vocalization at all. Not even a whisper. Everybody thought I was faking that. I started carrying a small note pad and a pen around with me to communicate.

After a week of not being able to talk I became more than concerned as I began thinking I could kiss a career in radio good bye.

We went on a twenty mile march to bivouac in tents. My temperature was normal, but every few minutes from the marching, I'd start convulsing and choking and be on my hands and knees coughing out the unbelievable amounts of congestion. When I would recover I had to run forward to get back in my place in formation and continue the march until I had another attack.

That night we were in two man tents on a wooded hillside. The temperature dropped into the low thirties and my convulsions got bigger, louder and longer. Two sergeants came to my tent, pulled me out and told me they were taking me to the hospital. I could tell my temperature was way up again. They put me in the front passenger seat of a jeep and one of the sergeants drove me to the hospital. Here's the kicker to that. The windshield was folded down for the thirty-five minute ride.

We got to the hospital and I was admitted, this time with my highest fever. While in there I wrote a note requesting to see a throat specialist about my lack of vocalization. I was told I'd have to make an appointment at a later time. After two days my temp dropped below one hundred and they sent me back to my company.

Between my bouts with pneumonia and time away from training to rebuild my 201 File, I was in danger of being recycled back through the two months of training.

I finally got in to see a throat specialist about my inability to utter even the smallest sound. It turns out my vocal chords were frozen open. The doctor could not come up with a logical explanation for it. He said that, in time, they would slowly return to normal. I asked that he put it in writing on a note to my commander. After all the crap I had gotten over four weeks by the cadre and troops, I needed them to know the truth.

Turns out that was a good idea. Because of that note, and the fact that I had made a genuine effort around my illness to do the training, I was not recycled.

At the end of training the various battalions put on their dress uniforms and marched in graduation ceremonies on the Camp Parade Grounds. During our ceremonial march, I fell out twice and wound up on all fours hacking and coughing up congestion. Each time I ran forward to rejoin my place in the marching formation.

My 201 File was far from being rebuilt so following the two months of training, I was sent to what is known as a Holdover Detachment. This was a catch all for those waiting the beginning of a training cycle like helicopter flight school, or special Military Police training, K-9 Dog School, persons like my self needing to complete administrative files and at the bottom of the pile, persons awaiting Court Martial for minor infractions.

I mentioned some pages back that checking those two bags at Cincinnati's airport on January first just may have saved my life, here's why.

Having to rebuild my 201 File kept me at Fort Polk an extra two months after my Advanced Infantry training was over. Because of that I did not get to Vietnam until mid June. Had I gone with my training group, I would have arrived in Vietnam just after the Tet Offensive of 1968. It was one of the bloodiest times for Americans during that entire war. That's not to say that my tour was any cake walk, but it has always given me reason to pause and be thankful.

Just after I got to the Holdover Detachment, I was given a two day Pass to go to Lake Charles, Louisiana. I got into an old hotel, but it was clean. I went straight in to the bath to take a much wanted civilian shower. After the luxury of a long, hot soapy shower I walked into the living room where there was a full length mirror. I had only seen my neck and face in a small mirror for months in the latrines on the Fort to quickly shave. I dropped the towel and saw my body head to toe. I was shocked. I looked like an Auschwitz victim. I was skin and bones. I'd been thin at 160 pounds, six feet tall for years. There was a scale in the bath and I went right in to get a reading. I was 128 pounds. I had been on the mend from the pneumonia for just over two weeks. I still had some congestion coming up in small amounts from time to time, but was getting better and I had partial vocal ability back.

All I could think was, if I looked this bad now, how thin had I gotten, just how sick had I been?

One morning just after I got to the Holdover Detachment we were in formation in the company street, our head, Sergeant Montgomery, asked if anyone in the group could type. I immediately raised my hand. "Good", said he. "Go up in the office. I'll be there after I send these guys on their details for the day".

The Holdover Detachment had a roster of about forty men on average. There were daily changes as orders would come in sending men on to their next duty stations, while new additions arrived throughout each week.

While awaiting assignments, Holdover members got sent out daily on work details across the Headquarters area. Some of that work was truly a pain in the ass.

Becoming the company clerk meant no guard duty, no work details. I had banker's hours from 7am to 4:30pm. I did all the typing, paper work, kept up the files, answered the phone, and dealt face to face with officers who would stop by without warning just to catch us off guard, which was no big deal to me. I was a Private E-2, meaning zero rank, couldn't command anybody, yet, had total control of the entire operation.

Sergeant Montgomery was a veteran of WWII, Korea and Vietnam. A really good man who was staying in the Army long enough to retire on his thirtieth anniversary which was coming up within two years.

After a few weeks as clerk I decided to go into Leesville for the evening. There were Fort busses that ran once an hour in each direction. It was about a twenty minute ride. Dress khaki's were required and the last bus returning to the Fort left the town around midnight.

Leesville was a typical Army town in the South in the late 60's. I say Army Town because, without For Polk, Leesville would not have been there. It was maybe two city blocks long with trashy bars, eateries and damn little else. I got there this particular Saturday night around 7 o'clock. It was my first trip to the hell hole. I wandered in one bar and the bartender offered me the house specialty. It was only two bucks. I tried it.

I remember very little else the rest of that night.

Couple of days later the phone rings at my desk. I answered it to find I was talking to The Clerk of Court of the City of Leesville. In his very southern drawl, he explained he was looking for me. He wanted to know why I failed to show up in Court that morning.

Suddenly sweating I asked why I was required to appear. He said I had been arrested Saturday night and had to appear to answer to the charges of the arresting officers. He then went on to say that I could appear that afternoon at one o'clock without penalty for missing the morning court. I said I would be there and hung up the phone.

I asked myself what the hell happened after that drink.

Sunday morning I had awakened in my bunk sick and with a major hangover, but had no memory of dealing with the Leesville Police, or for that matter, any remembrance of anything after that bar drink.

I went right to Sergeant Montgomery and told him about the phone call.

Montgomery rolled his eyes. Get in your dress khaki's. I'll take you in for your appearance. He told me to take all the cash I had and he then handed me five twenty dollar bills saying, "You may need these and you'll pay me back".

I sat with the Sarge in the courtroom and waited for my name to be called. When it was, I walked up and stood at the podium where a clerk held up a bible on which I rested my right hand while holding up my left swearing to tell the truth, the whole truth and nothing but the truth, so help me, GOD.

A Leesville police officer was opposite me at the other podium. We exchanged glances, head nods; he then smiled like he was going to laugh and then looked up at the Judge. I figured the fix was in and I'm about to get "walked down the path".

The Judge asked the officer to explain the charges against me. I was curious because at that moment I had no idea why I was there.

He proceeded to tell the judge that he and his partner had first encountered me when they rolled up in their patrol car along side me as I was walking down the double yellow line on Main street singing at the top of my lungs. He asked me if I would get in the car to which I said very nicely, (his description), "I'd be happy to, officer". They drove me to the police station, got my information and because I was so nice, they released me to the Fort Polk MP's who drove me back to my barracks.

The judge asked the cop if I had made any attempt to resist arrest. His response, "no, your honor".

The judge said to the officer, "Then it's simple public intoxication, singing loudly and both without malice?" Smiling, the officer said,

"Yes, your Honor." The Judge looked at me and said, "That will be fifty dollars for public intoxication, and twenty-five dollars court costs". He wrapped his gavel and I sighed with relief.

As an Army private in 1968 I was paid a whopping one hundred dollars a month. It was just after my birthday and because of some birthday cash I actually had seventy-five dollars. I thanked Sarge Montgomery for his help and handed his twenties back to him when we walked out. That was important to me because I knew he didn't have that kind of money to throw around. We were from two very distinct different backgrounds, but had found common ground where we shared respect for each other.

Chapter Five / Good Bye Fort Polk

By May one I had finally completely rebuilt my 201 File. I knew it was just a matter of days to weeks before I would get my orders for Vietnam. I would get thirty days to go home on leave first. The orders came Monday, May 13th. I was to report to Oakland Army Terminal thirty days later on June 13th. I called my dad at his office to say I was flying home that day and I would call later with details.

Next I called Stan Reed at WPFB and let him know I was headed home and wanted to work as much as possible and gave him the dates of my availability.

I stayed real busy at WPFB that month. I saw as many family members and friends as was possible. I didn't talk with anyone about what I was feeling having to go to Vietnam and to war in the infantry. I probably should have talked about it with someone, but I never brought it up. Everyone around me talked about ANYTHING but where I was going or what I would be doing.

During that month I came up with an idea. It was to send back taped reports from Vietnam. These were not to be battle reports of the war. I was going there as a US ARMY Infantry Soldier, so to have done that would have gotten me in hot water and possibly even Court Martialed. Rather, what I wanted to do, when I could, was mail back taped reports of how the men were doing over there. How the war and events here at home were affecting us there. I named it VIETNAM PERIODICAL. (*More on VNP later*).

At Cincinnati's airport I hugged my mom, gave her a kiss and turned to my dad, hugged him, looked into his tearing eyes and kissed him on the lips, (which was not a usual form of our father-son expression of love, but seemed right at that moment). I said whatever one says when one's emotions have taken over, turned and walked outside towards the plane.

I flew to San Francisco where I was picked up by cousin Lloyd with Nan who took me to
their house for the night before I had to report to Oakland Army Terminal.

As I mentioned before, Lloyd was my first cousin, but a full generation older than me. He was a combat Captain in the Army Engineers working just ahead of General Patton during World War II. Because of him and others like him, Patton had roads and bridges to move his men, equipment, and materials across Europe. He was amazingly quiet and supportive for what I was going through in those few days before disembarking.

I had been in Oakland two full days waiting to ship out when; I got a six hour pass from 3pm to 9pm on Saturday, June 15th. I called Nan. Lloyd said they would come get me and take me back to their house in the hills of San Mateo to have dinner with the family and then he and Nan would take me back to Oakland before 9pm. That's about forty minutes each way. That is the kind of man Lloyd was. That supper with all of them and Nan meant a lot to me.

Sunday, the 16th at Oakland called for falling into many formations as time got closer to my departure.

Suddenly there it was in my hand a simple piece of paper for a ticket/boarding pass. Our duffel bags were loaded on to a truck and we got on buses headed for Travis Air Force Base. It was close to midnight when we got to the Entrance Gate at Travis. The MP's motioned us right through without slowing down. We went through a few more gates passed the flight line where rows of various Air Force planes were parked and then through one more gate on to the tarmac. We rolled up to the left side of a TWA 707 with portable stairs fore and aft. We were instructed to board the aircraft as fast as possible for we were due to depart in mere minutes.

When I stepped from the bus, I could hear the jet engines on the other side were already running. We ran up into the plane and took our seats. When the last man sat down, the doors were sealed and we began an ever accelerating taxi right straight to take off.

There were roughly two hundred of us on the plane which was set up with six seats across from front to back. Fortunately I had a window seat. I was glued to the sight of the lights of the California coastline as they became smaller and smaller until they were gone. I said a prayer and took a deep breath.

The entire crew aboard our plane volunteered to work the flights in and out of Vietnam. We would be together for almost twenty four hours hop scotching our way across the Pacific stopping only for fuel, food and water. They were wonderfully helpful with their upbeat, positive energy.

We were given headsets so we could listen to music channels as we flew. Some tunes are forever burned into my memory tied to that flight, "DON'T SLEEP IN THE SUBWAY", being a prime example.

From California we flew to Hawaii, Guam, and then an odd turn northwest to Okinawa. From there on to the South China Sea just off Vietnam's coast over which we were met with a pair of Air Force F-100 fighter jets, one on the left and one on the right, just off each of our wing tips.

Our Captain came on the intercom and told us to secure any loose items immediately and to tighten our seat belts as much as possible. He explained that we would be on the ground at Bien Hoa Air Base in mere moments and to hold on.

We were still at a cruising altitude of thirty thousand feet when, mere seconds after the Captain's words, we dipped steeply to our left and dove like a fighter bomber towards the ground. The F-100s stayed right on our wing tips all the way to wheels down at Bien Hoa. When we were on final approach, the F-100s started shooting their forward firing machine guns. That was a wake up call! We had just completed the roller coaster ride of our lives in a 707 with the perfect finishing touch…gunfire.

We found out later that our plane had been hit with six small arms rounds just before landing. Viet Cong were lying down in the marshes under the final approach slope firing their AK-47 Assault Rifles into commercial aircraft, like our 707, hoping to create a disaster which, in turn, would have a major impact on American troop morale.

Chapter Six / Vietnam

There was more than a hush inside that 707 as we rolled to a stop. I think we all collectively exhaled and gasped for air. But now we were on the ground in V I E T N A M !

In training all we ever heard, over and over, was protect yourself from a 360 degrees, all around you point-of-view. You could "get it" from any side, anyway at anytime. The minute you let down your guard, that's the minute you'll be killed.

We sat on the plane for what seemed for ever. There was no air conditioning with the engines powered down. Finally an MP came on board and spoke to us on the intercom. He said they were waiting for our buses to take us to the incoming personnel processing center in Long Bien.

Looking out my window I saw our pilot on the tarmac walking around and under our left wing with several Air Force men who were carrying clipboards and writing as our pilot was speaking and pointing at a place under the wing. There was a lot of head shaking, looks of anger and some obvious swearing.

It was a silent movie for me with no concrete information, but I assumed that what I was watching was connected to the small arms fire we took on our final approach into Bien Hoa.

From the lie of The Gulf of Tonkin Resolution on, this was a weird "war". World Wars I & II were all out wars. Everybody who could go and fight did. Every American was involved in the effort in their day to day life. The combat went on until there was a victory and then everybody went home.

Here I was beginning twelve months as an infantry soldier in this "war". If I managed to live through the next twelve months, I got to go home and that was it for me. My home, America, was still there fully in tact, with everybody going about their business. Vietnam was something they saw for a few minutes nightly on Huntley-Brinkley, or with Walter Cronkite, and then they had dinner, watched TV and went to bed.

Sitting there I was now sweating my ass off with two hundred other guys on this 707 that had been shot at before we even got on the ground. We didn't know if we'd get shot getting off the airplane, or riding in the bus to report for duty.

All this mental soup was building in my mind culminating to: "You are now a target". For this real life game, you have one course of action: Run as fast as you can for a year. If you're still running in a year, you get to go home and resume your life.

Resolute: I came to two resolves at that moment on that hot and sweaty plane. First; I was going home alive, walking and talking. Secondly; I would not place any other person in jeopardy so that I could fulfill my first resolve. Blind Faith…I was in God's hands.

Orientation to Vietnam came in many forms. There were Army do's, don'ts, and some advanced combat procedures learned the hard way by those who had preceded me.

Being an infantry grunt, new in country, I was the lowest of low…expendable. In that milieu, you gained respect by doing what you were told and living through another day. Literally, the longer you were in country going through all the shit, the more respect you had from everybody. None of the guys that had been on line for a half year or more wanted to invest time in getting to know newcomers because they were the ones to most likely make a mistake and get killed.

It was a strange psychological twist. Those who needed the most support in learning the ways to survive in this extreme, hostile environment did not get it on a one to one, personal level. There were exceptions to this general practice, but they were rare.

The experienced and often hardened guys had gone through too much emotional pain from the accumulation of personal losses from the deaths and maiming of their buddies.

When not out in the boonies, most, not all, of the grunts would spend what free time they had consuming anything to deaden their pain. The Army made alcohol very available in the forms of booze and beer. The Post Exchanges (PX) had it in quantity and it cost almost nothing compared to prices back home in the states. There were also the stone heads who would acquire marijuana from the Vietnamese. Many guys combined the booze and the smoke to "stay smooth".

In my twelve months in country I can count seven fingers worth of nights that I imbibed. I am far from a teetotaler, but I've never been a regular drinker. I don't enjoy the feeling I get from alcohol. My mind is always working and in that state, sobriety is very compatible and comfortable for me. And yes, there were singular nights when I tied one on to excess.

APO: New in country. My bones followed the paper trail assigned to them beginning with Military Assistance Command Vietnam (MACV), then the First Infantry Division, who assigned me to The Third Brigade, who sent me to The First of The Sixteenth Infantry Rangers Battalion, where I was assigned to the Charlie Rangers Company and wound up in the First Platoon.

At each step my next move was determined by the holes that existed within the ranks. In short my new blood replaced the old.

It took about four days to finally reach Charlie Company. Once there, I had to kill a few days until the next Brigade Jungle School course began. This was a mandatory week of up to the minute training on current tactics that were currently in use in the field.

During those fill days before Jungle School I got sent out every day on a work detail. The first day I was sent to attach explosive warheads to rockets that would be loaded on to helicopter gun ships. If I remember correctly, once assembled together the explosive rocket was around five inches in diameter and about five feet long. I had no idea how to properly handle them and was given piss poor instructions except to "put together as many as you can, as fast as you can". We did just that and made a messy pile of them as there was no proper place to put them where they would be secure. I was real glad to get away from that area of the heliport for I was convinced that pile would unravel and one of those rockets would detonate and set off the several hundred other rockets we'd put together.

Two of the detail work days I was sent to the Brigade laundry which was located at Third Brigade Headquarters. The First Infantry Division Third Brigade Headquarters was located in Lai Khe, a small town thirty-five miles north of Saigon up Highway 13. The Brigade Headquarters building had been the plantation house for what had been one of the largest rubber tree plantations in the world. The entire complex had been designed and run by French businessmen for decades until they were run out during the French-Indo China war in the early 1950's.

When I got to the laundry, which was in a distant corner of the Plantation House, the sergeant there said I wasn't needed because his equipment was broken. He told me nicely to get lost. By now, I knew how to take the rest of my day and make it my own without getting into any trouble.

I was curious about the Plantation House, but the main building was just too busy militarily to hang around in plain sight all day. I needed to make myself less visible. I saw a stand alone building that had no action in and out of it a mere fifty yards from the main plantation front door. I went to check it out.

Entering I found two large rooms with fifteen foot ceilings. There several large desks with chairs. Book shelves covered all four walls and were filled with large leather bound volumes that appeared to be ledger books. The place was dusty from lack of use, but was not really dirty. What writing I saw around the room was in French. I pulled one of the large books down and took it over to a desk and sat down to see what was in it.

I had never studied French in school, but had spoken it fluently, even better than English when I was three and four because my mother was brushing up on her French during my informative language learning years. Beyond that I had studied Latin and Spanish, so I would at least be able to read enough to get a flavoring of what was in these volumes before me.

All entries were in ink and written by hand. Not only were there ledger books for the Rubber Tree Plantation, but there were also accountings of all the comings and goings of every French employee and executive plus their family member travel plans to and from France through Saigon. The information included ship, shipping line, or airline, dates, times, costs and length of visits. If they were important people, they had suites or rooms at the Plantation House.

The actual financial ledger books showed the costs, expenses, profits, sales all in French Francs which have always confused me.

Overall, the most interesting thing to me was that all the entries ended in the middle of the writing of them in April, 1954. Literally the entries stopped in the middle of sentences, and/or financial entries. That would coincide with all the French Indochina War developments as the Vietnamese had been fighting for years to drive the French out of the country.

After completing jungle school, I was put on all night perimeter guard duty at the edge of Lai Khe the night before I was to be sent out in the field to join Charlie Company which was with the rest of our battalion at a Night Defensive Position (NDP) many miles north.

This would be my first taste of being out and exposed to the enemy. From my limited experience I was going where we could be over run by Viet Cong (VC), or the North Vietnamese Army (NVA) before the dawn's early light.

My apprehension was with good reason. Mere months before during the Tet Offensive, Lai Khe was hit regularly and the NVA did break through the perimeter and intense fighting took place. Like all American installations in 1968, this one was subject to incoming enemy rockets at anytime from any direction day or night.

Lai Khe was the home of Third Brigade, several wings of helicopters, a fixed wing air craft landing strip; Chinook and Sky Crane heavy lift supply helicopters and several batteries of 175, 155 and 105 millimeter Howitzer artillery guns. I can only guess, but I would think the military part of the village was maybe two miles by two miles. All the way around it they had plowed under anything green and growing in a strip at least a football field in length. There were rows and rows of barbed wire along with trip flares, anti personnel mines and other deadly surprises for any VC or NVA who would make the mistake of trying to cross this "no man's land". On the inside edge of this bare, barb wire covered earth were large watch towers dotted all the way around the perimeter about fifty yards apart. These towers were twenty-five feet high and gave a clear vision looking across no man's land.

Between the towers were dug in the ground fox holes surrounded with sand bags to protect the men inside from small arms fire.

Though there had not been large attacks since the days around Tet, make no mistake, Lai Khe was a regular target for the VC, mostly for harassment, but none the less deadly. If not intercepted further north by our units, the NVA were always a potential for an attack.

Every company at Lai Khe had a section of the perimeter to man every night. Guard Duty was important as the welfare of all inside relied on it being handled with due diligence.

I wound up in a fox hole near one of the towers. When it became dark it was primetime for watching and listening for what was in front of me towards no man's land. The goof balls up in the tower had brought a regular radio and were listening to Armed Forces Vietnam (AFVN) out of Saigon. (AFVN was like listening to a good stateside rock and roll radio station at the time). This was strictly against standing orders, but they were not alone that night. I could hear the delay from the radios at distant positions on either side of me up and down the perimeter. It was both soothing and rattling to my new in country nerves to hear tunes I knew, but at the same time they prevented any of us from hearing the small scruffy sounds in the dirt that would tell us we were being invaded.

Around one or two in the morning AFVN played Jimmy Hendricks's ALL ALONG THE WATCH TOWER. The perimeter came alive with nearly every radio turned up...way up. Talk about surreal. Total darkness except for shadows of the towers against a star lit sky.

It would have been a perfect time to get hit, fortunately "Charlie", as we referred to the VC, chose not to hit us that night.

09:00 hours the next morning I was out on the helipad waiting to be flown to join my company at the battalion's forward Night Defensive Position (NDP) many miles north of Lai Khe. The battalion consisted of four infantry companies, a medical detachment, Supply (S-4), and one 105 MM Howitzer Artillery battery made up of three 105 MM Howitzer artillery guns.

These NDPs were set up in completely undeveloped parts of the jungle where military intelligence had compiled information that led them to believe the NVA were active close by. The hopes were that being that far north in South Vietnam the US units would be able to intercept NVA units and their supply routes headed south towards Saigon and other targets.

Typically one company of infantry would occupy and defend the NDP for a night or two while the other three were patrolling day and night within several miles. They would swap positions on a rotational basis so that every seven to ten days or so, a company would get a night or two out of the boonies and provide security for the forward battalion headquarters. Additionally, at least one mortar platoon from one of the companies would be set up within the NDP. The composition of an NDP was according to the anticipated needs at any given moment due to enemy activity in a given area. Everything in Vietnam 1968 was subject to change without notice.

*As I have noted earlier, the Vietnam "War" was not a war in the classical sense where everybody at home was concerned and involved. But, for us at our do or die level out in the boonies, it was **war** and we were determined to bring as many of us home alive as we could.*

I was put on to a large Chinook resupply chopper to go out to the NDP. Our company was securing the NDP for the day and night. I had a packet of mail for the guys and some other logistical paperwork for our First Sergeant. The chopper was loaded with a

potpourri of items to include: C-Rations, food for the forward
Mess Hall in the NDP, ammunition, compound four plastic
explosives, boxes of explosive hand grenades, smoke grenades and
some uniforms to replace those torn and lost. Externally hanging
underneath was a very large netted sling bag holding tons of
artillery and mortar rounds. I I was told Chinooks could carry
12,000 pounds slung underneath in addition to their internal load.

We were the First of The Sixteenth Infantry Rangers Battalion in
the Third Brigade of the First Infantry Division. I write all that
because General Keith Ware, our Division commander made it a
point to see to it that the men under his command would have one
hot meal a day everyday no matter their assignment, or location.
That is why there was a Mess Hall in the middle of the NDP.

Chapter Seven / Into the fire

It took nearly fifteen minutes to fly from Lai Khe to the battalion NDP just south of the border with North Vietnam. Looking down as we flew, the terrain was hilly and the forest-jungle was very thick. The chopper Crew Chief came over to me yelling above the engine noise to let me know that we'd soon be landing and that when the rear door dropped I should get off the chopper quickly moving straight back until I was clear of the rear rotor blades. Made sense to me, those rotor blades could make mince meat of me in one second.

This NDP was now my home of the moment. It was centered in a clearing surrounded by high trees and lower, a thick overgrown jungle. In the center was a sandbagged area in which was the Tactical Operations Center (TOC) for the battalion. Above it several tall poles with radio transmission antennas on top. From within it I could hear radio transmissions, but the content was drowned out by noisy little gas powered generators just outside the TOC. A sand bag's throw from the TOC, the so-called Mess Hall was preparing a meal. I couldn't tell if what was cooking smelled good or bad, but smell it did.

The uniform of the day was damn little due to the intense heat and humidity. Everyman was dirty, sweaty. Beyond our jungle kitchen, was the artillery battery. Three 105 millimeter howitzers completely ringed with a double thick layer of sandbags just over three feet high.

Everywhere I looked were one and two man sized areas surrounded with sandbags. Dirty uniforms were stretched out over sandbags drying in the intense sun. Jungle boots caked with drying mud were atop sandbags next to their owners who were cleaning their weapons while bullshitting with a buddy.

I turned around and walked back towards the TOC looking for anyone who appeared to be in charge. I had to report in to the battalion before doing the same at Charlie Company. Out of the sandbag covered TOC walked an older sergeant smoking a cigarette his head facing inside the TOC finishing a sentence. He turned, saw me and said, "new in country?" I responded that I was, gave him my rank, name and said I was reporting for duty with Charlie Company. I held out my paperwork which he took as he introduced himself. He then told me that he would do everything he could to keep me alive as long as I returned the favor. I told him that worked for me. He smiled and pointed behind me saying Charlie Company was over there. I thanked him, turned and made my way across the NDP.

Approaching a circle of half naked, raggedy looking, burned out appearing troops sitting around on mud covered sandbags, I asked if they were Charlie Company. "Yeah", said one looking at me through bloodshot eyes, a mop of sun bleached hair atop his very tanned head. "Welcome troop" he said. "I'm Dale Young. Drop your stuff there and grab yourself a soda and tell us about yourself".

Dale turned out to be my squad leader. He'd been in Vietnam seven months and despite his actual twenty years, he seemed very much like an old man. This contrast stunned me and comforted me all at the same time. I got it right away that he was operating totally on instinct. He had a big heart, had seen too much in his seven months and wasn't talking about it. He didn't bother with telling me what not to do; he went right into what "to" do.

It is fact that I would not be here writing this book had I not met Dale Young.

We would be going out that night as a squad of six to set up an ambush position for the night. Along with many other squads from our battalion, we would spend the night in a likely position to ambush a unit of the NVA on the move. They moved troops and materials at night so as not to be seen by US units in daylight from the air, or on the ground.

My heart was pounding as we reached the perimeter of our NDP. It was an hour after sunset and in the waning moments of light we were going to a holding area roughly a mile from the NDP to wait for total darkness, after which we would move quietly to our all night position.

As we went outside the barb wire perimeter of the NDP we locked and loaded ammunition in the chamber of our M-16s, but left the triggers on safety. There would be little, if any words between us...only simple sign language and eye contact. Footsteps were careful ones avoiding unnecessary sound with each step.

We got to our holding position and sat down. Young looked at his watch, looked at us, held up five fingers and pointed to his watch. In five minutes we would move into position for the night.

Dale had found what appeared to be a trail through the jungle growth. We set up fifteen feet off of it. We put out claymore mines between us and the trail and strung the detonating wires back to where we were going to spend the night.

If you have ever been awake at night in the darkness, whether in your bedroom, or camping out, you know how in time the darkness can play tricks with your vision and your mind. Now add to those thoughts being in a dark jungle, far from anywhere, there are just six of you. You have been told that thousands of enemy NVA are known to be all around where you are sitting. They move large units many miles every night down trails like the one fifteen feet in front of you. Squads just like yours have been wiped out many times by the well trained and disciplined NVA.

I was scared shitless. It may have helped to be able to talk it out right then and there, but that would surely have gotten all six of us killed. Voices carry long distances in the quiet of the jungle at night. The NVA were very good at stealth movement. If they heard us they would do one of two things: First; they may decide to avoid us and go around so as not to be detected and giveaway that they are in the immediate area, or Second; they might encircle us and hit us. I got to keep my feelings to myself for that and every night for that year. How's that for a daily practice of healthy psychology?

For our part we were there to sit quietly awake all night, report any movement, and if we lived through the night, return to the NDP.

If only it were that simple. That first night I was somewhere between seeing nothing and seeing everything that wasn't there. The artillery would periodically fire off flying flares in approximate areas where ambushes were set up in the hopes to expose NVA units moving in the darkness. Depending on weather conditions, these flares would be flying across the sky at maybe one hundred feet for seconds to a minute or two. The actual flare was under a small parachute. The light from them would cast an eerie moving shadow on all the jungle in front of ones vision. Sometimes I could actually see the mosquitoes I heard, and whose bites I felt, all night as the occasional flares drifted by over head.

We returned to the NDP in the mornings early light. As we got back to our squad area, our First Sergeant walked over and told Young to come see him about the operation for the day.

Young returned expressionless and told us to quickly grab some grub over at the Mess line because the whole company was going out on a three or four day Search and Destroy Mission in thirty minutes. He then added be sure to have twice the normal ammo, C-Rations and water. He did not say why.

My mind was racing. None of the preparation process was routine to me. The guys who had been in it for a while quickly grabbed what they knew they would need and ran to the Mess line. I was trying to think my way through what I would need and still be ready in time to move out. The basic amount of gear required along with ammunition, weapon, and hand grenades left little space for water and some C-Ration canned food. I have always been a big water drinker and two canteens at a quart each would last me a few hours in the hot jungle. I had much to learn about my needs and stamina in that paradigm.

When going through jungle searching out the NVA, we did not walk on trails or paths. They would be booby trapped with every possible hidden device to hurt or kill us. Additionally, if they had a base camp in the area, they would have manned ambush positions around it to hit us if we were stupid enough to be walking on an established trail.

Attrition in numbers of personnel for a combat unit came in many forms. The best was guys receiving their orders to go home. Second to that was getting assigned to a non combat activity while still in country. Every other form of it was not wanted.

For months my company had been on regular assignment in this northern region of South Vietnam near An Loc and Loc Ninh. The Killed in Action (KIA) and the numbers of wounded had been consistently high. Whereas we should have been on line with a field strength of around 110 men, we were lucky to be operating with 80-85 men spread across the three infantry platoons in Charlie Company.

The lack of five or more men per platoon makes a big difference in fighting capacity. But the bigger impact was on the morale, the feelings of each man.

I'm not a Pollyanna, and I am more likely to be in a positive state of mind most of the time. One of the first things I noticed when I joined my squad that first day was how sullen, down and quiet they were. They had been subjected to repeated intense combat and had had many of their buddies sent home in body bags while many others were in hospitals from Saigon to Japan, depending upon the seriousness of their wounds.

I had much to learn to stay alive and to appreciate where my new comrades were in their heads. I kept my mouth shut; my eyes open and when told to do something, did it NOW.

My First Platoon was on rotation that day to "Cut the Point" for the company progression through the thick of the jungle. The point unit was the one most likely to get messed up if contact was made with the NVA. The platoon leader, normally a First Lieutenant, would put his best squad leader out front. Experience was needed at the front in order to recognize pointers that we were getting into enemy territory. There was a lot of starting and stopping of the column as various potential indicators were evaluated.

Being new in country, I was expendable. Therefore I was third man from the front the first half of the day. The man at the very front, (The Point Man), did so with purpose. He wielded a machete cutting through bamboo and other jungle growth with authority. Young was right behind him with compass and funny paper, (our term for a map), keeping the direction going according to plan. Despite my understanding of maps and a good sense of direction, in that thick jungle I had no sense of the angle of the Sun, and was disoriented about which way I was headed. In that I found out I was not alone.

Young signaled to pause in our forward motion. Putting a "silence" fore finger to his lips, he looked at me and then pointed towards the ground right next to us. I saw nothing but ground, leaves and dirt. I shrugged my shoulders in a "what?" shape. He crouched down and pointed to a collection of pungi sticks in the ground. When I grasped what he was pointing to, I got down to get a closer look. They were thinly cut long pieces of bamboo. The NVA or Viet Cong made them to hurt us. They would take the sharp pointed ends and dip them in shit, (human or animal), and then push the other end into the ground. If stepped upon, or worse fallen upon, the spear sharp point would pierce the skin and the fecal bacteria would infect the victim. There would normally be a cluster of eight or more pungi sticks in a group. Getting pierced with them required being sent to a hospital for cleansing of the wound(s) and a long term treatment of various medicines, without which a victim, would more than likely eventually die, or wish they were dead.

The thing I kept learning was that in war a determined enemy will do everything to win. They not only want you dead, they want you incapacitated, out of action and away.

We Americans knew this when we went to end British rule over us.

The sad point regarding Vietnam for America was that despite all our advanced training, tactics, hardware, expense, the one thing that defeated us was the lack of spirit. Fighting to the death for anything requires it.

The reality of the pungi sticks woke me up. I was feeling major fatigue from the hours of drudging through the dense jungle, the intense humid heat, constantly being tripped up by all the growth at ankle height, the no sleep nights out on ambush, and the vigilant, incessant peering in every direction for an NVA ambush.

Young stood up, he muttered, "those pungi are fresh, they're close". He then turned to our Point Man and waved him to continue.

It was early afternoon when the Point Man asked for a break. He had been hacking away at all the bamboo and growth non stop for over seven hours. Young turned and handed the machete to me. Willing to try, I took it and let him know that he would have to keep me directed in the right direction as I had no idea which way was North.

Talk about "a babe in the woods", and now I'm thrashing about with this extremely sharp machete. I was dangerous to everyone starting with myself.

All that green stuff called jungle growth is tough stuff. Not only does hacking through it take strength, it takes restraint. What looks easy to cut isn't and visa versa for what looks hard to cut. The freshly severed branches would scratch, or cut my arms as I progressed forward, the sweat I had worked up in the day's heat intensified with all the wielding of the machete. The frustration mounted as I tried to cut the green shit. I swung wildly and the cutting edge got stopped, not by my arm muscles, but the upper half of my boot. (Don't ask.)

Young kept pointing me in the right direction adding a guiding word on my cutting from time to time. The jungle thinned slightly for a time and I started making some headway. Feeling some degree of accomplishment, my energy picked up a bit. I was about to cut yet another branch when straight ahead of me about twenty feet ahead, stood an NVA soldier. For a split second we made eye to eye contact. His weapon was raised and he was going for the trigger when Young's M-16 opened up and cut the man down. Dale was so close to me that the hot, empty shells flew all over me as he emptied his ammo clip.

61

We hit the ground as, the jungle in front of us came alive with weapon fire. The searing sounds of the mini missiles piercing the air inches away was new, frightening and surreal. The deafening sounds of all the weaponry firing from both sides was now being mixed with men screaming in pain as some of those missiles ripped their flesh. Other screams were of commanding orders to move here or there for better return fire.

I have no idea what happened to that machete. Amazing it didn't cut me in half as I hit the ground. My M-16 had been harnessed on my shoulder in order to cut point and had it not been for Dale Young in that split second, I would have died right there my first day in the bush.

The NVA eventually pulled back and abandoned that one position by the end of the day. There were multiple dead and wounded on both sides when it was over. They would pull their dead and wounded out with them as they departed a position. It made it harder for us to establish actual statistics. Sweeping through what had been their position, the amounts of blood in spots and the trails of blood leading away were indicators for the amount of damage that had been incurred. Human carnage is not a pleasant sight. Suffice it to write here that I was sickened by what I saw this first time.

I did not cut point after that. I volunteered to carry radio instead. I had observed the various men carrying radio and came to a quick decision that that would be my form of soldiering. I needed something to keep my mind occupied. It was obvious to me that though carrying the radio along with extra batteries and more would be physically taxing; it was the right thing to put my abilities to good use.

There were many levels to achieve in radio carrying. I would have to start at squad level, and once perfected, advance through platoon, company and then battalion radio. Along with paying attention to immediate surroundings, radio operators (RTO's) had to be adept at fast, clear and concise communications which were common to other RTO's. The lives of everyone relied on there being very fast radio work to get help in all its forms immediately when needed.

We stayed out that night and several more before returning to the NDP only to find that the entire battalion was packing to return to Lai Khe. I came to learn a phrase well known to those of us in the infantry; first in, last out. The infantry always had to enter a new area of operations first to secure a landing zone (LZ) for everyone and everything that followed. Since men and material were brought in by helicopters, it was organized chaos as everything was plucked from the jungle and flown back to base. Of course the minute we would pull out of a location, the NVA, or VC would immediately reclaim it. Somewhere in the back of our minds that part kept chewing at us with the resultant thought, why did we bother?

Being in the First Infantry Division, we frequently would be teamed up with mechanized units. Besides large battle tanks, there were what are known as Armored Personnel Carriers (APCs). Mounted on turrets on top them were fifty caliber machine guns, which could do a lot of damage in short order to structures, not to mention enemy personnel unfortunate enough to be within their gun sights.

These heavy, armored vehicles were not really practical out in the jungle. Our job was to be on foot alongside on the left and right of their column as they advanced slowly forward. "Slowly" being the operative word here. (Nothing against my mechanized brethren, for they were just like us trying to stay alive and go home).

We always felt that operations with them were more dangerous for us due to their girth, slow movement and noise level in that environment. Plus if one of them threw a track, (the drive belt on

which they traveled versus tires on a truck), it could be hours for them
to repair it, during which time all the mechanized and infantry stayed in place to provide protection while those poor bastards busted their collective asses to fix it. The NVA loved to hit us when we couldn't maneuver around as needed to effectively execute combat.

On July 20th we were on a combined operation with a mechanized unit when we came up against a unit of NVA. When the combat began we were not sure from which direction the hostile fire was coming. The APCs were moving around as were we on foot trying to ascertain to where we should effectively return fire. There was combat chaos as the popping gunfire with green (there's) and red (ours) tracers flew all around us. One second I was flat on the ground, the next up and running to hopefully a better position then down again. The screams of those hit quickly became more numerous and louder. One of the APCs positioned in the middle of my squad suddenly lunged in reverse twenty feet and made a right turn and stopped.

The battle for that patch of jungle and mud was one of, if not, the bloodiest. I was in my third week on line. I had been trying to find the few guys I sort of knew from my platoon after the hostilities had ended. It was late in the afternoon daytime dark because of the dense jungle canopy overhead and a heavy layer of cloud.

I walked around the APC and found one of my new friends, Roosevelt Sherman on the ground, his eyes open. I got down close to see if he was just dazed and motionless, but no, he was dead. He had been so animated, a happy soul with music in his heart and laughter in his stories.

We had come into the company within a day of each other. Being new, we were often treated to extra dirty duties. We took them in stride and together put some spirit to our drudgery. We enjoyed that about each other, and boy did it help to make those miserable moments less so and pass quickly.

I looked into his now lifeless eyes and cried. I tried to determine if he'd been shot. Maybe the damn APC had backed over him in the chaos. I have never known. I got one of the guys to help me carry him to where the KIAs were being placed for eventual recovery by helicopter. I had never carried a dead man before. It was very upsetting to be doing so and more so because this was my friend Roosevelt.

It was getting to be night and raining as we put Roosevelt next to the others. I stood over him and prayed and added that I would not forget him. Feeling empty and raw I backed away slowly and felt something tugging at my pant leg. It was Roosevelt's gas mask, cover and strap. I reached down picked it up and held it to me. One more look at my dead friend and I walked away.

I spent that entire night cold in a downpour sitting waist deep in water clutching his gas mask, silent, rocking ever so slightly back and forth aware, yet stunned.

Chapter Eight / A Welcome Change

A day or two later we were back in Lai Khe. The company clerk told me I had a rather large package that had come in the mail several days earlier while we were on patrol. I sparked as I was sure it was from my dad, and if that was the case, I knew exactly what had come.

I ran over to the Orderly Room and waiting there was a large box with my dad's handwriting on it. I thanked Paul Widzowski, our clerk, for safe guarding it as I picked it up and ran back to my barracks.

My dad had wrapped the box in a heavy, multi layered paper in the middle of which was a thin layer of tar to keep out moisture. That was my dad always thinking of how something would be used and preparing for the options. In this case he was protecting the audio tape recorder I had asked him to buy and send me in order to record my features for WPFB.

We had talked about it before I left for Vietnam and agreed that once there I would be better able to determine the features needed.

Among the items on the list for the recorder: it had to record at the professional tape speed of 7.5 inches per second, accommodate 7 inch size reels of audio tape, had to take D-cell batteries for power because they were easy to get from Supply (S-4) as they were needed for flash lights. As long as they were new, the batteries were reliable to make recordings with a speed that would play back correctly at WPFB.

He sent one hell of a perfect AIWA tape machine. It had all those features plus it was a stereo recorder-player with two microphones.

It could play prerecorded stereo music tapes, which though hard to get, some did appear along with tapes sent from friends at radio stations at home. As I was looking over the features of the tape recorder it struck me that it had been made in Japan, shipped to the US, purchased in Cincinnati and then shipped to Vietnam. Somehow that seemed a little whacked, but a sign of the times.

As I wrote earlier, I went to Stan Reed, my boss at WPFB, while I was working on air there the month before I left for 'Nam and told him I wanted to record human interest stories about how the war was affecting those of us fighting it. He said it sounded to him like a good idea and he would air them if I turned in good material. I assured him that they would surely be "airable". The only problem would be the regularity in delivery of tapes. I would be a soldier and would have very little free time. I suggested calling the series VIETNAM PERIODICAL. He liked my idea, the name I'd given it and encouraged me to do the best I could under the circumstances.

I needed this. It gave me things to think about all the time. Everything I saw, every feeling I had. My mind was in "record" around the clock.

I may have been in the war, but I was mentally able to step out of it all the time as I stashed away memories of my observations, to later jot down in notes which I eventually would organize into a script and then secretly record on tape in stolen, solitary moments away from everyone usually in the middle of the night when we would be in out of the field for a day or two out of fourteen.

I knew I wasn't doing anything wrong making my recordings on how the war was affecting all of us, but I was in the military and I did not want to find myself trying to explain what I was doing to my commanding officers, or others above them.

As soon as a PERIODICAL was recorded, I mailed each tape to WPFB and the hand written script to my parents. Reed sent the tapes to my parents after he made a copy to put on the air. I have all thirty-one of the tapes I sent in the fifty-two weeks I was in "Fun City East", (one of the printable surnames we gave Vietnam).

Unlike our instant information world of the internet today, it was hard to get timely information then. AFVN did run hourly newscasts so we could get headlines of American and international happenings when we were out of the field and our private radios were available to us. But there were many gaps throughout my year there where things happened elsewhere and I, we, did not have a clue. There was STARS & STRIPES, the military's daily newspaper printed in Japan. But there were just so many copies to go around and we did not get them at all in the field. Editorially both AFVN and STARS & STRIPES were understandably bent the way the Military Assistance Command Vietnam (MACV) wanted on all stories that were reported, and some others were left out period. To be clear, when you're in the military you're under military law and not civilian law. Your rights are also different, very different.

Chapter Nine / Back to the Carnage

My three weeks in country became six. Charlie Company carnage was all too common. We never went out with full troop capacity and by the end of day one in the field, between the wounded and the dead; we would be down ten or more before nightfall.

I was now carrying, or, as we called it, humping radio. It gave me a way to use my abilities to communicate quickly, accurately and to hear what was going on immediately around us near and far.

After yet another few disastrous days up north near either An Loc, or Loc Ninh, what turned out to be our final day on that mission, that day, July 20th, we got hit hard. After the battle was over we got the wounded and then the dead dusted off in Medivac helicopters. After our night in the rain, they flew in a bunch of choppers and brought us back to Lai Khe, I think much earlier than they had planned.

I did not know what to do with the input that was becoming all too frequent and disturbingly familiar. People I would meet begin to make friends with and then suddenly, violently they were dead...gone.

Some of the guys were not willing to invest their hearts in getting to know anybody new...they'd lost too many over a few months. They were burying their feelings in substances to numb their pain when ever they were out of the field.

I just didn't have it in me not to connect with those around me. Admittedly some more than others, but then that's how we are with close friends, isn't it?

We continued to operate as an infantry company at two thirds to three quarters of the troop strength we should have had each time they put us on choppers and took us north to go up against the NVA. Morale was lower than low. I was now carrying radio in the Charlie company command group.

In the midst of all of this, we got sent out. On this particular day I was assigned to be with our First Sergeant, James George. He did not normally go out on operations as his main responsibility was to oversee the administrative workings of Charlie Company. There was a lot to plan for and coordinate to keep one hundred combat soldiers fed and supplied with all they needed when they needed it. He ran a good operation without the sense of an iron fist. A combat veteran of our mess in Korea fifteen years earlier, Sergeant George was a career Army man, who had a keen sense and understanding of the makings of good men and how to support them at being the best at what they do.

On this day Sergeant George and I were purposely separated from company commander Captain Ferris in case of enemy contact. It was procedure not to have all the command and control group members in close proximity when on patrol for obvious reasons.

As you may recall reading earlier I stated that there were a handful of days in my entire year in Vietnam when I imbibed. I had consumed five, maybe six beers the night before this mission. Half a dozen brews is nothing for a regular drinker, but for this light head, hoo-boy...I got sick. I had mixed the beers with chocolate. A lot of chocolate... I don't know why, I just did.

There were four radio carriers for the command group. Only two went out on the average mission, two would stay back. When on patrol, we were essentially on duty for the full twenty-four hours of any one day. I knew by rotation schedule, I was due to be in the next day when the company went out. For some dumb ass reason, for the first time in a couple of months, I had the beers and once into a few of them, got into chocolate, then a few more beers and long before midnight was feeling sick as a dog. I puked until I couldn't. It wasn't pretty.

At sunrise I was awakened to be told that I would be going out to carry radio for First Sergeant George who suddenly decided to go on the patrol. I was still sick and now hung-over. I had forty-five minutes to get my shit together. For all appearances I had to seem fit for duty. I flushed as much water through me as I could. Washed my face, shaved, brushed my teeth, put on a clean uniform, got on my gear and radio and headed for the company Orderly Room to stand by for departure.

Because of my self inflicted "illness", it was "show time" for me that morning. I had to appear normal, ready to go.

First Sergeants are usually called "Top" in a unit because they are, in fact, the top ranking Sergeant.

Once outside the Orderly Room, I got a cup of water and drank it down quickly. All I could think of was to flush my system. Top came out of the Orderly Room door all decked out in patrol gear carrying his weapon. I'd never seen him dressed for patrol before. He was always seeing us off, or welcoming us back from patrols.

Top had these bright, smart eyes that could look right in to you and get what was going on with you in a split second without so much as a word. He told me we were going along so he could see how things were when the company was on patrol. I let him know that whatever he needed to do I was with him to make it happen.

Three platoons got choppered out that morning and began patrolling. I was struggling walking behind Top. I probably was as green as my fatigues, but was not about to let Top know it. Just after mid day, we got hit by NVA. It was costly as three or four of us were killed and seven or eight were wounded.

The actual battle was over after half an hour, or so, although we were never really sure how long actual combat lasted. With adrenaline flowing like water from a fireman's hose, your sense of time is completely warped.

A med-i-vac dust off helicopter took the most seriously wounded first. After a short time another arrived to take the less critical and the dead. Top and I helped move the KIA's on board then got out of the way so the remaining wounded could get aboard. Once they were on, standing at the door he motioned me to get on and then he too got on. The choppers crew chief waved his hand "no" and said there were too many. Top looked at him and said, "this is it…let's go". Sliding the Hueys door closed, he waved a "go" to the chopper pilots.

A Huey chopper normally had a crew of four, and could safely accommodate five, maybe six average weight battle equipped soldiers. I've never been sure of the total on that one that afternoon, but my guess is there were ten of us plus the crew of four. There was no room to move. I was on my knees, but compared to the men behind me who had died within the hour and the others wounded, I had nothing to complain about.

That bird was way over weight. As the turbine whined up to get the rotors moving fast enough to lift us off the ground the entire aircraft began to vibrate, shuttering like I'd never felt or heard a helicopter do. I could see the instrument panels left and right in front of me. We were at maximum RPM, barely getting lift with the slightest of forward motion. The entire craft was shaking from the turbine and rotor blades overload, yet we were clear of the ground by inches to maybe a foot with some forward motion.

It was not the clearest of landing zones, but the closest for evacuating everyone as fast as possible. The chopper Captain "threaded the needle" with his expert dodging of nature's obstacles of low plants, bushes, rocks and the like, anyone of which could have flipped our bird as it trotted to get fully airborne. Had a tree line been too close we would have crashed into it. Little by little we got more forward air speed and with that improved lift we headed towards the field hospital at Lai Khe.

Most Infantry Grunts like me flew in Dust Off helicopters because they were either wounded or dead. That was my one and only flight in one, thank God. My heart ached as I looked around me. The wounded guys were hurting, but not in immediate danger for their lives. They were field bandaged and quiet. The four KIA's were on stretchers up the back wall of the choppers cabin. At that point I wasn't sure who they were. The silence among us, beyond the sounds of the choppers turbine, was deafening and sad.

Because of our casualties, Top had much administrative work to do back at Charlie Company. The rest of the company was pulled out and returned to Lai Khe within a few hours.

Once in the Field Hospital, I radioed back to Charlie Base to have Gary Jones, our jeep driver come pick up Top and myself. As I finished the transmission I saw our CO, Captain Ferris with his head bandaged. I was shocked and concerned and up to that moment had not known he had been hit. I never got close enough to speak with him as Top came up to me and we began a hand written list of the names of our wounded and dead. Some of the extremely injured would either go to Third Field Hospital Saigon, or be sent on to Japan. Those decisions were made by the Army Medical Corps and were determined by the severity and nature of the wounds.

Too many M-16's standing on end, bayonets affixed, stuck in the ground with the dead man's helmet sitting on top, all in a neat row with the rest of us at parade rest listening to the Chaplin speak religiously about our dead buddies as tears wetted our checks, shirts and hearts. This was our "next day back" ritual which sadly had become routine. We were full of sorrow and anger all at the same time. Some didn't know what to do with their rage.

When will this shit end? It kept rolling around my head. The only sane answer I could come up with for myself was June 16th next year, if I live to see it.

Again that haunting, this isn't real part of being in Vietnam. If you lived through to your prescribed time, you got to go home...for you the whole thing was then over, but many friends you had made there would still be in it getting wounded, dieing and for what? The question that couldn't be answered...the question that kept taking a bigger and bigger piece out of me every day.

Chapter Ten / Our New Commander

Captain Ferris never returned to lead Charlie Company. Our new Commanding Officer (CO) was one Warren Judge Goss. This was his second tour of Vietnam. He had been a Lieutenant and a platoon leader and, therefore, came to us with combat experience. From my first meeting with him I immediately had a sense of mutual respect. He was tall, built strong, not like a muscle builder, but decidedly in shape. There was an old soul about him, truly wise beyond his years. He was highly intelligent. His intelligence was an on going tool, not a weapon. He was keenly aware of his surroundings and the people who populated them.

Captain Goss was a graduate of Howard University. He was part of a whole new growing cadre of black officers who were making their marks in America's military. I would come to find out that Warren Goss had the attention of the highest brass in the US Army.

We were damn near a week without going out on patrol. Captain Goss got a sense of the company; we got much needed replacement troops to bring our roster closer to a proper field strength. Overall we had a few days to lick our collective emotional wounds.

On our first mission out with Goss, that very afternoon I got a radio call from above for Captain Goss. I always wore headsets on my helmet so I would never miss a call and therefore heard every word radioed in or outbound. I did not recognize the Commander's call sign, but could tell it was from a helicopter and by the chatter between Goss and whoever it was that this guy was up there in the command.

Goss completed the radio call, handed back the handset and said that General Ware, the First Infantry Division Commanding General, would be coming down to talk in three minutes. We were already in a fairly large clearing as Goss got on the company radio and had the platoons quickly secure a wide perimeter around what would be the landing zone for General Ware.

I heard the distinct chop-chop of a Huey helicopter not too far off as my radio came alive asking me to pop smoke to identify our exact location for the landing. I threw out a purple smoke grenade, they identified same and within seconds the Huey was blowing us around in its rotor wash as it touched down. Goss stood up and started moving toward the chopper and I followed him. The General and his Executive Officer (XO), a full bird Colonel, hopped out along with a magnificent German Shepard. A quick greeting all around and they walked away from the chopper so they could talk without having to yell over the noisy turbine. (*I'd seen many Command and Control helicopters up close by this time and I'd had never seen one so clean, immaculate and crammed with communications equipment.*) It was interesting to note that the chopper never powered down, but sustained a moderate RPM in order to be airborne in seconds if required.

I stayed close behind as a radio should never be far from a commander in the field. The gist of the conversation was that General Ware wanted to know how Goss was doing in his new post, the general condition of the company and then they quickly discussed the mission for the day.

Ware told "King", his German Shepard, to get on the chopper, the Colonel turned to the pilots and spun his index finger at which point the turbine increased RPMs. Goss, Ware and his XO shook hands, parted, the two of them bent low under the spinning rotor blades moved quickly to the chopper and climbed on board. Goss and I went to our knees preparing for the rotor wash as the Huey came to full power and lifted off.

I told Goss that that was a first. To my knowledge, the company had never had the Division Commander pay us a visit. He said that he and the General had known each other for some time.

Combat wise August was not a good month for us.

Captain Goss proved to be a good leader of men as he earned respect from all the ranks in the company. He did so by being genuine in every moment. His respect for the Chain of Command came out of conscious consideration for every man up the Chain and down. He did not profess it, he lived it.

August 27th would be yet another violent day for Charlie Company in Binh Long Province. After the disastrous day of combat we were returned to Lai Khe.

In our company Mess Hall that night I was walking with my supper to sit down to eat when I ran into members of my old platoon whom I'd not seen since early morning. I stopped to ask how they were and if they knew where our friend Tim Cottrell was. They looked at me blankly and then told me that Sergeant Cottrell had been killed that afternoon. I said nothing, put my food tray down, walked out of the Mess Hall, went to First Platoons shack, sat down on a foot locker and starred over at Tim's bunk area. We had gotten on well together. Now he too was gone permanently.

It wasn't but a week later that we got word that our entire battalion was being transferred from the First Infantry Division to the Ninth Infantry Division down south and west of Saigon in the Mekong Delta. We did not know if this was a good thing or a bad thing. The one thing we did know, it would be a different thing.

Chapter Eleven / We Move

In the military movement is a constant. To transport an entire Battalion some sixty miles was a project not beyond the Army to pull off, but still complex and a lot of work in a short amount of time. There would be a convoy of heavy five ton trucks loaded with all the big stuff and deuce and a halfs with everything else except us. We would fly down in KC-130 and KC-123 fixed wing cargo planes. Of course there were delays and a lot of sitting around on our day of flight, but we got down to the Mekong Delta and the Ninth Division before sunset.

Our new base of operations was Dong Tam, a two mile by two mile square literally carved out of the jungle by the Army right on the Mekong River slightly east of the Vietnamese city of My Tho. It was the Ninth Division Headquarters and a real military hole. It was also a target for the VC as they would regularly fire rockets and mortars into it from every direction. It gained the nickname "Rocket City" because of the frequency of the incoming hostile fire. Since it was strictly US Military and not attached to a civilian Vietnamese village, it was always open season as a target. But, hey, it was "home".

Up north we got plenty wet, but down in the Delta, we were regularly submerged and climbing out of chest high water-mud-muck full of leeches and water moccasins. Thank God Captain Goss was strong as he was forever pulling me out of the that delta shit in which I would sink more than most due to the radio, batteries and other gear that weighted me down. I hit the scale around 160 pounds (still do), so I was far from being over weight, but with all my gear, I was more like 200.

Dong Tam was our "home" for September, October and early November, though we were seldom there as our Battalion, now known as the 5TH of The 60TH Infantry, operated out of a forward Fire Support Base. Named Moore, it was a lavishly appointed series of sand bag circles with lean-tos, tents and one bunkered "building" in which was the Tactical Operations Center. From Dong Tam, Moore was about a half hour long dirty, dusty ride in the back of an open deuce and a half winding through village after village on a sort of dirt road.

It was at Moore, on a sandbag wall around Charlie Company's Command tent that, while drying out my over soaked, rice paddy fungus infected feet one hot October afternoon, I voted for the first time in my life by absentee ballot. It was the 1968 Presidential Election. From my immature, distorted point of view, thousands of miles from home, I voted for Richard Nixon thinking that maybe a change of party in the Executive Branch would be good for the country. Kennedy and Johnson had helped lead the way to the build up in Vietnam following (the lie of) The Gulf of Tonkin Resolution and I did not want to see more of that thinking manifest itself where I was. *Hey, it was long time ago and I did grow up...and wake up.*

Keeping up with my WPFB Vietnam Periodicals was difficult during this time. I was not at a loss for ideas or material to report about, but I needed to be in Dong Tam to record them and we were seldom there. I was scribbling down subjects as they came to mind and squirreling them away in plastic bags hoping to have them still readable when I did get back. Once in Dong Tam I would hand write the scripts and then record them on audio tape in the middle of the night away from anybody who could hear me.

On the jungle camouflage cover on the side of my helmet I printed: "WPFB MOBILE NEWS" and under it: "We're so mobile, we're lost".

Lost was more than a joking matter. Think about it…why was America so committed to this "war" in Vietnam? That was the question that kept circling in my little P-brain the entire time I was there. There were hints right in front of me everyday, yet despite my observations of them individually, I did not put all the pieces together in a mosaic and view it as a whole until some years later looking back on it.

Government dollars, into corporate profits.

I was twelve, not quite thirteen years old when President Eisenhower wrote and presented his Military Industrial Complex speech. I watched it but my depth of understanding the workings of Washington was too limited as a Seventh Grader. Despite my good history teachers, not one of them had us make a study of the insight and significance of Eisenhower's brilliant foretelling.

Our operations were different around the Mekong Delta. For the most part we were dealing with the Viet Cong, a loose nit group of vigilantes who came in all sizes, ages, and sexes. They were mixed in with members of the villages and hamlets. Visually there was no way to distinguish between the villagers and the Cong.

Up north we were primarily up against the NVA, a highly disciplined, well equipped, uniformed army. The Viet Cong were no less deadly, but in the Delta we were always on a 360 degree full circle high awareness level. There were Vietnamese civilians all around us much of the time.

The surreptitious nature of the Cong meant our lives were in jeopardy every minute. We could be walking through a village square full of people going about their daily activities, have a woman brush by us and suddenly explode killing herself and killing or injuring anyone unfortunate to be too close. It happened to us more than once.

I fought the urge to mistrust every face I looked into. This part of the survival conditioning in which I found myself living was contrary to who I am. But it became second nature for the sake of all of us. Constantly looking for that first indication that the person I was watching had a weapon, or was bundled up with a satchel charge of explosives preparing to detonate it. It made me sick at heart to think I had to do it; but even more, I did not want to be the one who missed a signal and thus got any of us injured or killed.

Around the hamlets and villages were field upon field of rice paddies each surround by mounds of mud better known as dikes. The rice paddies were normally full of water about half a foot in depth into which our feet would sink with each step. It was easier and from a mobility sense, faster to walk the dikes and a lot more dangerous. It was easy and common for the Viet Cong (VC) to bury pressure sensitive anti-personnel mines in them. Step on it and one to several of us would be killed and, or badly injured. It wasn't always the first guy in a line who hit the mine. The wrong part of a single footstep could trigger a mine after twenty guys walked by and then the damn things would blow up. Along with all the other hazards, just walking was unnerving.

The VC would farm the rice paddies by day and go on military missions at night. Who was the hard working farmer, and who was the VC acting like a farmer? We got to spend our days and nights wondering that. All too often we found out the hard way.

We were the front of what became known as the Pacification Program. The object was to go into the hamlets and villages and befriend the local Vietnamese to cause a reduction of the rebellious nature of those who would take action against us or the South Vietnamese government. For this effort every company was assigned an interpreter in order for us to speak directly with the civilians.

Our first interpreter was college educated, smart and was an urbanite raised in Saigon. He knew very little about the lives of the hamlet dwellers. I never knew if he was an actual member of the South Vietnamese Army because his uniform was devoid of any patches suggesting affiliation with a particular unit.

I don't remember his name, I think it was Huaong. *For the sake of what I write here, he's Huaong.*

The action in and around the Delta did permit a bit more social time among those of us working around Captain Goss while we were out. As part of the Pacification Program we were to get to a village during day light, befriend the villagers, try to get the gist of what was going on with them, as in had there been any VC traffic lately. Further, we would let them know we wanted to spend the night in and around the village for their security. Sometimes we would offer to pay them to cook a traditional meal.

Goss was very careful through Huaong to make it clear we were not forcing ourselves on them. Some responded with openness and others did not. Either way we all knew any of them could be a VC, but while watching closely, this was an opportunity to show consideration, kindness and perhaps win those who were on the fence over to our side.

We had Goss, our Medic, (who we called Doc), our artillery officer and his radio operator, a company radio carrier, Huaong and me carrying the battalion radio in the CP group. One good night we were welcomed by this very nice family who cooked up a couple of fresh chickens, some rice and the seven us and the four of them sat around their long table in the middle of their thatched hut and exchanged ideas as best we could through Huaong as we ate. It was a great opportunity to talk at some length with the other men in the CP group. I had gotten to a good personal connection with Goss. We completely understood and appreciated each other. Doc was a Conscientious Objector, which meant that he did not have to carry a weapon, but could serve as a Medic. He had wonderful insight into alternative thinking for the resolution of disagreements, versus killing someone who thinks or wants something different. He was a true pacifist.

Besides working hard all day and night to keep each other alive, we were getting to know each other. As good as it felt to grow connections with these men, having lost guys I had let in, I was sadly wary of putting my heart out there.

The whole company was dispersed all around the hamlet that night which passed without incident, save one for me.

For sleep, we moved outside the huts to be in defendable positions within the hamlet. I took the first watch as my other RTO caught some shut eye time. As the Command Team RTO's we would run all night series of Situation Reports (Sit-Rips) by radio to the platoons and squads throughout our deployment. Every few minutes we would call and they would respond. It was a way to ensure a part of every element of the company was always awake and on watch. Likewise, we got regular Sit-Rep calls from Battalion all night. All that activity along with a sense of responsibility kept me upright and functioning through those dark hours. This night I woke my partner around four in order to catch some shut eye. I awoke before dawn lying on my left side on the dry earth. I was nicely warm on my backside. Once fully awake I came to find that a large pig had lain down behind and up against me. *OK, I hear your jokes.*

Chapter Twelve / We Move (Again)

Early in November word came that we were moving again. We would leave scenic Dong Tam and move into Rach Kien, a village roughly twenty miles south and west of Saigon.

The army had apparently bought half of the village a year or two before. It was a real lash up mix of vintage Vietnamese brick and mortar houses and small business buildings with a few scattered wooden military bunkered buildings built by the Army Engineers. The long term plan was to raise all the old buildings, but that would be a year or two in the making. The unit based there ahead of us had sand bagged and bunkered the existing old buildings to make them reasonably safe in the event of incoming rockets or small arms fire.

Charlie Company had the western most end of the US part of Rach Kien. On the other side of a Security Check Point Gate was an ARVN compound and beyond that the civilian section of the village.

Many of the locals worked during the day throughout our battalion areas. The workers were issued ID cards. At the Check Point they were fully frisked, and bags checked before entering or leaving the US section.

It was a refreshing change to have what had been an eight room home suddenly become our barracks. Understand there was no glass in the windows, but only two or three of us to a room and to a degree it felt very unarmy like.

The first night was bizarre. We got there as darkness was setting in. As we were assigned to our sleeping quarters, we went in to claim our spaces. We weren't in our house more than minutes when we had a couple of Vietnamese guys with air mattresses and a couple of pretty Vietnamese girls trying to entice us into "shortiming" them for five dollars right there on the floor. They did not belong inside our compound and certainly not to solicit prostitution. They presented a security and therefore a safety breach. We gathered them up and took them right to the check point and let the MP's deal with them.

Apparently things had been loose around the former unit and this was a common practice. We were men and we were hungry, but we were not stupid.

We fell into a couple of weeks of routine operations with, I am happy to write, few calamities. We radio carriers were in our usual rotation of going out every other mission. Captain Goss was in the process of moving on as he was getting promoted to Major. We were happy for him but, selfishly, not so for ourselves. We kept our feelings within our tight circle.

I went out on a mission with his replacement and knew all day into our deployment for an overnight that this guy really did not know what he was doing. I was relieved to see the sunrise and later to hear the inbound flight of Hueys coming in to return us to Rach Kien.

The following day, December 6, 1968, I awoke remembering that my brother Jim's son John was one year old. I recalled how one year earlier I had managed to get to an outdoor phone booth in a downpour at Fort Benning that night to call Jim with my congratulations for becoming a father. There would be no phone call possible for his first birthday, but my nephew, my bother and his wife Sue were in my heart that morning.

It was my turn to stay in and my friend and fellow RTO, Norm Prance was going out. Captain, now Major Goss had decided to go out with Charlie Company one more time to aid in the transfer of command as he wasn't comfortable with his replacement.

When the company was out there were always two radios on speakers in the Charlie Orderly room. One was monitoring the Charlie Command push, the other the Battalion Command push. Top had had special antennas rigged so that we could receive even far off transmissions from the field. We wanted to know at all times as much as we could about what was going on with our men. Plus on the Charlie Company push information could readily be transmitted to or from the field for supplies or logistics.

I had agreed to accompany my friend (our former Third Platoon Leader), Lieutenant Bob Cooper, who was now the Head of S-5 (Civil Affairs) on a little pacification visit to a nearby hamlet. I had obtained a military Drivers License and therefore was a legal jeep driver when necessary. I went down to the Tactical Operations Center where the S-5 office was to meet up with Lt. Cooper. All the battalion jeeps had radios on them so I would be able to keep an ear on Charlie Company no matter where Cooper wanted to go.

I checked in with Lt. Cooper and then ran the jeep down to S-4 (Supply) and loaded it with fuel. It was the ultimate in self serve. There were these large black bladders lying on the ground that were flown in by big Chinook, or Skycrane helicopters. Some were marked Diesel and others Gasoline. When you say pump gas, in this case that is exactly what you did. It was literally a hand pump. I loaded the jeep tank and the spare 5 gallon strapped to the back. We may get a flat tire, get hit by an ambush, but one thing I was certain of, we would not run out of gas.

It was a pretty sunlit day. Lt. Cooper met with some village leaders and everything I'd monitored on the radio lead me to believe that Charlie Company was out on what seemed a routine patrol. I was enjoying driving Uncle Sam's convertible out with Bob Cooper. It was mid afternoon and we were headed back towards Rach Kien.

Chapter Thirteen / NO!

Suddenly Norm Prance's voice came over the radio. The company was pinned down by enemy weapons fire. I snapped a look over at Cooper and he reached behind me and turned up the radio. My heart began pounding. Next I heard from the radio… not a voice but, for a few seconds, the sounds around Norm…sounds I knew all too well…rifles firing, men shouting and then Norm bringing the handset to his mouth and in a breathy, strong voice said, "Charlie Six is KIA". "NO" I screamed. "This isn't fair…this isn't fair!" I was sobbing uncontrollably. "Not Warren Goss" I screamed through my tears. "He wasn't supposed to be out anymore!" Cooper yelled at me to pull over. Through my tears and upset I realized I was driving wildly and way too fast for the conditions. I regained some control and assured Cooper that I'd be OK behind the wheel.

I felt terrible in so many ways all at once. The loss of Warren Goss was devastating to me. I loved him, knew he had so much to give in the years to come. I felt so bad for Norm having to experience Goss's death so horrifically. *It was not a conscious awareness on my part at the time, but I found later that I carried a sense of guilt that I wasn't the one out with Goss that day.*

Fighting tears and listening to the follow up radio transmissions I drove fast, but in reasonable control until we reached the Battalion TOC, parked the jeep and went inside and just stood in the TOC staring blankly at the room. TOP was in there. We said nothing because the tears in our eyes said it all. The TOC guys knew I was Goss's RTO and let me be. I was sore inside…empty…I was in the room, but out of phase with everything and everybody around me. I'm not sure how much time passed…minutes, half an hour…I don't know. I walked out of the TOC and found that I'd parked the jeep rather poorly, saw that my M-16 was still on the floor next to the driver's seat, (*a no-no, you never leave your weapon like that*), I picked it up and started walking towards Charlie Company area. If I could remember what happened the rest of that night, I'd write it here.

When I woke up the next morning Norm was across from me in his bunk asleep. I looked at him long and hard. I prayed in silence.

The Memorial service for Major Goss was the following day in the Battalion Chapel. Norm had been quiet and was sleeping a lot. I gave him space to just be.

As one of his RTO's I agreed to hold the American Flag throughout the service at the front. I decided to audio record the entire service on my reel to reel tape machine. I secured a new set of eight D cell batteries from our S-4 and took my recorder over to the Chapel to assess things and get set up. There was a podium so I taped both microphones in there table top stands to the podium, secured the wires down the podium stand and back to where I had the recorder sitting. I wanted everything neat, orderly tied down without a chance of getting messed up. I was recording in stereo and it would be around for posterity for ever. I connected the output of my tape recorder to an amplifier in the chapel which fed speakers outside so that the many dozens of guys in Charlie Company who couldn't squeeze inside would be able to hear the service. Attending was voluntary. Many guys in the Battalion outside of Charlie Company who knew Goss also showed up.

The service was short. The producer in me wanted it to be more than it was, but in retrospect it was perfect. Throughout the ceremony, the artillery battery directly across the dirt road we called Main Street, had a fire mission in support of one our units actively in combat. The Battalion Commander flew back from that ongoing enemy contact long enough to say some personal words for his friend. After a three gun salute, the Chaplain said one more prayer for the survivors and it was over. The chapel was shrouded in silence as everyone quietly walked out.

Norm missed the whole thing and was sleeping when I returned to our room with my tape machine. I played the tape for him and he began to open up a bit and talk.

The weeks that followed leading up to the holidays were a blur of in one night, on patrol the next. There were minor skirmishes, fortunately without much consequence as I remember. I had reasonable opportunities to get caught up on my Vietnam Periodical tapes.

I caught Joey Bishop during a USO tour in Rach Kien. He was kind and took a few minutes off stage and recorded an interview with me for Vietnam Periodical.

Chapter Fourteen / The "Holidays" in Vietnam

Not two weeks after our loss of Warren Goss, Norm and I drew lucky straws to go to Dong Tam for Bob Hope's big show being recorded for his Holiday with the Troops special for NBC. The headliner with Hope was Anne Margaret.

The Army had built sort of an outdoor amphitheater in the southeast corner of Dong Tam right next to the Mekong River. I would guess there were maybe ten thousand of us there to yell, scream, laugh and, for those precious two hours, forget where the hell we were.

My seat was in a perfect location for my TV production head. I could watch the on stage show and see what the crew was doing just to pull off the production. I knew these were the best Hollywood had for such ventures which made for a great experience of study and entertainment for me.

I had grown up watching Hope's Holiday shows for GI's around the world. I never missed one and now here I was a GI attending one. In my young little heart I pinched myself to realize where I was more than once.

Ten years later, working closely with Hope at CBS in Hollywood, I had the opportunity to thank him for coming and putting on our show in Dong Tam. He was humbled and appreciative of my thoughts and words.

Part of Hope's show was upstaged by the Viet Cong across the Mekong River who attempted to fire rockets at the show.

Helicopter light fire teams made short work of them and the show went on after that brief hiccup of intervention.

As I mentioned before, Rach Kien had a substantial civilian section west and south of our Charlie Company Security Checkpoint. Depending on intelligence reports, there were periods of days to weeks when the village would be on limits, meaning if we were off duty for a few hours we could wonder down there, buy a soda, meal, snack, or for some of the guys, sex. There was brothel-bar owned by a rather flagrant Vietnamese lady named Madame Phuc. Always smiling, warm and welcoming, the center of excitement, she was one of those characters you read about, but never come across in life.

Phuc's was the biggest house in the village. She had music, girls, a bar and a large indoor-out door open living room where the drinks and girls were handy and playful. You could go there and hang out as long as you kept buying beers and drinks. If you wanted more, well, that was a matter of negotiation between you and the shortime girl you were with. There was a separate building to act on the outcome of the "negotiation". Some guys were there every free moment they had. Others never saw the place.

Trucemas was announced just days before Christmas. The idiot, so-called Peace Talks going on in Paris that were supposedly going to draw up agreements to end the Vietnam War, did manage to come to one resolution, that there would be a twenty-four hour truce commencing at Midnight, Christmas Eve. It was never officially named Trucemas, but you know how creative service men can be with the obvious verbiage right in front of their eyes.

Christmas Eve day the village children were invited to a couple hours of fun, games, candy, ice cream and a fly in of Santa by helicopter, who along with his local "Elves" had a wrapped gift of some sort for each of the village kids. It was actually fun and gave a hint of family feeling to the day. I took random pictures. One of a little boy enjoying ice cream moved me because no matter who, where, or the conditions, kids are kids and they deserve to be happy.

That night at midnight "Main Street", the only road through the center of the US part of Rach Kien, came alive as all the GI's loaded up the street with colorful smoke bombs, purple, red, yellow as they yelled "Merry Christmas" and/or "Trucemas", sang Christmas songs at the top of their lungs as some others scattered throughout the compound were firing their M-16's loaded with red tracer rounds up in the air looking much like a red string fountain against the night sky. Out across the visible rice paddies the VC responded by firing their AK-47's in a like fashion up in the air creating a green flow of tracers. The stench of the smoke bombs lingered for some time as the combining cloud of colors blew its way in and around the buildings.

I had Charge of Quarters (CQ) for Charlie Company that night from Midnight to 06:00, so my time to be on duty certainly began with a bang, perhaps more like a series of bangs for about fifteen minutes. The celebrating took off a minute or two after I got to the Charlie Orderly room to relieve my predecessor. Not a minute passed and the ring down landline phone rang from the TOC wanting to know if there was a problem in our area. "No" I responded, "Just a little celebration for Trucemas". The voice at the other end said, "Carry on, but stay alert". I assured him we would.

The celebration demonstration lasted maybe ten minutes and then everyone retreated to their various hootches to continue in a variety of ways I didn't want to know about.

I had brought my music radio because AFVN had promoted playing Handel's Messiah beginning at 1am. I knew that by then there would be relative peace and quiet in order to enjoy it while maintaining my Watch responsibilities.

I got out my many scribbled notes and subject ideas for VIETNAM PERIODICAL. Having to be up all night at a desk and typewriter was a perfect time to write my ideas into scripts. At one o'clock I turned my radio up for the Handel concert.

About fifteen minutes into the Messiah, the Watch Commander for the night rolled up in his jeep. It was Delta Company's CO. He was a good guy, who stood around six feet five. He knew me from all the joint meetings with Captain Goss over the months. I offered him a soda, a comfortable chair and The Messiah. We sat there quietly listening for a quarter hour. He looked over at me said, "Thank you". "You are welcome, Sir and may the next holiday season be at home".

Chapter Fifteen / A Break

I had been in country now for more than half a year. Because of all the changes, moves, turn over of guys due to death, injuries, those going home, the constant new blood coming in to replace those who had left; all this mixed in with the mental and physical fatigue that continued to build each day. My first six months seemed to have both taken forever and gone by in flash.

The Pentagon set up a system for Rest & Recuperation (R&R), a concept that had been carried forward for members of the US Military since WW-II. The basic concept: to give members of the military some time away from a hostile environment to, as the name implies, provide time for the mind and body to rest and recuperate. In theory, it pays off returning an individual in an improved mental and physical condition in which to function better at waging war. During the Vietnam War after an initial period of six months of service in country, a member of the armed forces could apply for, and once approved, was provided an airline seat to and from the distant location. Once at the location all expenses were the responsibility of the individual.

It was time for me to put in for my R&R. This was a cherished week long break where you could put in to visit one of many tourist locations around the Far East and Hawaii. Bangkok, Tokyo, Sydney, Australia and Honolulu were among destinations offered. There were only so many allocated trips throughout a month and, if you were eligible, you could put in for a destination. The way it was set up you could enter any of these countries on the paper of an official US Military R&R, but they were limited in numbers per month per location. I wanted to go Sydney, but those R&Rs were taken, but I could go there on leave with a US Passport.

I did not have a Passport, but I could take a day and go to the US Embassy in Saigon and get one. Cool, I get to go see what Saigon is all about. The trip to Saigon fell together and I went with a few other guys from Charlie Company. It would take two days with one night in a Saigon hotel. An older Sergeant knew where we could get a room for the price of a carton of Salem cigarettes. At the PX a carton of Salems cost maybe two bucks. I frankly don't remember exactly, but it was truly peanuts. The carton would go into the dollar-a-pack black market on Saigon's streets where the mentholated cancer sticks were in demand. For that one night the dirty trade of Salems for a room worked for me.

The main road going into Saigon from where we were in Rach Kien was Highway 4. To get to it took about fifteen minutes going due North. The road was about a lane and a half wide. When dry, it was hard dirt and dusty if you were behind another vehicle. When wet, it was slippery mud.

For our sojourn the road was dry. There were rice paddies for parts of it and frequent small villages and hamlets. Our supply trucks drove the route to and from Saigon every day and never knew when they might get ambushed, or blown up by a mine buried in the road. Once on Hwy 4, it was two lanes and asphalt. On this very busy road we passed US military, South Vietnamese Army units, hundreds of civilian busses, motor bikes all being driven too fast and a vehicle called a Lambretta, which was like a three wheel motorcycle only it had a minibus body on it inside of which were sometimes as many as eight or more Vietnamese crammed in like sardines. These damn things putt-putted along looking like they would tip over. Most of the vehicles burned kerosene in their diesel engines making for a lot of dirty, black smoke everywhere.

What the Hell, this was a day away with new sights...oops, about half way on Hwy 4, not a mile off to our left a US unit in a rice paddy was in contact with VC and getting helicopter gunship

96

support. We could both see and hear the on-going combat. We and everybody else on the Highway sped up.

As we got to the outskirts of Saigon the traffic thickened. We passed more and more buildings. On our right I saw the many transmission towers in the heavily secured communication center of Military Assistance Command Vietnam (MACV). It was the direct link for US Forces back to The Pentagon. I wanted to stop and call home. So did the other half a million of us.

As we got into Saigon it was obvious how much of an influence the French had left behind. There were roads, but more so; I was struck at the numerous long, very wide boulevards lined with trees among the buildings. Everywhere I looked there were blue and pale yellow vintage Renault taxis scurrying about with their passengers. People, lots of them in all sorts of attire going about their lives and work. For just a moment I had to think, where's the war…certainly not here, not to these people.

One of the guys knew of a steam bath on Tan Son Nuht Air Force Base. I was all for that after six months of bathing in the cold, rusty trickles of dirty water at our various company areas. There were plenty of steam baths throughout Saigon, but most, if not all were run by one of the Vietnamese mobs. There were too many stories of guys getting rolled, their money stolen and worse. All we wanted was a safe place to boil out the dirt of Vietnam for an hour, or two.

Following our "boil out", I was taken to the US Embassy to begin the process of getting my Passport. The Embassy was a very impressive place on Embassy Row, just down the boulevard from the Presidential Palace. Our Embassy had had a lot of damage during the Tet Offensive, but there was no evidence of it when I got there almost eleven months later.

Once past the MPs, I was directed to where I would begin the Passport process. A very attractive young American woman greeted me and gave me the form to fill out. How refreshing to see and talk with an *American* woman after nearly eleven months out in the Vietnamese jungle and villages. I hurried through the forms and walked back up to her. She asked if I had two identical photos of myself to which I answered no.

She told me there was a photo shop in a house within walking distance where they would take the picture and have the right size prints for me in minutes for just a few dollars. She gave me directions to the shop and added that I should be able to be back at the Embassy with the photos within an hour.

I thanked her and walked out of the Embassy following her directions. Within a few minutes on a side street I found this small gray house in front of which stood a small, hand painted sign "Pics for Passports". As I walked up on the porch to knock on the door, from inside a man's voice called out, "Come GI". Before I could reach for the door a small Vietnamese man in black silk pants and an oversized open collar dress shirt with the sleeves rolled up above his elbows opened the screen door smiling, bowing his head repeatedly he said, "I take Passport picture, give you two copies five minutes, five piasters".

I smiled, bowed my head and said, "yes". In what had been the living room of the older somewhat run down house, in front of the fireplace was a large white card for a background, a few feet from that an old, I guessed German camera on an older tripod. He pointed to the decrepit stool between the white card and the camera. I removed my military bush hat and sat down. Off of a table next to the camera he picked up a negative plate and shoved it in the camera. He then held his left hand up like you would to stop something and said, "still" and then pointed at the lens with his right hand and counted, "1, 2, 3", and then he clicked the lens open, still holding his left hand up in the stop position, I heard the lens snap closed and he dropped his stop left hand. He never took his eyes off of me. I got it that he'd done this a few ten thousand times.

Smiling and again bowing his head quickly, he said, "four minutes". He turned pulled the negative plate out of the camera and went in the next room behind a raggedy, black curtain.

Not knowing what to do, I just sat there on his little stool. I could hear things happening in the next room, but could not truly discern exactly what was happening. By my watch at almost exactly four minutes he reappeared with a still wet fully developed piece of photo paper with two images of my twenty-one year old mug.

He held them up for my approval. I shook my head yes and pulled out my wallet and got out the five Vietnamese Piasters and gave them to him. He put the money in his pocket, shook the water off the page of prints and handed it to me. Surprisingly the top where the pics were was almost dry. Thanks between us and I was out the door looking at them. They would surely work for a Passport picture, but they looked like they had been shot in 1869, not 1969. The vintage camera put a whole different look to it. In a quirky way I liked that.

I went back to the Embassy, made my way through Security and to my lady clerk friend. Seeing me with my oversized photo sheet, she laughed, "They always come back that way. No problem, I'll trim them…and look yours are dry already". "I waved them in the air as I walked back so they would get dry", I said to her.

She looked at my application and wrote in large red letters at the top, "Expedite, active soldier", looked up at me, smiled and told me to come back the next day to get it anytime after noon. I thanked her profusely and left. As I walked away a short thought crossed my mind to ask her to dinner, but then I thought in a thousand quick flashes how much I did not want the pangs of an impossible relationship at this point in my life. I was still hurting over Barbara, when I let myself feel it. I kept walking towards the exit.

I reunited with the other guys late in the afternoon and we went to this just above Flea Bag level hotel and checked in with my pay-in-advance carton of Salems.

We went up to our rooms with a plan to go eat in an hour. I entered my room which consisted of a rather large, stark room, ten foot ceiling, a double bed, a bare table and chair and a bathroom, also of good size, a shower and a toilet! You don't realize how wonderful a flushing toilet is until you spend nearly seven months without one. No dirt, no sand bags to squat over the stench and efforts of the last fifty guys while you try to do yours. Just sit down on a nice, clean seat. Do your business and then reach around and pull that beautiful handle and FLUSH…it's all gone! Now that's luxury!

Out my open, large hotel windows three stories down was a busy street. I sat and watched the show. After living in the jungle and dodging every fatal device man could conceive of, this was better than a movie.

Looking at my watch I got up from my "movie" seat and went into the bath to brush my teeth at a real sink with running water. It was OK to brush my teeth with Saigon city water, but I knew not to drink it, rather to drink only bottled water.

There was a knock at the door just as I finished brushing. Two of the guys with me walked in, but one was dressed as a Lieutenant Colonel. He was the older Sergeant I mentioned earlier who knew about the hotel we were in. I had known him as an E-7 Master Sergeant, the head of Charlie Company's Mortar Platoon. He'd been in the service a long time and always had angles going on. I didn't care one way or the other about his deals and he knew it. He explained that he was a Lieutenant Colonel in the Army Reserves and would be seeing friends from his Reserve unit away from us after we ate dinner. He said he would appreciate it if I kept this under my hat. I said matter of factly, "sir, your business is your business and has nothing to do with me". He laughed and we left to meet everyone else.

Out after dark in the lights of the Saigon night was an adjustment. For the last seven months I had become conditioned to watching and listening defensively in a three hundred and sixty degree constant sweep of my immediate area, especially after dark. Here I was out and about walking down the street like it was no big deal. It was. My heart was racing. I was excited to see the lights, cars and people and fighting my acquired fear that danger was about to come from any direction. It looked like a busy city going about its normal early evening's business, but this was Saigon at the height of the Vietnam War and yes, we were carrying our weapons.

It was less than a ten minute walk to our restaurant, which turned out to be a Vietnamese run mix of French-Italian cuisine. It was obvious that the multi-generation run establishment had been there for some time. The smells as we entered told me immediately that this would be a good sit down dinner no matter what I ordered. There was an obvious pride exhibited by everyone who worked there. They spoke fluid English with us and a mixture of French and Vietnamese among themselves. White linen on the tables, a lit candle in the middle with linen napkins and nice stainless completed the individual settings. The recorded music playing at a comfortable background level was a mix of French and Italian.

I was pleased to read the menu and find that the prices ranged from affordable for me to very expensive. The clientele around us was a mix of middle class working civilians comprised of Americans and Vietnamese along with Military of the same origins from the various services. In jungle fatigues, we were obviously the out-of-towners in that setting, but no one seemed to notice. The other military wore holstered weaponry, where as we had our M-16's leaned up against the table right next to us, with the exception of our Lieutenant Colonel for the night who wore a shoulder holstered 45.

I enjoyed an absolutely splendid hand made pizza with a small side of spaghetti and an American can of coke. (Coke had a Saigon bottling plant, but not canning. We had been warned by the Army to stick to the US version).

After dinner everyone else was going out on the town. Not this boy, I headed back to my third floor room to have some quiet time, watch my live "movie" out my windows, take another long, hot shower and go to bed between sheets, (what a concept).

I awoke the next morning and took yet another long, hot shower knowing it would be my last for weeks, if not months. I got dressed and went downstairs checked out and then partially footed and then taxied my way back towards the US Embassy. The guys had agreed to pick me up there shortly after noon.

On the way I came across a French-Vietnamese bakery. Entering, I was overtaken by the wonderful smells of all the baked goods and pastries. I bought some croissants, some amazing pastries and a cup of coffee. It took two trips to carry it all to a small, round table outside among probably a dozen others like it all surrounded by a low black iron fence…very French like. I knew I was not too far from the Embassy and Embassy Row based on the clientele and those walking by on the sidewalk. Checking my watch I had plenty of time to enjoy the sights and the abundant amount of carbohydrates I had purchased.

In that part of Saigon there were few, if any jungle fatigued out-of-towners shouldering M-16s like me to be seen. Lots of men in suits, with and without ties, non Vietnamese ladies were dressed for the office. The military folks were in starched, non combat uniforms, if not in full dress uniforms representing whatever service they were in. Everyone in uniform had a holstered weapon. The Tet Offensive less than a year prior had taught them a hard lesson; always have a weapon on you. Many died because they were not armed and therefore unable to defend themselves or others with them.

My 150 pound, six foot tall self finished the last of my splendid thousand calorie breakfast of croissants, pastries and coffee. I then waddled the rest of the way to the Embassy.

I arrived around a quarter to twelve and made my way through Security and back to see my lady clerk friend who had been so helpful the day before. There were two people ahead of me, but when she saw me she looked me right in the eye, winked, waved and held up one finger "I'll be with you in a minute", with a smile. I smiled right back and thought to myself, "Hey, Dumbo, you missed an opportunity yesterday/last night".

She turned the two waitees ahead me over to someone else and then, still smiling at me, motioned me to an isolated part of the counter. As she walked she picked up what turned out to be my file and completed Passport. I followed like a good dog.

"Well, Mr. Breidenbach, (she said it right) what part of The Queen City did you grow up in?" "Walnut Hills-Hyde Park", I answered without pausing, but then added, "You know Cincinnati?" "No, but another lady here is from there so I asked her if she knew you or your family". "Turns out she doesn't, but then she told me to surprise you by knowing the nick name". "Well you did and that was very sweet of you", said I.

We both stopped, still smiling, looking straight into each other's eyes. She's very pretty I thought, still sharing our eyes. I stumbled verbally, " I, I messed up yesterday". She wanted to know why and I told her that I had had the thought to ask her to supper, ice cream, anything, but didn't because I was a combat soldier and would have virtually no chance to see her again after getting my Passport.

She smiled, reached across the counter and laid her hand on mine. "Bless you for what you're doing and please be safe", still looking into my eyes, she verbally stumbled and tried to say, "Yes, that's what I would have said, yes… (long pause)…yes". Slowly she withdrew her hand and picked up my file. The whole time we remained locked on and in each other's eyes. She told me my Passport was ready. All I had to do was sign it and the filing papers to indicate that I had received it. She handed me a pen and I scribbled my signature where appropriate.

I told her that I was being picked up outside in minutes and had to get back to my unit down in the Delta. "Back to the war", she mumbled, still looking in my eyes. Nervously I shook my head yes. Another long pause…she reached up and touched her right finger tips to my cheek softly, but quickly, "be safe Peter Breidenbach". She broke our look and backed away from the counter. "Thank you. You too", said I. One more shared look and reluctantly I walked away not knowing what else to do. That hurt so much I couldn't bring myself to take one look back at her. I went outside saw my buddies waiting in their jeeps and we were off to get back to Rach Kien before it got dark.

If you're wondering if I ever did get her name, the answer is no. That remains an oddity as all my life I've been the guy who wants to know the names of people with whom I speak. She and I made a fast, extremely deep connection to the depths of our beings and then gone. I had a name in my "I hurt" department; Barbara. At that point it was nearly twenty months since she'd called it off and I was still too raw in that part of me to add to it. In the case of my Embassy lady, she was easier to let go.

The drive back to Rach Kien went without incident. My friends all had hangovers and looked a little beat up from their night. The Lieutenant Colonel was a Sergeant E-7 again.

As we drove the reality of the combat zone we really lived in closed in on all of us. The Sun was setting, leading to darkness and we were still driving. We entered the Rach Kien North Gate Security Point at dusk. Once again covered in dust and dirt from the road, that wonderful CLEAN experience I had just hours before in Saigon was nothing more than a faded memory, more surreal than real.

I checked back in at the Charlie Company Orderly Room to find out, no surprise, that we had an operation at first light and I was up to go out. I sat down and immediately wrote up my request for a Leave to Australia, checked the "Yes" box where it asked if I had a current Passport, signed it and dropped it in the correct box knowing that for that I had Seniority in the company and that I would get notice on it in days, not weeks.

I went to my hooch to check and prepare my gear. I filled my four canteens with water, loaded two olive green socks with canned fruit and tied them to my radio pack frame, put a fresh battery in my radio and did a Como check with the Battalion then turned it off. Next, I secured and tied two new, extra batteries under the radio and checked the condition of my long and short antennas. I took the heavy plastic bag that the new radio battery had been in and put it over the handset and sealed it. I got my double headset out of my locker and connected it to the radio. It was large and heavy, but having it straddling the front of my helmet, with the headphone hanging over immediately above my ears on each side allowed me to hear every radio call to and from the Battalion which enabled me to keep my CO apprised of situations near and around us at all times. My insistence to get the headphones and use them that way saved lives. Their extra weight on my helmet and liner bouncing up and down on my head all day and night definitely put a crunch in the vertebrae of my neck, but hearing those radio calls was crucial.

Chapter Sixteen / Back to War

Somewhere in this time period we had a horrendous overnight securing a hamlet somewhere in the Mekong Delta. Our latest Commander, whose name I don't remember, (and it's a damn good thing I don't), had the company poorly deployed considering the layout of the terrain and the pattern of the buildings. I'm not trained in such matters but after seven months on line setting up five and six nights out of every seven, you get the idea of what's safe and what is not. On this one night, the company was dangerously vulnerable from more than one angle of approach the minute we set up. (Combat Think, if you will, teaches that it is imperative to always be concerned about potential avenues of approach by an adversary, as well as your own avenues of escape from a location).

Here we were, the Company Command group literally out in the open and as vulnerable as we could be short of setting up immediately in front of an enemy bunker. I made up my mind that I would spend the night sitting up, wide awake, with my back against a solid object so as not to get shot in the back. That left me only three directions to watch for approaching trouble all night. Our deployment was deplorable.

First Platoon got hit hard by RPG's (Rocket Propelled Grenades) and small arms fire around 03:00 hours. Three guys were KIA and another four were wounded. They should not have been placed where they were. The Viet Cong that hit them disappeared into the night and though attempts were made to pursue them, it was fruitless. They had obviously planned a hit and run. In the confusion, darkness and the efforts to come to the aid of the men who were hit the two or three VC got a way.

There was an unusual occurrence for my company at first light. A squad from First Platoon went over to do a sweep of the hamlet next to where we were about a half mile away. They were searching for signs that VC had stayed there recently. After about fifteen minutes, as they were returning I noticed a lot of smoke rising on the horizon in the direction from which the squad had returned. It wound up that a great deal of that hamlet burned to the ground. Our acting Commander said and did nothing about it.

I fault myself and everyone else for not reporting the incident. It was wrong. I do not know the particulars beyond what I have written here, but like me, I am sure you can read between the lines.

That hamlet incident would not have occurred with our late Captain Goss in command. More importantly, the company would not have been deployed so vulnerably as to create the opportunity for the attack that befell the First Platoon at 03:00 hours.

Chapter Seventeen / R & R

My Australian Leave papers arrived and I was on my way to the Rest & Recuperation Center at Tan Son Nuht Air Force Base.

The way the process was set up Leave papers meant that you were then eligible to be at the R&R Center to, in my case, wait for a slot to Australia to open up due to a no show by an individual who had an R&R for there. If, after waiting a day, at most two, no slots opened up, then you could get on the list for another destination. Australia was a popular choice for Americans, but most of the slots were taken because the Australians who were serving in Vietnam would apply for the R&R's in order to go home for five days to a week. There were no R&R's to the States because it was too far and took too long for the transit time alone. There was a concern that many would go Absent Without Leave (AWOL) and not return to Vietnam. There were R&R's to Hawaii for married men only so that they could meet their wives from the States. The cost of the wives travel was on the couple and not the military, but many of the airlines offered reduced fares in that circumstance.

My second choice was Tokyo. A slot opened right away and I was out of there.

Once we were off the chartered 707 at an Air Force Base in Japan we were bused to the R&R Center for an hour of: Welcome to Japan; here are the guidelines for visiting in Japan plus valuable information on where to go, where to stay and more. I chose Tokyo and learned that Tokyo at night in 1969 was a dress up affair. For this they had a rental center where one could rent dress shirts, ties slacks, sport coats, suits and dress shoes. Coming from the infantry in Vietnam I had none of that. (My dress clothes were home in Cincinnati waiting for me).

I wasn't too keen on renting, but decided to look and then decide. To my surprise the selection was of good quality, in like new condition, in my sizes for all of it, and best of all affordable. They even provided a good wardrobe bag to transport it.

I chose to stay at The New Otani Hotel in Tokyo. Located near the center of the city, it's just minutes from The Imperial Palace, The Ginza, Tokyo Tower and many other great places to go. The hotel is on the grounds of a very large, beautifully maintained four hundred year old Japanese Garden.

I should point out that I went there in January, 1969. The value of the American Dollar versus the Japanese Yen was amazing. It was only twenty years since the complete rebuilding of Japan following the massive destruction incurred during WW-II.

As my cab drove up to the New Otani I was pleased to find that it was as opulent as I hoped. After seven months in the filth, mud, dust, dirt, cold-rusty, trickling water attempts at bathing every few days, I was ready for five days close to anything called luxury.

I checked in and went up to my room. Not sure what to tip the Bellman, I give him in Yen what equaled an American dollar, he about fell over himself with appreciation. I thought I'd better sit down and figure out in my head an easy way to convert mentally what I was spending before I spent it. I was beginning to get to that when there was a knock at my room door. I wasn't expecting anyone, hell, at that time in my life I knew no one in Tokyo.

Opening the door I was flabbergasted to find three, beautiful, tastefully dressed Japanese women standing there. A fourth woman stepped in front of them and speaking in perfect English asked if they could come in for a moment. They did not look or act like hookers. In fact quite the opposite so I welcomed them in.

I was introduced to each of them by the lady who spoke first. She explained they were tour guides to help me see Tokyo, they spoke perfect English and anyone of them would be happy to show me around. I asked what the charges would be and was told as long as I covered out of pocket expenses during the excursions, there would be no charge.

I thought there had to be a catch somewhere, but what the heck; I'll take it one step at a time. One of the ladies seemed more refined than the others and I went up to her and asked if she would show me some of the nicer places starting with a fine restaurant that night for dinner. The other ladies interrupted long enough to wish me a good evening and departed.

Her name: Sumiko, which means, child of clarity. I would find it to be an appropriate name for her.

After they left, I went on to suggest a low key place where it was possible to converse, enjoy a good Japanese cuisine along with some quiet, but good music. She asked if I dressed up when dining out. I replied that I did and she let me know she knew the perfect place and would make us a reservation. We agreed on a time when we would meet in the lobby and begin our evening.

I know what I'm about to present will seem hard to believe and you are welcome take the info and do whatever you want with it.

I assumed prostitution fell into this equation somehow, I didn't get it yet. I was happy to have apparently met an intelligent, refined young woman with whom I could spend the evening sharing a pleasant time. That's all I wanted. I was starved for some female companionship, some conversation.

Any coupling would come out of mutual interest, not out of payment for services. My head and heart were too sore for that.

I had a couple hours to get unpacked and get my things organized for the week.

I wanted to call my parents in Cincinnati. It would be the first opportunity to have a conversation since calling them on a pay phone from Oakland Army Terminal the night before I left for Vietnam. It was great to hear them like they were across town, not across the Pacific. We caught up on family and each other. I didn't want to end the call, but we found a good getting off place and hung up.

I took an extremely long, hot shower, shaved and got ready for my evening out with Sumiko.

It felt so good to be in a suit and tie. The entire ensemble fit as if it was mine, and the quality matched my taste as well. You might say that I felt like me for the first time since Cincinnati before shipping out to Vietnam seven months before.

She was waiting in the lobby when I walked from the elevator. She was prettier than I remembered. She too had changed for the evening looking as refined as she had earlier. I walked up stopped in front of her, smiled and bowed. She smiled and returned my bow and then asked where I learned my Japanese greeting custom. In San Francisco I told her. She laughed, (but not the nervous Japanese giggle we've all seen in all too many movies).

I complimented her on how beautiful she looked. She took my arm, we walked outside and the Doorman signaled for a taxi.

The evening panned out nicely. She had made reservations at the best Japanese Traditional Steak house in Tokyo. The drive from the New Otani down Chao Dori, the main boulevard through The

Ginza was most impressive. An amazing display of lights and large buildings as impressive as New York's Times Square. We turned off Chao Dori and within a few blocks the taxi pulled up in front of our restaurant. A door man opened the door and once we had exited the vehicle, showed us the way to the entry which led to stairs to a second floor greeting area where our reservations were checked. We were led to a place to check our shoes and then directed to a wide, carpeted tunnel through which we crawled on all fours for about fifteen feet passing some others who were laughing as they departed.

The end of the tunnel opened into a beautiful, large room finished in a very traditional old world Japanese décor. We were immediately immersed in a potpourri of wonderful, smells of the various Japanese dishes being prepared at each table. The tables were at floor level with a very wide path down the middle of the rectangular shaped room. There were private rooms leading off the main room. Every table was surrounded with patrons on their floor pillows actively enjoying their time. At the end of the room opposite the entry was a small stage about a foot off the floor. Sitting crossed legged in the middle of the stage, a young woman in a magnificent period costume was playing a string instrument. The entire staff wore traditional Japanese outfits. Tables were large with preparation and cooking areas each one at a different stage of dinner.

We were led to our table where we were greeted by our hostess. We arranged our pillows and sat crossed legged next to each other across from her. The hostess was very sweet, spoke no English, so Sumiko kept the dialogue moving along.

As we worked our way through the many, wonderful courses, there was what seemed a genuine interest between us about the other. She was in her third year of advanced studies of language arts. Born in post war Japan, she was around for the worst beginning stages of the rebuilding; she was too young to have much memory

113

of it. Her parents met trying to put their lives together. Her father was a medical technician and her mother a nurse.

I chose not to ask about the escort work out of which we had just met. I would leave that to her to discuss voluntarily.

I told her about growing up in Cincinnati, my television and radio work and having no real choice about being, or not being in Vietnam. I did not speak about Vietnam and she did not ask.

The evening was as I hoped filled with interesting experiences of Japanese cuisine, entertainment and warm, friendly company.

She was pleasantly surprised that beyond a small glass of wine while we dined, I drank only tea and water. She noted that, to her experience through out her life, that most men, no matter the nationality, became intoxicated when out for the evening. She said that Japanese businessmen were particularly inclined to over imbibe socially.

Sumiko filled me in on some things to do in Tokyo as we taxied our way back to the New Otani. It was obvious that we had enjoyed each other's company throughout the evening. I asked her to ask the driver to pull over for a moment before getting to the Otani Entrance.

I put into words my appreciation of her and her company for the evening. I told her that, if she was interested, I would like to see her again. Day, night, or both, I was up for any and all of it. She said she too would like to share more time together. She had classes over the following couple of days, but would have some afternoons and some evenings free and would leave me a message with the Front Desk the following day regarding her availability. I told her that would be fine and that I looked forward to hearing from her and more so, to seeing her gain. We had the driver pull up to the Otani Entrance. He told me what I owed and I gave him four times that, turned to her and told her he had been paid to take her home. We looked at each other, she touched my cheek warmly and I squeezed her other hand, which I was already holding. I slowly pulled way, the Doorman opened the door, I stepped out, still looking at her I bowed slightly, she smiled and tilted her head in return.

I stood and watched the taxi drive away. I waved and she waved back in the rear window.

It felt good to feel so good, if only for this brief moment's break in my twelve months of Vietnam.

I went in and up to my room. I had sent every piece of clothing I hadn't worn that night to the hotel cleaners. I was pleased to find it all beautifully cleaned and already waiting in the closet and on the dresser. The Otani was living up to its reputation as a high end hotel.

The hotel is on a hilltop and from my room on the eleventh floor; I had a beautiful view over quite a bit of Tokyo. Below me on the extended grounds of the hotel I could see part of a famous four hundred year old Japanese garden and I promised myself I would venture into it the following day. It had been a good, but long day and I went to bed.

Being January, it was considerably cooler than what I had left in Vietnam. Fortunately I was ready with daytime and evening attire suitable for the conditions.

The remainder of my visit to Tokyo was a potpourri of trips around town to include: a visit to Tokyo Tower where, on the Observation Deck I met several groups of Japanese school kids who wanted to try their English out on me as we shared some funny moments; a couple of late nights to the Roppongi District for great jazz; some on foot day trips into interesting, off beat areas where they only spoke Japanese and tourists just did not go, but in which I thrived.

I saw Sumiko one more time. We went to an early dinner and a wonderful all Bach concert at the Nessei Theater. It was a very good evening we shared and it was nice we both could have pleasant memories of our two nights out together. There were reasons to consider pursuing an on-going relationship with Sumiko, and there were even more reasons not to. The foremost reason to forego a connection was that I did not want to be back in the war zone with my heart panging away over her, or anyone else. In the seven months I had been in Vietnam I had seen too many guys fall apart over relationship problems with wives and girlfriends. I was only twenty-one, immature in the relationship department and I knew it.

All through my trip to Japan I packed away mental notes that would make good material for my Vietnam Periodical series. It all boiled down to the break the R&R gave me from the stress of being on guard 24/7. It was too little time to truly relax back into a non war daily life, but it served one valuable service for me and that was knowing that if I was fortunate to live through the next five months in Vietnam, I would be able to once again live my life away from the stress of being on guard for my life 24/7.

Chapter Eighteen / Back to Combat

I got back to Vietnam, Rach Kien and Charlie Company without incident from my R&R. But I arrived to major devastation within my company. While I was away the company was ambushed and, except for my close friend and fellow radio operator, Norm Prance, the Command Group was wiped out. In all seven members of Charlie Company were killed.

Due to the circumstances when the ambush occurred, and in order to save lives, Norm initiated actions that resulted in the redeployment of the company, the demise of the enemy and source of the hostile fire, thus preventing further losses for the company. For those vital moments he acted as a commander.

Because of his expedient and accurate reaction and actions with respect to the immediate hostilities and the subsequent saving of American life, the next day Norm was promoted to the rank of Sergeant, E-5 and was personally given The Silver Star for Heroism by Ninth Infantry Division Assistant Commander, General William R. Kraft.

All this had taken place four days before I got back. Prance had already moved out of our room in the hooch and moved down to Headquarters Company where he was now billeted. He had been moved to serve in the Battalion Tactical Operations Center (TOC) as a Duty Sergeant, a perfect and logical move due to his understanding and experience in the field.

I went to find him and to see how he was doing after all that he had been through. When I got to the TOC he was in the middle of a conversation with the Battalion Commander, so I backed off a bit until they were finished. As the Colonel walked away from Prance, I exchanged greetings with him and proceeded towards Norm. We shared a very quick, but meaningful hug. He explained that we'd have to talk later as he had a lot to do right then. I too had to get right back to the company as we were being sent out for the first time since the disaster of four days prior. Norm and I would find our time. It was important that we had reconnected face to face, if only for that moment.

Back only two hours from my Japan sojourn, I hadn't unpacked but was at the hooch prepping my radio and packing for the new mission. TOP Sergeant George wanted me to go out. Being the Senior RTO, he wanted me to be out with the new Company Commander on his first mission along with the rest of the new Command Group.

Japan was already a foggy, was it real, vague, distant memory in my mind. I went through my prep and packing like some sort of automaton. I'd done it so many times over the months that I found myself consciously checking back in to where I was and what I should be doing.

I became emotional thinking of the men who had died while I was away. We had been through a lot together in a short time. It was not easy to contemplate they were dead.

My thoughts kept going to Norm and what he had gone through, and done, to prevent matters from getting worse only days before.

I knew that doing what we did out in the field always meant being very present, in the moment. In the infantry we were dependent upon each other to stay alive. In our position as the commander's RTO's, we were the company's connection to getting any and all support when disaster hit. Thinking and reacting correctly, in the "right now" moment saved lives and Norm had done that.

Now I had to go out with a totally green Commander, who I did not know. It would be incumbent for me to "tip toe through the tulips" learning his strong and weak points in lightening time. I would have to know if his decisions were sound for the safety of the company. If not, I got placed in a position of double jeopardy. Poor deployment decisions by him that I knew were potentially disastrous should be circumvented. If I were to take action contrary to an order from him, I could be Court Marshaled. If I didn't take the action, men could die.

I prayed for divine guidance…no, I really did pray. I prayed frequently in Vietnam…I remain thankful to this day for the direction and, I feel, the divine interventions that occasionally occurred. *Without the latter, I doubt I'd be around to write this.*

That initial mission was, I guess, a practice one. We were not sent into a known on-going hostile setting. Once back in Rach Kien, going to sleep that night, considering the attention given to us overhead by the Battalion Commander, Lieutenant Colonel Cutello, I got it that they wanted us to have time in the field to congeal as a unit before being subjected to the real tests of combat again. I was grateful for that, but as I lay there replaying the day in my mind it was obvious to me that our new Captain was not at the level we needed for optimum readiness. Knowing that and more, the feeling in my bones made for a sleepless night.

I got up the next morning having come to two conclusions: If I stayed on line, my chances of surviving for the next four and a half months were greatly diminished; my change to off line would have to be by a natural progression of circumstances and could not originate out of a manipulation on my part.

I decided to catch Norm before either of us was tied up with our duties for the day. I had another mission with Charlie Company with an estimated departure from the helipad at 10 Hundred hours. Having completely packed my gear, I took it to our Orderly Room dropping it off with Top in his office at 09 Hundred telling him I was running down to the TOC to get a map and that I'd be back in 30 minutes.

I found Norm just back from breakfast at the Mess Hall about to read some mail from home. Before I could say anything he asked about Charlie's new Commander (CO). I told him about the prior night and the many deficiencies in deployment and practices. He shook his head saying, "sounds like what we went through last week when you were in Japan".

This was our first private time to talk at any length since Norm had survived the massacre (my words) that had befallen him and the rest of the Charlie Command group. I asked how he was feeling. He smiled and shrugged it off. He wasn't going there verbally and I did not push him.

He went on to say they offered the job in the Battalion TOC and he took it without hesitation. He indicated that had they not taken him off line after that experience, he just may have disappeared as he had no intention of going back out on patrol. I echoed his feelings for I was now looking to find a place to serve my last four and a half months in country off line. He said he would let me know if anything opened up where he was.

I looked at my watch and said I'd talk with him later via the radio from the field. He shook his head and I left.

The operations were a bit intense over the following weeks as we went through the one year anniversary of the big Tet Offensive of a year earlier. Our entire battalion kept getting helicopter'd up to an area on the map known as The Plain of Reeds. This was on the NVA's many routes for troops, but even more, supplies to the Viet Cong in the South and the Mekong Delta. During the infamous Bombing Halt, the NVA moved tons of weapons, munitions, rice and other supplies quickly. We Americans can be dumb as a box of rocks at times. The Bombing Halt was a prime example of our stupidity. The Halt was not a military decision. We can thank the politicians for it and all the American lives that were lost subsequently because of it.

Chapter Nineteen / The Panic Palace

I was offered a job in the TOC early in March roughly six weeks after Norm moved there the end of January. Everybody working in the TOC had been on line and had a complete understanding of the immediacy of attention and action in support of units suddenly in combat. I found that I would relive a combat experience the second the radio would light up with the undeniable pitch of a voice under hostile fire. The adrenaline rush was the same for us, the only differences, we weren't actually under fire, and we had specific actions to take in order to get them the correct assistance in the shortest time.

Our list of responses included: Artillery fire support; helicopter gunship and light fire team support; moving in additional troops if we still had helicopter flight time; helicopter Med-i-vac Dustoff of the wounded; to name only four. Based on Situation Reports (Sit-Reps) from on the ground commanders, we could determine what would help them in the most expedient way. We had one primary rule: appropriate and fast. There were no set rules of *what* to provide. Due to our many months of field combat we were always anticipating and working ahead of their needs.

Not long after I started working in the TOC, Top Sergeant George from Charlie Company stopped by to see me. He wanted me to know that he had put me in for promotion to Sergeant E-5. At first I reacted weirdly to his thoughtful act. I knew that in a matter of months I would be out of the Army. I had never thought of myself as a "Sergeant" and in an embarrassed way told him so. He reasoned with me to say that I certainly had earned the rank over the previous nine months with my due diligence to service at all times. He added I get more pay as well. Grateful and humbled by his thoughts and words, I thanked him and accepted the raise in rank.

All during my year in Vietnam I had been saving what money I earned for two completely separate reasons. First, I would need to buy a car when I got back to Cincinnati. I knew with the pittance I was earning in the Army that my monthly pay could only add up to a reasonable down payment for a vehicle. During Basic Training back at Fort Benning I had signed up to buy a $25 Savings Bond every month which was automatically mailed to my parents address. The bonds were stacking up in my office/room at home and when the time came would be put towards a car.

My other reason for saving was to purchase the main components for a high end sound system. Due to the amazing exchange rate of the US Dollar versus the Japanese Yen at the time, combined with the US Military Pacific Exchange Service, thousands of dollars worth of very good Japanese audio gear could be obtained at a fraction of the market price. It could be shipped stateside without any Customs Duty or sales tax. I methodically chose and ordered each item throughout my year in Vietnam. Piece by piece over the fifty-two weeks, they arrived at my parent's and were safely stored in my room. My Christmas '68 would be celebrated in June '69, assuming I got through my year in "Fun City East". (*If not, then my brother would have one hell of an audio system*).

My radio series, Vietnam Periodical was being well received at home with many airing multiple times due to listener demands. Now that I was off line, for my few remaining months in country, the seven day a week noon to midnight schedule I was working made it easier to get them written, recorded and mailed in a timely manner.

Nine months on line and suddenly I was what we on liners called a Rear Echelon Mother Fucker (REMF). It was an entirely new perspective. I found that, as much as I had spent those nine months wanting to be one, I felt awkward about our men going out day and night with their lives in jeopardy. True, any of us on the ground in Vietnam were targets for the NVA and the VC, but my chances of survival were greatly improved being, as Prance and I were, in the embunkered Tactical Operations Center. I had to keep reminding myself that as veteran on liners, we were best suited to support our on line comrades. Sometimes my rationalization worked in my head, sometimes it did not. That's the fun of being one who gives a shit.

A common practice all of us sent to Vietnam had was to count the days left before we could get on our Freedom Bird and go home. Some counted every single day over their year. I decided when I first arrived in country that there was no point for me to do that. It was too depressing to compare my many days with the guys around me who were down to low double digits, or less.

As my remaining days were now down to two digit numbers I found, like many others, that I became increasingly more and more cautious about what I did, when, where and why. Hell, I had gotten this close to going home, I wasn't about to let my guard down.

The old "Situation Challenge" as I call it, often sticks it head into life at a time like this. I think it appears just to test us, (or get us killed if we happen to be in a combat zone).

My "Challenge" came when I had about fifty-five days left before going home. Colonel Cutelo's RTO, Jim, was going to be away for a few days. I walked right up to my commander and volunteered to fill in when ever needed. The Colonel thanked me and said we'd be flying the following day while Delta Company was on a ground operation. I had a love of flying and that part I looked forward to, but flying with him meant I would be out in the field with him. Command and Control helicopters were targets for the NVA and the VC. I had to be prepared to land and maneuver on the ground with him, should that become necessary. It went with the territory of being the Colonel's RTO. Recent operations for the Colonel had been almost entirely from the air, so, though I would be prepared to ground pound it, I felt I would spend the time flying and not walking.

Norm told me I was nuts to go flying and possibly find myself pounding the ground again so late in my year, and told me to "watch my ass".

While we did get assigned a full wing of Hueys to insert Delta Company where the Colonel wanted them to be, the Command and Control Huey assigned to that wing was grounded so we wound up with a four seater Hughes 500 LOH. That meant on board would be the Colonel, the battalion Artillery Officer, the pilot and me. A version of this bird still flies today. Pilots have described them as the Porsche of rotor wing aircraft.

My helicopter experience throughout my year had been hundreds of flights in Hueys going in and out of areas of operations and a few flights in the large Chinooks. This four seater LOH would be a whole new experience. Part of me was excited, the rest of me was dumbfounded that I wasn't scared to "test the fates" so close to going home.

Always wanting to be informed as much as possible, after prepping the radio and my backpack, I put my helmet on with headphones for the first time in two months. I was struck at how heavy the headgear was. I had worn it for nine months and never thought anything of it. All geared up, I went into the TOC to learn as much as possible about Delta's mission. The Colonel was surprised to see me studying the map of where we would be putting Delta when he came in the TOC. He then noticed I had complete combat RTO gear on, smiled and said, "Glad you're with me today, Sergeant. Let's go".

Room in the LOH was limited so I threw my radio backpack on the floor between my feet where I could control it, pulled the headphones off my helmet and put them on my head so I could be in sync with what was going on by hearing all the transmissions on the Battalion Push. I placed my helmet on top my radio. We landed two different times to talk directly with Delta's CO. I just put my head into serving the Colonel while keeping my awareness level high on a 360 degree angle. The second time we landed the LOH pilot left us for almost an hour as he went to refuel. I just hoped like Hell that he would not have a problem and leave us out for the night with Delta Company. The chances were fifty-fifty. Happily he did return to continue the day's work in the air and then dropped us back at Rach Kien at days end.

Duties in the TOC at night were a mix of prepping for the following days planned missions which took many forms. A constant activity was the updating the Area of Operations (AO) map with the locations of our units that were out as well as potential spots on the map where units might be inserted. Our AO map covered one whole wall. A smaller one on the long desk under the line up of two-way radios made for quick reference when talking on any of the five radios we used for: Logistics; Battalion Command; Brigade Command; Medi-i-Vac/Dust Off Control and the fifth for encrypted secure transmissions when needed.

Units that were out for the night were kept awake, on their toes and aware of their hostile surroundings with radio calls we made to each regularly throughout every hour. Being tired, dirty, on the hard ground in the dark after patrolling all day made it difficult for those guys in a Night Defensive Position (NDP) to stay awake, I knew, I'd been out there almost every night for nearly nine months. Keeping them awake would mean keeping them alive. An NDP found asleep by the NVA, or VC, would not see the Sunrise.

One night we had a non responsive NDP. After ten minutes of trying to raise them on the radio, I turned to our Artillery Sergeant, gave him the coordinates of their location and asked him for a "Celestial Wake Up Call". Smiling, he knew exactly what I wanted him to do.

The Artillery had what they called marking rounds. These were used periodically to set a point of detonation for High Explosive (HE) rounds. These rounds were composed of white phosphorus (WP) which, when it exploded overhead, did so in a blinding white flash of light. If the sleeping boys on the ground didn't have a heart attack when it detonated just one hundred feet over their heads, they were wondering how to get the shit out of their pants.

This was not an authorized way to wake up a position that had fallen asleep. In 1969, those WP rounds cost about $500 a piece. Having the artillery battery fire a gun would literally wake up damn near everyone in Rach Kien.

The Colonel came out of his quarters which were just behind the TOC and wanted to know why and what the artillery fired on. I told him the truth and he just looked at me for about ten seconds. I couldn't read his look, was he pissed, or what? Not breaking his look at me he uttered in a low tone, "don't make a habit of that, Sergeant". "Yes Sir", I replied and he went back to his quarters. That was the only time I did that in my three months in the TOC. Oh, that patrol NDP did stay awake the rest of the night!

Chapter Twenty / Another R & R?

I was now down to less than two months left in country. I was getting what we called very "Short" in time until going home. TOP Sergeant George came by the TOC and asked me if I wanted to take another R&R. He explained that they only got so many allocations per month and that if they weren't all used, the company would get less the following month. All the other eligible guys in the company had taken the rest, but one was left with no one back in the company to use it. He said it was to go to Tokyo. I had just been there in January and had had a wonderful time doing everything first class and I'd met Sumiko. I was now on a major spree of saving money for going home. But then I thought, what the Hell, I may not get another trip to Tokyo for a while; I thanked him and took the papers.

I had to be in Saigon at Tan Son Nhut for departure on April 30th. That was just five days away.

We got to the in-processing center in Japan to find out that they were not offering any services off the US Military Base as it was May 1st and that meant that the Red Guard would be holding mass demonstrations all over Japan that day and particularly in Tokyo where they could get the best Press coverage. No US Military would be allowed off US facilities in uniform. We would be permitted to go where ever we wanted on our own on paid public transportation, but they recommended we wait a day and offered billeting on the base.

I decided that I would make an adventure of it and get myself to Tokyo that day. Once again I rented good looking civilian clothing, cleaned up and got dressed in slacks, tie and a sport coat, grabbed my luggage and with hand written directions started walking off the base towards a railway station not far away.

I got to the train station and walked up to the ticket window. The ticket man smiled and bowed his head. I returned the bow and then said "Tokyo". He wrote some numbers on a piece of scrap paper along with the word "Yen". I shook my head "yes" and gave him that amount of Yen and he handed me a ticket printed in Japanese. I bowed and said, "thank you". He bowed in return.

From the ticket window there was a pedestrian bridge over the two train tracks. Several trains sped by in each direction without stopping. "Expresses" I guessed. I walked over the bridge to the other side and down to the trackside waiting area. The area was rural and beautiful. I was alone for a few minutes until a nice couple came across the bridge and joined me. I smiled a greeting, which they both returned. I reached in to my coat pocket and pulled out my ticket and said aloud, "Tokyo". The gentleman with concern on his face waved his hand back and forth indicating "No" and pointed to the track on the other side and then said "Tokyo" pointing in the other direction from what I had somehow assumed was the correct direction.

Shit! I was on the wrong side! I pantomimed a "Thank You" and ran like hell back up over the bridge and down to the other waiting platform. Damn good thing I did because not a minute after I got there here came a train and it was stopping.

My ticket was checked by a white gloved uniformed employee as I got on, so I knew I was on the right train. There was no where to sit down, but the car was not crowded. I put my luggage down and took hold of a train pole and got ready to ride. It was late afternoon and the train moved faster and smoother than I expected. It was not their famous Bullet Train, but a commuter that made more and more stops as we got closer to Tokyo and then went underground. We kept taking on passengers and nobody was getting off. I picked up my luggage to keep control of it. We were quickly becoming human sardines in a moving "can", if you will. The Public Address announcements for each station stop were in Japanese and one identifying word in English. I could hardly breath we were packed in so tightly. The scenes I had seen in news clips a few years before of the white gloved train conductors pushing people in to close the doors was, for now, my immediate reality.

Out of no where discernable a very tight fist hit me in the ribs. At first, I thought someone had lost their balance. But then I got hit again in another rib and this one was harder. Another hit came to my right shoulder. Had we not been "sardined" at the time I would have been knocked off balance by that hit. I got two more hits before I recognized the word "Ginza" from the Public Address system. I decided it was time to exit and the Ginza would be a location that once on the street I could taxi my way to a hotel. I plowed my way off the train taking yet another hit, this one in the stomach. Because I was moving that blow was diminished by being off angle. Now off the train I was in a sea of human movement towards up escalators. It took some time for my train had come in on the bottom of five levels of train tracks. I towered over almost everyone which was a help for my navigating, but it also made this very American looking Goy Boy an easy target for the Red Guard sympathizers to take a swing.

I got up to street level in time for the afternoon going home commuter foot and vehicle mass movement. I managed to acquire a cab quickly and told him to take me to the New Otani. I didn't have a reservation, but figured I'd be able to get a room. I was wrong. They were completely booked.

I had a list of hotels and wound up at a much smaller boutique hotel. It was fine with me as it was half the price of the Otani.

The week went by quickly. I did not see Sumiko. I had no phone number or any other way to reach her. That was OK with me.

We'd had our two pleasant nights out in January and they were enough.

I kept to myself during that visit to Tokyo. It was a very introspective week. My year in Vietnam was within mere weeks of being over. In a span of too few months' time so many good men had died. Men that I had come to know like Warren Goss, with whom I had shared many thoughts and feelings on life over the many hours of day and night we were together under some extremely dire situations. I was not surprised that Generals came to talk with him. He wasn't even thirty years old but lived and spoke with the insight of a weathered guru, yet his vernacular was comprehended by whomever he was addressing. He never talked down to anyone. He spoke to be understood and did so with respect. He may have been the Company Commander, but the respect he got was for his person, not for his rank.

I went to the top of Tokyo Tower to just stand and look as far away as I could. Several hours passed and in the distance where I had been looking Mount Fuji became faintly visible. My thoughts wandered a lot over those hours.

As I looked over the massive, active city of Tokyo I thought how much they had done in just twenty-four years. The city had been reduced to rubble in 1945. The war had finally ended and American and Japanese people banned together to rebuild lives, relationships and a city. Talk about resilience, wow.

Walking near the Ginza a sudden, loud explosion sent me crashing my chest to the sidewalk as I looked in every direction in a split second. When reality of time and place sank in I was soaked in sweat. As it was happening, it felt like five minutes. I could see every second like a series of movie frames one at a time. I got off my chest and sat on the sidewalk and cried. I wasn't in Vietnam, it was in me.

Chapter Twenty-One / The Wind Down Begins

I got back to Rach Kien a few days later and went back to work in the TOC. We kept sending our units up to The Plain of Reeds where they kept getting messed up with land mines, booby traps and sporadic combat with small numbered units of NVA.

While there, one of the companies came across one of the largest buried cachets of weapons, munitions and rice ever captured requiring several long days and a lot of man power. Many large Chinook and Skycrane helicopter sorties were needed to haul all that shit out of there. Meanwhile it had to be guarded 24/7 by our infantry units so that it wouldn't be recaptured.

One of the largest problems was communications with our units when they were that far north of Rach Kien. The Plain of Reeds was right on the edge of our radio transmissions. We had a one hundred foot tower on which were hung the five antennas for all the radios we had in the TOC. The Command Push for the Battalion was placed highest for obvious reasons. There had to be some physical separation between each antenna to avoid crossover and, or interference among the channels. The distant units could usually read our transmissions, but we frequently could not read the transmissions coming from the ground units up there. During the days while the cachets were being extracted we frequently had to have helicopter crews relay messages from our units on the ground. We sent some longer pole antennas to aid in their communications to us as well as a lot of radio batteries which they were changing every six hours instead of the usual twelve in order to have the strongest transmissions back to us. It was a matter of life and death for those men. They needed to be able to reach us immediately for any and all assistance. The added bitch of it was that if they got hit by NVA, being that far away it would take a while to get whatever support they needed to them in time to be effective. I was relieved when that operation closed.

Giving a damn about all the men brought about an inner conflict. I wanted more than anything to get the Hell out of Vietnam and go home. Within the same breath of thought I was worried they wouldn't get the concentration connection to the level of help that Prance and I had given them daily. Having been in the thick of it "out there", every time anything happened to a unit, it was like we were there in it with them. We relived our desperate moments and worked to get them whatever they needed ASAP!

Do not misinterpret my feelings. I did not have some warped sense that I was irreplaceable. There were plenty of good men around me who also had combat experience and would continue to give the fighting units 110% support long after Norm and I went home.

It's hard to give up an activity that is in direct support and supply of the help needed by people you care about.

It was one thing to take a few days away for an R&R knowing I was going back to the TOC to continue my involvement in the support effort. My mind was adrift in a different mental place as I contemplated leaving permanently knowing all this death and destruction would be continuing and I wouldn't be there to help.

I had spent most of my year longing for the day I would climb into a 707 and fly away from Vietnam. I was winding down to my final days and had not anticipated the feelings that were growing in my gut. It did not matter whether I knew anyone still on line, or not. My concern was for everyone. It always had been that way. But now this added twist inside about leaving them and going back to "milk & honey" while they continued to dodge, bullets, bombs and death. How could I be comfortable and OK at home while they were still there?

Norm Prance had arrived before me and it was now time for him to "Get the Hell out of Dodge". We had shared a lot of shit over our year and had become true friends. We already had exchanged addresses and phones back in the states and knew we would maintain a relationship for the rest of our lives thus his departure was not a "Goodbye", but a "talk with you soon". I was so happy for him that he was leaving. He'd been through a lot over the twelve months. That he was still walking, still talking was in many ways a miracle. I know the Colonel shared a fair amount of expensive Bourbon alone with him the night before he left trying to get Norm to "Re-Up" and become an officer. He respectfully declined the Colonel's solicitations and rode off the following morning with a hangover.

I got a bit mischievous with some of my decisions in my final days in the TOC. For one I knew enough that if I instructed wings of helicopters in certain ways during an operation they would burn up our allocated wing hours faster in a given day. Doing so would bring our troops back to Rach Kien earlier and would get the chopper crews out of the sky sooner. My intended result: the ground troops and the chopper crews would spend less time being exposed to lethal danger. I was walking a fine line and I knew it. To be clear, I never usurped an order by any of my superiors.

My few, small acts of shortening time spent in the field by our units began painting a picture around the person responsible…me. Before my series of "Operations" became overly apparent, late one night before going off duty, I was offered an operation of a different type.

Chapter Twenty-Two / Vung Tao

It had been decided that I would leave the next day on a three day in country R&R at the sea side center at Vung Tao, and then return in time to out process from the Battalion and get shipped home on my scheduled departure date of 16 June 1969. I was handed the necessary papers and told to be ready for departure the following morning at 08 hundred hours. Believing the old adage, "Never stare a gift horse in the eye", I smiled, said thank you and left to pack.

The countdown to my big "Freedom Bird" home to the States was now five days. I rode with the supply guys to Saigon where they dropped me off at Tan Son Nhut Air Force Base to catch a small fixed wing to Vung Tao. You may, or may not, remember that Australia had a military commitment in Vietnam. While smaller in size to the numbers of Americans, it was still quite substantial in men, equipment and material. I mention this because once processed through the in country R&R Center, I along with a handful of other GI's, was directed to cross the tarmac and board an Australian Air Force two engine Cayuse.

We get to the aircraft and the Aussie crew greeted us with smiles and "welcome aboard Yanks. Find a seat; we'll be off in mere minutes". Cargo planes when empty of large crates of cargo are like large empty rooms. On this one looking forward there was a wall with six steps dividing it in the middle. At the top of them I could see the flight deck and the Pilot and Co-Pilot who were going through their pre-flight regimen. On the right side of that forward wall was a colorful, well painted drawing of a kangaroo in the airborne segment of a hop under which was written, "This is a Wallaby Flight". Typical of the Australians, who in my brief experiences with them, had always been professional, yet managed to have a sense of humor behind almost all aspects of life, a trait that I had come to admire, and actually expected of them.

We get ourselves belted in our seats, the rear loading platform door closes as the engines are cranked and we taxi out for take off. The Cargo area attendant who had been standing on the forward steps chatting with the pilots stepped down and took a seat and belted himself in facing towards the rear as he said, "We'll be off in seconds". We had come to a stop and the RPM's on the engines increased and then I felt the brakes released as we began to move as the engines got louder and we rolled for take off. I could tell we were close to getting lift and then the forward landing gear wheels left the tarmac as we got rotation and the front of the aircraft lifted. The wing gear wheels on either side cleared the ground and then a POW came from outside the left side and the whole plane spun around and slammed on to the ground sliding, but on its wheels because the gear had not been retracted yet. There was smoke outside and the smell of burning oil and other like smells. Excited, yet orderly, emergency procedures were being yelled back and forth along with some swearing by the pilots and the aircraft came to a stop. Two seconds of total silence and then one of the pilots yelled back, "Are you blokes OK back there?"

We were OK. The left engine had blown when fully throttled and the aircraft had begun to fly. Seconds later and higher in the air would have made for an entirely different outcome. Lucky for all of us, this wallaby had only just jumped and landed on its feet. We were towed back to the hangar area, grabbed our things and boarded another Cayuse and fifteen minutes later with the same crew, we took off successfully and flew to Vung Tao.

Vung Tao had a French-European Riviera Sea Resort feeling about it without all the opulence. There was a very nice beach there. I ran into a couple guys I knew from the Battalion, so I made the most of the two plus days. It was still Vietnam and once dark hostilities were both visible and audible less than two miles away in the hills.

Chapter Twenty-Three / Good Bye Susie

I returned to Rach Kien without incident on the fifteenth. I reported directly to the Charlie Company Orderly Room for my departure paper work. As I walked in Paul Widzowski, a good man and the company clerk, was sitting shirtless at his desk as he had everyday for most of the last year. He smiled and handed me my going home papers. I grasped his hand and gave it a hearty shake with a "thank you". In the next room TOP Sergeant George yelled out, "Breidenbach get your ass in here!"

Smiling ear to ear, I ran in, snapped to attention, whipped a hand salute at him and said, "Sergeant Breidenbach reporting, TOP Sergeant!" He cracked up and retorted, "At ease, asshole!" We both laughed and then looking at each other we stopped. It had been a long year experientially.

Widzowski joined us in a silence we three shared. The moment was not awkward, rather it was reverent. We looked at each other and then I said, "There has been a supportive circle for me this year and you two have been half of it. The other two members were Norm Prance and Captain Goss." (Another brief silence) "Thank you from the bottom of my heart". TOP said, "My feelings too". Widzowski echoed, "Yeah".

Right on schedule as we said our good byes, "Susie", the Company Beagle wandered in, looked up at me, walked over to my feet, sat and rolled over on her back. She always loved a chest and tummy rub and this would be the last from me and I told her so. Whether it was a response, or Susie being Susie, she made little whining sounds along with her usual "that feels good" grunts and snorts.

After finalizing my goodbyes with TOP and Widzowski, I went across to our Supply Office to turn in my M-16. I would be weaponless my final twenty-four hours in country and though the thought of that after carrying it every where all day, every day for a year seemed strange, I was ready to do it.

I walked back down the dusty lane and a half wide Battalion "Main Street" towards the TOC. As I got to the little Chapel, I paused and remembered the service for Captain Goss six months earlier. I wanted to cry, but found myself turning numb. I looked up at the tiny steeple and the sky behind it. "God Bless you" I said to Captain Goss and walked on down the street.

I walked into the TOC to find them having a quiet period in the middle of the afternoon. Delta Company was out on a Pacification Program outing in a nearby village basically handing out candy to children and propaganda to the adults.

The Colonel saw me and waved me over to him. "I thought you left already, Sergeant." "Sir", said I, "I would never be so rude as to leave without a Good Bye". "Thinking about it, Breidenbach, you're right, that would not be you, not without a final word," he chuckled. I laughed too on that. He thanked me for my service to Charlie Company, the Battalion and in particular to him and my work in the TOC. I thanked him for his good judgment in his command of the Battalion and that it had been an honor to serve under him. I meant it and he got it as he stared me right in the eye and then said, "Thank you and good luck back in the States." "Thank you, Sir", said I as I snapped to attention and saluted him. He returned it with a smile, offered his hand and we shook as he said, "Now go pack, that's an order". "Sir, yes sir", said I.

After making my rounds to say bye to the other guys in the TOC, I went back to my bunk, and locker to pack for the trip home.

I had finished my last Vietnam Periodical and mailed the tape before I went to Vung Tao. Having put the word out that I was selling my audio tape recorder, I was happy to discover that there was an eager buyer. He had left a note on my locker saying he had the cash and would be by later to get it. I had two great audio tape decks at home and to attempt to drag this one along for the journey was not going to happen. It was like new and had very few hours on it, so he was getting a great deal. The last item to get rid of was my large battery powered Panasonic AM-FM radio. I had listened to news and music from AFVN, Saigon during my free hours on it for most of my year when I wasn't writing, or recording Periodical. It kept me sane in a way.

The programmers at AFVN were smart enough to know that if they made the radio station sound like those on the air back in the states, it would help to maintain a subliminal "connection" with home for the several hundred thousand GI's in Vietnam.
It was a transitional time in rock radio programming. Running from 1965-1970, the Drake-Chenault "BOSS RADIO" phenomenon happened on stations coast to coast. It was sandwiched between the end of Top 40 Radio and what would become (Underground) FM Album Oriented Rock Radio.

I had promised to give my radio to a guy in my barracks when I left. I was not willing to be without music until I jumped in a vehicle to leave.

The steps of out processing from Vietnam were much more enjoyable than the in processing I had endured one year earlier. I did not care what they wanted me to do. If it moved me along just that much faster, I did it. We were completely processed and were an hour or so away from getting on buses to go to Bien Hoa Air base to board or Freedom Flight home when some jerky Lieutenant appeared, looked at the group of us and announced, "If your hair is too long, you will not be allowed on the aircraft". He then pointed to a Barber Shop and walked away. Half of us jumped up paid the two dollars and had our already brief military locks made even shorter.

Among the contrasts from twelve months prior, the buses that came to take us to Bien Hoa were new, air conditioned and had heavily tinted windows. The divided highway we traveled on likewise was new with landscaped dividers between the lanes. The road looked like Mission Viejo, California, not Long Bien, South Vietnam. It was all very abrupt and quite surreal. The bus was the first air conditioned vehicle I'd been in since before leaving the States a year earlier. Suddenly, there was this separation from the heat, smell, sounds and dust of a Vietnam road. All those everyday things that had become common and matter of fact in my day to day life experience were behind glass, removed from tangibility.

We arrived at Bien Hoa and stepped back into the heat one more time to walk from the covered, open air gate area out under the hot Sun and onto the tarmac to cross to our waiting FREEDOM BIRD. I felt an amazing smile come to my mouth and face. As I climbed the stairs to that 707 I could not keep up with the fast-forwarding thoughts racing through my consciousness. My first thought: I made it, I was going home and not in a box. Faces of men I'd left behind both alive and dead streamed by like the windows of a train speeding by up close at a hundred miles an hour. I thought of my mom, my dad, and my brother…all that before I reached the top of the stairs. I made my mental picture parade pause when I got to the landing at the top. I turned and looked back at Vietnam, took a deep breath of the air through my nostrils, one last smell I thought. Large tropical, white thunderheads were off in the distance suggesting that Monsoon season was nearing. I would be glad not to have to go through that again. "Good Bye Vietnam", I said out loud, then turned and entered the plane.

As the plane rolled down the runway, lifted off and cleared the ground there was a very large cheer from end to end. Everyone on board was returning to the States. Some were going home to a month's leave and then their next duty station. Others were going home for leave and then a return to Vietnam. Then there were guys like me who were returning to end our term of active duty and get out of the Army.

This may seem odd, but other than being treated royally by our all volunteer flight crew, I remember nothing from that flight, absolutely nothing. *It was a military charter meaning no booze, wine or beer which was just fine with me.*

The Army had introduced a policy which effectively said that if a soldier returned from Vietnam with less than five months remaining on his term of duty, and he had a clean record, he would be terminated from the service with full credit for time served. For me, returning on June 16, 1969, I got a four month drop. The policy developed out of necessity. Many men had returned stateside with only a few months to complete their term of duty. The majority had become discipline problems as they were, in their minds, "killing time" until they got out. It turned out to be better for The Army and better for the men to return them to civilian life.

We flew into McChord Air Force Base outside of Seattle. I deplaned and walked down the stairs. At the bottom I got on all fours as my feet touched the tarmac and kissed it.

What followed was a bus ride to Fort Lewis where I would spend the next twenty-six hours going through a non stop, highly organized marathon of out processing from the Army.

Once we got to Fort Lewis we were given time to call our families to let them know we were back safe and on American soil. I woke my folks up, but they sure didn't mind my middle of the night call. It felt good to hear them.

We were clustered into a group of some fourteen men. We had to go through all the processing together. We were not permitted to

142

move on to the next step until all fourteen of us were ready for it. We were tailored into a new full dress uniform with all the proper decorations and trimmings. No off the rack dress coats or slacks were permitted. There was a team of tailors and seamstresses that measured each of us altering to the measurements until they were right. We were sent on to the medical detachment while the uniforms were being put together.

The medical part was the most involved and took up the most time. We were inducted into the service following a battery of tests that determined we were physically healthy and therefore fit to serve our country. Now that we were leaving the service, it was the responsibility of our country to return us to our civilian lives in the same physical condition. They picked, poked, probed and tested things until we were ready to scream.

Many diseases had infected Americans serving in Vietnam. Some were due to chemicals spread systematically across large areas of Vietnam like Agent Orange, designed to defoliate the jungle vegetation. *(We're still today, in 2014, discovering many new maladies that are a direct result of our men being exposed to it in Vietnam and that includes me).* Some strains of incurable venereal diseases (VD) never seen before in America were appearing in some of the men. The worst of the VD when discovered in an individual resulted in quarantine.

At about hour twenty-one of our marathon out processing, we were each given a cup and sent to a latrine to provide a urine sample. We were so tired, yet determined to work together and finish the process. We got in the latrine and I was the only guy who needed to pee. We all had to walk out of that latrine together each with his own urine sample in his cup. My own pressure to pee had reached the critical level. "Fuck it, guys", I said, "Line up with your cups and I'll fill 'em". They did, and I did. I walked out with my cup wondering what I had let in the country. I knew I was healthy, but what about any of the other guys?

143

One more interesting, potentially disastrous personal note about me came out of the medical processing. At Fort Benning twenty months earlier as I entered the Army, my blood type was determined and my Dog Tags were stamped with: Blood Type: A Positive. Dog Tags were worn around our necks in the service so that we were identifiable if killed in action, or if injured and incapable of speech our identities were known along with our blood type for immediate life saving transfusions. I went through my year in the infantry, in combat wearing those A Positive Dog Tags. A lab specialist called me out of the line to ask me my blood type. I grabbed my dog tag still tied with a boot lace around my neck too tight for me to read it and held it up to the lab tech saying, "What does it say?' He was astonished to read A Positive. He thought it was a misprint on my paperwork. He then went on to say that he checked the vials containing my blood twice to confirm it was A Negative. There I was just hours before getting out of the Army to find out that my blood type in fact was A Negative. Had I been injured and been given A Positive blood, that alone would have killed me, without the wound.

The final step for getting out of the Army was to get into my new dress uniform, collect my DD Form 214 and head for the Seattle airport. I was twenty-two and a FREE MAN!!!!

Chapter Twenty-Four / Out of the Army!

As I rode in a bus heading towards SEATAC, (Seattle's airport), I remembered a conversation I shared one year earlier on my first night at Charlie Company in Lai Khe. I was with four other new timers just before we went out on our first all night perimeter Guard Duty. We promised each other that if any of us managed to live through the year and get back to the states, we would make the most of returning alive to honor any of us who didn't make it back. I thought of Roosevelt Sherman Jr. and fought not to cry out loud.

I had military rate plane tickets to San Francisco and then a few days later to Cincinnati. In order to use the tickets I had to be in uniform while flying. I had arranged to spend a few days with cousin Nan and her family in San Mateo.

I was excited to see Nan. My mind had moved on to that anticipation and the damn bus could not go fast enough to get me to that plane.

As I walked into to SEATAC and up to the ticket counter, I was greeted by a very nice ticket agent who immediately said, "Just back from Vietnam?" I said I was. She let me know she recognized The Combat Infantry Badge on my uniform and then explained that she knew others who were still over there and prayed for them every day. I did not know what to say so I just looked at her. She picked up a phone and dialed four numbers as she checked my luggage and placed it on the conveyer belt. I heard her say to someone on the phone, "There's a military ticket on your flight to SFO, please move him up front". She hung up the phone, smiled and gave me my ticket, told me the Gate Number and pointed me in the right direction. I smiled in return, thanked her and walked away.

I wasn't twenty steps from that ticket agent when several people roughly my age walked by giving me dirty looks and then one pretty young lady yelled, "Killer". I was completely caught off guard. I didn't know what to feel, much less what to say. I stopped as they walked away and gazed at them puzzled. One looked back at me, gave me a dirty look and a big Thumbs Down gesture.

I turned and connected visually with direction signs to check the path towards my gate. I took a breath and continued my walk still trying to reconcile what had just happened.

I found myself walking straight, tall with a quickness in my step. I began looking, albeit briefly, into the eyes of many who passed in an attempt to get a read of their reaction to me in my uniform. There were saluting head nods, some looks of either sympathy, or sadness, (I wasn't sure which), and occasional angry stares from people roughly my age, fortunately not all my age were of that sentiment.

I had not even made it to my gate and I was already wondering; what had I come home to? What was going on in my country? Was this just unique to a few people in this airport, or, was this a microcosm of America in June of 1969?

This seven minute walk to my planes gate had my head full of many questions and no answers.

I checked in with the Gate Agent who let me know it would be fifteen minutes before we boarded. I thanked her and looked for a refreshment stand. There was one less than a minute's walk down the hall. I headed towards it.

With my awareness of the people around me now very keen, I was astonished to find everyone had some sort of reaction to me in uniform. I felt out of place. I did not want to feel that way. I'd just spent a year dreaming of coming home and just being me again among everybody else.

As I walked to get a soda I thought, the Vietnam War was unpopular, I knew that. Hell, it was unpopular with all of us while we there. But the U.S. involvement in Vietnam was not the fault of the men in the various services who were sent there.

There I was in a uniform just made for me; Technically no longer in the Army, not even two days out of Vietnam and feeling like a pariah within fifteen minutes of being back among Americans.

I bought a Coke with a lot of ice and walked back towards the Gate. Sipping on the straw I was taken aback at the fresh sweetness of it versus what I had tasted out of cans in Vietnam. The good feeling reality of being back in America returned to my mind.

As I got near the Agent's Desk at the Gate, I noticed that the Agent had been joined by a flight attendant. They were involved in a conversation. The Agent saw me and waved me over to the desk. She asked me if I would like a window seat. Still sipping on my Coke I nodded my head "yes". She asked for my ticket. I handed it to her. She put a sticker on it marked F and then she wrote 2-D next to the F and handed it back. The Flight Attendant told the Agent, "We'll take good care of him". She smiled at me and walked away towards the plane.

The plane to SFO was half empty. Through the kindness of those Western Airlines employees I was in First Class and got royal treatment.

Once in San Francisco's Terminal I again found myself to be the object of visual scrutiny. The glares of disapproval were more frequent and across a broader age range than I had experienced in SEATAC. Hippie dress was well into vogue. Several girls in tie-dyed blouses and beads looking like they were right off Haight-

Ashbury walked up to me and stuck flowers on me. One kissed me on the cheek and whispered "Peace" in my ear. The aroma of Patchouli Oil was all about her as she smiled and, with her friends, walked away. Not seconds later a long haired young man walked by angrily calling me a murderer and wanted to know how many Vietnamese women and children I'd killed.

Judging by the looks of those around this experience, there were many mixed reactions. I had already taken a defensive stance mentally which was to let it all wash over me without any outward reaction. I was obviously very alone, out numbered and did not need to escalate matters to a level I could not handle.

Nearing baggage claim, I saw Nan and for the moment forgot anybody else was around. Finally…a warm, loving, and familiar WELCOME HOME.

Once at cousin Lloyd's house I quickly hung up my uniform until I had to fly to Cincinnati. My days in San Mateo with Nan, and all my cousins was a recharge of my emotional battery.

We hit San Francisco, went down to the edge of Big Sur and watched the Sea Otters play. Out in public in regular clothes I was just one of the folks. I let my guard down *some*.

I woke early the day I was to fly home to Cincinnati. I wanted to go home and I did not want to leave Nan. She and I have shared a connection since we were mere babes. Nothing that can be easily explained, it was, is and always will be intangible, yet very real. On top of that emotional package I had to get back in my uniform and prepare myself for whatever was to come to me while wearing it.

I told Nan to just drop me off at the airport. I didn't want her subjected to any of the potential negative treatment my uniform would bring about.

I walked into SFO and got immediate reactionary looks. The little bit of relaxation I had for the couple of days with my cousins brought me to realize just how tired I was of having my guard up. I'd been that way for a year. I was feeling good and antsy at the same time. I was twenty-two and the people who were giving me the most grief were my age.

In my uniform I represented myself as a Sergeant in the US Army, but from my perspective it was much more than me. I represented all the guys who had stood beside me and now were six feet under. They deserved respect. The uniform represented all of us who had gone, no matter whether we came back dead, or alive. In that whole culture of respect, I felt I had to take the higher road by not lowering myself to respond with anger. I would not let them get under my skin. My guard was very much up in several ways. I had not anticipated having to deal with my fellow Americans like this once back in the states. We in uniform had become the victims of the terrible decisions in Washington to go to Vietnam and make war. Coming home we were the targets for the frustration and anger Americans had over the war.

One angry young guy came up to me as I was walking through SFO towards my plane to Cincinnati and demanded to know why I had not burned my Draft Card and gone to Canada. I continued to walk and he insisted I give him an answer. I inquired if he had a student deferment and he confirmed that he did. I told him that as long as he had that then he could not possibly understand the serious life changing decision one had to make when ordered to report for a physical knowing that if passed, it would mean immediate induction into the military. I went on to tell him that if he decided not to report, but instead to run, he would be running for the rest of his life and could never go home. He stopped walking with me and I proceeded to my gate.

As I boarded the plane to Cincinnati two flight attendants stopped me. One took my Boarding Pass and the other asked me if I was just back from Vietnam. I told her that I was. The other handed me a different boarding pass telling me that my seat had been changed and to please be seated in the seat number printed on the new Boarding Pass which was 3-F. I looked at her astonished. They had moved me to First Class, the same as the other flight crew had done in SEATAC several days earlier. Before I sat down they offered to hang up my coat for the flight and then asked me what I would like to drink. I told them that though in uniform, I was heading home, technically out of the Army and that I would like to buy a beer. They wouldn't hear of me paying for anything. They pointed out that I was now a First Class passenger and everything served was without charge. It was their small way of saying Welcome Home. In the four hour flight I splurged having three different brands of beer. The one before lunch was my first ever taste of San Francisco's Anchor Steam, tasty indeed. The second, with lunch was a Coors, another first taste of that Rocky Mountain Brew (Back then Coors was only available in Colorado). After we dined I toasted the mid west with a Black Label.

I felt beer number one as I had not had alcohol in any form since my second trip to Tokyo nearly seven weeks before. But the four course lunch and dessert following took a positive affect on my soberness. I was not going to return home pouring myself off the plane as I had heard the stories of what some other guys had done. In fact I had a nice cup of coffee about a half hour out of Cincinnati (CVG).

I was excited and anxious about getting home, seeing my parents, brother Jim and wife Sue, their baby, John, the rest of the family and my Boxer, Heidi, who had just turned ten.

Minutes before landing I went into the restroom to pee and freshen up. When I got back to my seat, one of the Flight Attendants brought my Uniform coat to me and insisted on holding it for me as I put it on. Once I was in it she was in front of me buttoning the buttons and straightening my tie. Once finished, she looked me up and down then hugged me, stepped back a few inches, looked me in the eyes with tears in her's.

She explained that her brother, whom she loved, was in Vietnam for another six months. He was in the infantry like me, which she had determined by the light blue infantry rope and the Combat Infantry Badge on my coat. I told her to keep her Faith that he would be OK and thanked her and her co-worker for their kind treatment during the flight. She hugged me again and this time I returned it. She was pretty and felt very good in my arms for that brief moment, but I was in no way ready to pursue her or anyone else for the time being.

Cincinnati's airport was still small and seemed more so after all my flying in and out of cities on our west coast and in the Far East. Looking at it out my window as we landed and taxied across the tarmac to the Terminal building it felt the way it should, like home.

As I walked down the rolled up stairs and my feet hit the ground the reality of "It's Over" flew across my consciousness. Here I was about to see mom and dad, when just one year before in exactly the same place I had said good bye to them knowing then that my chances of coming home alive were at best fifty-fifty. I never said it to them, frankly never said it to myself either.

The emotional wake of my "It's Over" was still rocking my conscious boat as I entered the gate doorway and saw mom and dad. Smiles dampened with tears as we came together hurriedly. Mom gave me a kiss and a hug. Dad said, "Hi, son", kissed me and said, "I owed you that". He was referring to the kiss I had given him when I left the year before.

I have no idea what was said, or what we did specifically besides the mandatory baggage claim and the drive home. I was going through wave after wave of feelings, thoughts, memories, wants, needs, regrets, good feelings and oddly enough grief. I was home, but for that brief time I was a duck out of water.

I had my parents go in the house first without me so that I could come in and surprise Heidi. I was moved as she looked at me and started to whimper. I dropped to my knees and opened my arms as she ran over. She was beside herself as was I.

Chapter Twenty-five / Home (and changes)

The initial days home were an adjustment. I was in a hurry to get back to WPFB and on the air. My job there was secure due to the laws at the time whereas an employer had to reemploy those who had been drafted into the military.

My first need once home was to buy a car. I had purposely bought twenty-five dollar US Savings Bonds every month I was in the Army with the idea I would cash them in early, and use that money towards a down payment for a car. I found a two year old 1967 Red Ford Mustang V-8 fast back with a black interior. It had low mileage, was in like new condition inside and out and was perfect for my 22 year old young man's ego.

The $260 from the Savings Bonds was more than needed to satisfy Provident Bank for the down payment and left me with a monthly payment under one hundred dollars.

Thus within five days back in Cincinnati, I had wheels and on day six went back to work at WPFB.

The staff at WPFB was warm and welcoming. Vietnam Periodical had been popular with the audience as many were repeated due to demand. It had kept me connected to the staff and the listeners.

I went to Stan Reed, the Program Director to discuss increasing my hours and also asked about getting some compensation for Periodical. In the year in Vietnam, I had managed to write and record thirty-one them. He asked me what I thought I should be paid for them. I asked for $310, which equated to ten dollars for each. He thought that was very reasonable and said he would talk with Paul Braden, the station owner and let me know. I had Braden's answer the next day: No.

Stan Reed felt bad and said so to me.

It was a lesson for me about the business side of radio, or any other commercial entity. I did not have a monetary agreement with WPFB before commencing Periodical; therefore in Braden's mind nothing was owed. Considering the success of Periodical and the attention it brought to the station, from the human perspective it was cold and inconsiderate treatment of a returning Vietnam War Vet.

I felt his decision was odd coming from a WW-II Veteran who had started WPFB with nothing fresh out the Army just twenty years before. Through the generosity of every broadcaster in Cincinnati and Dayton he managed to get started and within those brief two decades had become a multi-millionaire owning a handful of radio stations.

I immediately started job hunting and found a news anchor-reporter job in nearby Dayton at WAVI-WDAO. I called and got a meeting with News Director, Paul Burke. We met and immediately had a meeting of the minds. He had come from NBC owned WRC in Washington. As the center of NBC Radio and Television News in the nation's capitol, WRC had very high standards for news gathering and reporting. I knew this would be a valuable experience for me to work with him. He had been hired by the station's owner to polish a good news department to a great one. He had heard my work at WPFB and a couple of my Vietnam Periodicals. He was impressed that I had managed to deliver thirty one of them while being an infantry grunt during my year in Vietnam. After we talked he said as far as he was concerned I was hired, but I still had to meet H K "Bud" Crowl, the station's owner. That meeting went very well. I was hired to cover City Hall and the Courts downtown beginning late morning into mid day with on air live reports as news warranted. I was then to be in the news room writing up stories I had collected on my beat, and to edit any tape recorded pieces or interviews in support of those stories. I anchored hourly newscasts on WAVI and WDAO up to and including the midnight news Monday through Friday. Throughout the week I would find, write and record four to five human interest-feature pieces two to three minutes in length that both stations would use throughout the weekends.

WDAO was a fifty thousand watt FM power house that programmed R & B Soul music exclusively to an urban, black audience in Dayton with a signal that reached comfortably into Cincinnati and all the environs in between. WDAO started the format in 1965 and was the first FM in the nation to do so. It rocked southwest Ohio at 107.7 in Stereo Soul and its popularity brought great commercial success. Sister station WAVI was a daytimer AM that played MOR (Middle of the Road) popular music to a generally white audience.

Both stations were housed in a brand new state of the art, broadcast facility designed and built from the ground up to do radio. Looking around that day I was hired, I thought I'd died and gone to radio heaven. So many radio facilities were crammed into spaces that did not support the work that had to be done. Every where I looked the many processes that made broadcasting possible were supported with thoughtful design for each and how they integrated together. That alone was an education on how best to do things which has stayed with me ever since.

I wasn't three weeks out of Vietnam and already I was at my second radio job and moving fifty miles north of Cincinnati to Dayton, the city where my parents had grown up.

Chapter Twenty-Six / WAVI – WDAO

Moving to Dayton and working there was not a difficult change. I had a lot of family in and around The Miami Valley and had been going there all of my life. My mother's family had had a brewery in The Gem City. "Olt's Superba" was a popular brew before Prohibition hit in 1919, and managed to come back after the repeal of it in 1933. The family business died over squabbles within the family for power, and money.

My father's father had been a very successful baker of bread. Breidenbach's Bakery delivered fresh bread daily to homes all over Dayton. It ended abruptly in 1920 when my grandfather became ill and died. My dad was the youngest of six and was only twelve at the time. None of his older siblings, three of whom were brothers, had shared their father's passion for bread making. Since no family member became the baker, the business died with my grandfather Henry. After selling off all the assets of the bakery, my grandmother Emma, was able to buy a new house and move the family in to it. When the Stock Market Crashed in 1929 beginning The Great Depression, my dad's family had already been living it for nearly nine years.

I began my radio newsman career with gusto. The enjoyment of putting my thoughts to paper and then broadcasting them had become part of me. I felt my job at WAVI-WDAO was the perfect place for me to participate in a progressive atmosphere and grow as a person and as a professional.

In radio, morning drive time and afternoon drive time were, (and still are), the main time periods for the largest audience potential. Broadcasting pertinent news and information relevant to the moment rolled into a palatable mix that's interesting and entertaining are the keys to success. WAVI-WDAO were far apart on the entertaining content scale, but were same-same regarding the news and information content. Paul Burke had been smart on that issue. The two stations went to the news like they were picking up news from a network news department. Thus as newscasters we were encouraged to go for it writing and reporting. The main anchor-reporter, John Ury, had been there for some years. He was good, very good. He had the perfect news voice, authoritative and human, without going over the top and sounding like a characterization. I learned a lot from him in conversations about developing stories and observing how he cared, prepared and presented on air.

Burke demanded a lot and I happily gave it. We never re-read news copy. Though there may not be any new information on a given story, there was always another way to restate the facts as we knew them. Our typewriters were always going whether there were new stories to write and report, or not.

My ability to edit audio tape got challenged and subsequently advanced by the constant deadlines for air throughout my work day and night.

My mother's sister Janet was kind and let me crash on her couch for my first two weeks in Dayton while I worked and looked for an apartment. I found a perfect one with a living room, bedroom bath and kitchen. Compared to my accommodations the previous two years, this was heaven. I did not have any furniture and at that point I didn't care about that. All I needed was a bed and that was offered to me by my mom's other sister, Charlotte.

I borrowed the station's Ford Econoline van for several hours early one morning to go to my parents and pick up my clothes, dresser and all my audio gear, drove through Hamilton to pick up the bed I'd been given by my Aunt Charlotte, drove on to Dayton put everything in my apartment, showered, dressed and got to work on time to go on the air.

The previous renter had had a fire so everything inside the apartment was new. It was the east side of a single story duplex, so I had windows on three sides meaning refreshing breezes plus great trees all around making for shade. Plus the roof hung way out from the outer wall so that when it rained, I could leave the windows open when home. The ceilings were nine feet, and though there was no air conditioning, I was very comfortable that summer.

As part of my assignment was to report on court cases, I found myself covering the big trial in Dayton the summer of 1969. Six young men were being tried for reportedly raping a Dayton nurse. The young woman had to be in court every day for weeks mere feet from all six of them as each defendant was tried separately. The evidence was clearly against the six on trial, but their attorneys dragged it out as long as they could for each defendant's case. The victim had to endure repeatedly the endless questions of what she went through that horrific night. My job was to witness the proceedings and report. It really sickened me. I could not imagine what she must have felt as it went on and on.

Separate from the rape trial, in my covering various court proceedings I quickly learned the difference between what is legal and when justice is served. They are NOT the same. Miraculously sometimes they actually come out on the same side of a decision.

I had come home from Vietnam smoking Salem cigarettes. I didn't smoke even a pack a day, nor did I inhale. I had picked up the habit of burning them down working in the Tactical Operations Center my last three months there. I bring this up because of what happened late one night in the newsroom at WDAO. Some news story had broken and I was on the phone getting the basics before running in to broadcast the midnight newscast.

I was at my desk typing, phone cradled to my left ear by my shoulder, a lit Salem hanging out of my mouth. I was totally focused on getting the story down with a minute to go before I had to run into the on air studio. The smoke from the cigarette was winding its way up into my left nostril and eye; it was irritating the hell out of me. I told the person on the phone to hold on a minute. I stopped typing and pulled the cigarette out of my mouth, said, "fuck this shit" and with my right hand, using my middle finger flicked it fifteen feet forward where it bounced off a piece of hanging wire copy paper and dropped into a tall metal trash can. I excused myself for swearing to the person on the phone, finished getting the story and ran off to broadcast the news.

Some nights I would have the newsroom put to bed for the night as I went to do the Midnight broadcast. Right after the newscast I'd say goodnight to the WDAO DJ on air, walk out, drop my copy in a trash can, leave the building and go home.

Fortunately this night I had weekend features to record and headed back towards the newsroom. As I walked down the wide hall I reached a point from where the entire length of the newsroom was viewable behind four large panes of glass. I could not see anything inside because it was completely filled with smoke. I panicked. I ran up to the nearest door opened it and went in to try to assess how serious the fire was. Fanning the smoke wildly with my arms as I held my breath I got to the far end where all the news wire machines were running typing out stories. I found the "fire" was actually smoldering news copy paper in the trash can which had been ignited by the half burned cigarette I'd thrown nearly ten minutes before. I grabbed a half drunk can of TAB of mine and poured it on the smoldering embers putting them out.

Had I left for the night the station would have had a major fire. I'd never been a real smoker and that was my last cigarette. I've not touched one since.

News Director Paul Burke kept me very busy and was, in supportive, positive ways on my ass to constantly up my game. As a result, my writing got more concise, more direct and to the point. My on air delivery became stronger. He gave me free hand on my weekend feature subjects despite the fact that some were a stretch to hear about conceptually. Even those he questioned ahead of time gained his compliments once he heard them completed.

My creative juices were flowing and it felt good to get both immediate and delayed reactions. I liked all sides of what I was doing. The writing, being on the air live, out digging for the stories, recording and editing to make the reporting of a story complete and concise.

Burke was a responsible professional. He was not a blood and guts, report at any cost news guy. I would not have gone on staff if the emphasis had been on sensationalism. Paul was competitive in a city which at the time had some very good broadcast and print news organizations. That was fine with me and we definitely held our own in the Dayton market.

In the midst of everything the summer of '69, Dayton's two main newspapers, The Dayton Daily News and The Journal Herald were shuttered by a labor strike. Newspapers still held a high profile for readers to attain information at that time, thus in their absence it was important for us to double down on our coverage and reporting of both hard and soft news.

Burke and I got on well. He too had been in the Army and, fortunately for him, he missed Vietnam reaching the rank of Corporal by the time he got out. At times he would teasingly call me "Sarge" and act as if I out ranked him in the news room making for some good laughs as we reversed rolls.

I introduced him to The Ohio Valley Jazz Festival which was held in Cincinnati at Crosley Field. We double dated. I wasn't dating anybody at the time but asked one of the ladies who worked in the office who happily went along for a fun night.

I had many friends in Cincinnati and found in my brief off hours that I was feeling lonely. Here I was back from the Army and they were forty-five or more minutes away. By the time I got off the air at midnight, it was too late to see them, plus I was tired after my twelve hour day so I would go home listen to some music and go to bed. Saturdays I got off at two in the afternoon and would hit the road to Cincinnati to see my friends for the evening. Following that I'd sleep over at my parents, do some laundry, have time with my folks maybe join them for a meal and head back to Dayton.

I wasn't making a big living at WDAO-WAVI, but I was meeting my needs and growing by leaps and bounds as a creative newscaster-reporter. I was really happy in my work.

I realize in hindsight what a good place I was in professionally that summer of 1969.

Things were going just fine and then one day in August my friend Terry Donohue told me about this new nationally syndicated talk-variety television show he was working on in Cincinnati at Taft Broadcasting. It was hosted by Dennis Wholey a good interviewer who had gained the attention of a former producer from The Mike Douglas Show, one Roger Ailes. Ailes had been the key instrument in the successful campaign leading to the election of Richard Nixon to The White House the year before.

Terry told me how they were parading three to four national personalities in and out of Cincinnati daily for each show taping in front of a studio audience of over two hundred. The show had a great eight piece band as well. Guys I had worked with at WLWT, or had been in college with were working on the show. Everybody was having a lot of fun and making a hell of a lot more money than I was.

After baiting me with all of this over a couple of beers, he went on to mention they were looking for people immediately. All I needed beyond my experience and drive was a union card, which I already had from working at WLWT three years before.

The lure of the lights, show biz and a lot more money was too much for my immature, short-sighted self at that moment. I stayed over at my parents that Sunday night and went in for an interview first thing Monday morning.

Within an hour of the start of my interview, I was hired on to The Dennis Wholey Show. I agreed to start one week later.

Two and a half months out of Vietnam and I was into a complete career change and my third job.

Walking out towards the exit after my hiring, all I could think about was how would I tell Paul Burke that this coming Sunday would be my last day at WDAO-WAVI? I had a fifty-five minute drive to Dayton to think about it.

I had developed a very good working relationship with Paul and it was well on its way to becoming a friendship as well. Leaving abruptly after achieving a good level of success in such a short time would not go over well for Paul or the station. All summer I had gone home every night happy and full-filled as I honed my reporter-writer-anchor-on-air-communication skills. In just days all that would end.

There just wasn't enough time to really think this out. My mind was racing to make sense of what I was doing. I had a very real internal argument during the drive to Dayton. As I neared the exit where I used to get off I-75 to go to WPFB, I considered going in to talk with Stan Reed. I nixed that idea figuring I needed to deal with this myself. It would be a growing experience. I was feeling very alone and it was of my own doing.

I pulled off 75 just north of Middletown for gas and to think. After getting gas I drove to an isolated area of the parking lot and turned off the car and just sat there. As I had my entire year in Vietnam, I got quiet inside and asked God for guidance. I was lost and I knew it. I closed my eyes and just breathed. After about fifteen minutes of no conscious thought I opened my eyes, started my Mustang I got back on 75 for the fifteen minutes to WAVI-WDAO.

I was over an hour early for my normal start time and Paul looked up and gave me a strange look as I walked into the newsroom. I put my brief case down at my desk and walked up to him and asked if we could go in the production studio and talk. In his intuitive way he said to me jokingly, "you're going to tell me you're quitting, aren't you?" I faked a nervous chuckle as we walked towards the production studio.

I began by apologizing as I unwound my verbal resignation. He was supportively pissed about my leaving. He argued to get me to stay and to continue to develop my on air career. He said the growth he had seen me display in just over two months, if continued, would lead to a rewarding broadcasting career. I told him that I would give him my best week ever as a parting thank you for the opportunity he'd given me. He told me to go break the news to our boss as "Bud" Crowl would respect me to hear the news directly from me.

I found Bud Crowl in his office doing some paper work. He welcomed me and asked me to have a seat. I gave him the news and he raised his eye brows, looked me in the eyes and made it clear that I would be missed. He said that I had already brought good responses to him from commercial clients and that others had made positive mentions of my on air work to him. He allowed that he probably should have given me that feed back weeks before as it may have prevented my inkling to move on.

Crowl went on to say that he understood the itch in the crawl of a twenty-two year old single guy just back from the war. He could relate to a degree thinking back to his days after World War II. He asked that I help Paul and the news staff during this sudden transition. I assured him that I had already mentioned the same to Paul earlier. He wished me well and I returned the sentiment. I then ended the meeting by saying I needed to get to work. We agreed to chat again at the end of the week.

It was a heavy news week and I worked late every night and went in early every day. I turned in a lot of good work. Around work, at home, with what little time I had there I began to pack what was not needed for the few days I had left.

My apartment was on a month to month rental agreement. The end of August matched my need to move out. There would be no cleaning fee as it was still new in every way. I never cooked there, except for my bed and dresser, there was no furniture and I cleaned the place thoroughly every week.

The following Monday would be Labor Day the first of September and I was already scheduled to commence work at the Wholey Show on the holiday at double time pay.

Fortunately it was a sunny my final Sunday at WAVI-WDAO as my dad and brother Jim were meeting me at the station when I got off the air at two o'clock to then follow me back to my apartment. My bed and dresser went into the El Camino pick up my brother had borrowed from his brother-in-law and all my audio gear and clothes went into my car. Within half an hour we were headed towards Cincinnati.

The station was right along I-75 and we had to drive right past it after leaving my apartment. I glanced over at it and wondered if I was doing the right thing. I turned up Cincinnati radio station WEBN and drowned out my thoughts with Procol Harem's A WHITER SHADE of PEARL.

Chapter Twenty-Seven / Back to Cincinnati

I stayed a brief two weeks with mom and dad until an apartment was found.

The Dennis Wholey Show was being produced by Taft Broadcasting at their facility at WKRC-TV in Cincinnati. Before production even started, on paper there were many up hill start up problems doing a nationally syndicated talk-variety show this complex outside New York, or Los Angeles. First and foremost was booking guest talent. Most lived on either coast which meant flying them in and out, versus sending a car across town. Take that times fifteen to twenty talent a week, add in a hotel night in Cincinnati for many of them, plus expenses, well, you get that picture.

The next problem was the facility. WKRC-TV was a local television station and not set up in any way to handle the technical needs, or anything else required for such a production. Lighting, staging and all the video equipment had to be purchased, or leased. Since the show needed time to show a return on investment, leasing was an obvious choice.

All that made up the picture of what I walked into that Monday, September the first 1969.

Between the production staff and the technical staff, there were roughly sixty of us involved in putting the Wholey Show together. They had been at it for a month and a half before I got there. It was ever evolving moment to moment with a ceaseless, speeding learning curve through which we all struggled to avoid loosing control, much like the driver of a race car hitting a turn too fast.

For me it was Mecca for picking up everything there was to know about producing an informative, entertaining and progressive show.

My friend, Terry Donohue was part of the studio crew who shot the show and then following a dinner break, would edit the show. The editing was taking most of every night and therefore was not desirable to most of the crew because of the long hours. I sat in on a session the first night on my own time to get the hang of it. I liked it instantly. My interest got me on the edit team right away.

When I got there the show was being produced by one Roger Ailes. He had previously worked on The Mike Douglas Show as Executive Producer. At some point when Richard Nixon decided to re-enter the national political scene with The Presidency as his goal, he went on the Douglas show. In his dressing room during that guest appearance, the story later surfaced that Ailes basically told Nixon what was wrong with his public image and how he could get the hopeful nominee elected to The Whitehouse by repackaging his television image. The rest is history for Roger Ailes did exactly that. Richard Nixon was completely repackaged for public consumption and would not do anything in front of the media without Roger's involvement. That connection remained active after the election, but was not commonly known outside The West Wing at the time.

Ailes was the TV Wiz Kid at the time. On Wholey's show we were recording two and a half hour specials every day of the week. The stuff was wonderfully inventive, creative and entertaining. The problem was quite basic. We were to deliver a ninety minute show to many stations while others were buying only a shortened sixty minute version.

I should point out that at the time Johnny Carson's TONIGHT SHOW was ninety minutes long and was the common length for

168

talk-variety shows. It would be some years later that TONIGHT went to an hour in length.

Editing challenges were enormous as we were determined to have the shows come out finished having a natural flow with conversational content making total sense even though many minutes were cut out in order to fit in to the time constraints.

A brief note about the technology available at the time: We were shooting the show in color on Hi Band two inch video tape. The two AMPEX 2000 VTRs that had been leased for the project were the state-of-art in 1969. They even had EECO time code, which was a revolutionary, new way to reference recorded video down to a single frame of video, (which had a rate of 30 frames per second of time). The time code made it possible to make precise, frame accurate edits. A common home computer in 2015 could run circles around what we did, but computers for video editing had not yet come into the business. Time code was the bedrock for what became computer editing of video.

Some nights, or should I say mornings, we would walk out of the building only to go home, shower, shave put on clean clothes and go back to shoot the next show, etc…

Eighty hour work weeks were common with many reaching over one hundred of the one hundred and sixty-eight available hours in seven days. Due to overtime, double time and quick turn-a-round penalties, we on the editing crew were making a lot of money. But more than the dollar compensation, the education we were getting was priceless.

I was taking no time to feel what was going on inside me. I became this production-technical automaton focused entirely on the production and editing of the show. Looking back on it, I had replaced my seven day work week at twenty hours per day in

Vietnam with The Wholey Show. I was completely programmed to the schedule.

I knew something would change the way things were going. Ailes was commuting back and forth between Cincinnati and Washington many times a week. The phone calls into the Wholey Show office from The West Wing when Roger was in town were as if the office was merely down the hall. There was no formality about where, or from whom the calls were coming, but everyone knew.

Then one dark day that October the news broke about a new tell all book entitled THE SELLING of THE PRESIDENT 1968. A mere twenty-nine years old, Roger Ailes was all through it.

As I wrote earlier, the Wholey Show was being produced at the home office television facility of Taft Broadcasting. This was the broadcasting arm of the Cincinnati Taft family descendants of President William Howard Taft and Senator Robert A Taft.

Even though Roger Ailes was essentially the P.T. Barnum of television, and the Wholey Show was good television, the second that book was out and Roger was named as the packager of the standing President of the United States, he was gone. The show was without a leader.

We all rallied around Dennis in support of continuing the enterprise while the execs at the top quickly shopped for a producer.

We got a great replacement for Ailes in the person of Don Silverman. He had already won an Emmy for producing Dick Cavett's Show on ABC. With Don came the bonus of his wife Patty Silverman who had worked on Carson's Tonight Show and was well known in the talent booking community.

The Silverman's brought fiscal responsibility to the operation of the show while keeping the entertainment, creativity and talk/communication relevant as the latter was Dennis Wholey's strength.

My very long days shortened some as Silverman produced a ninety minute daily show very close to ninety minutes as it was recorded in the studio. It was absolutely essential that that happen for survival of the production.

This was yet another valuable learning experience for me. I got to see first hand streamlining of the producing while maintaining entertainment values, sale ability and ratings in the market place.

Because guest talent could not be booked too close to the holidays during the last two weeks in December, it was decided the show would go on hiatus for those two weeks. Therefore a small holiday party in the show offices was scheduled Friday after the last show was taped the week before Christmas.

I was still working seventy to eighty hour weeks and after all the months of long hours was more fatigued than I knew. We all had become very close making the show work and shared a fun camaraderie. There was a great spread of catered food, drink and some wonderful stories shared to and for all of us as a thank you for the hard work and to commence the holidays. I ate and had one drink and then went around getting the rest of the editing crew so we could get started with the edit for the night.

I found our other video tape tech essentially drunk on his feet leaning up against the VTR and the audio mixer had his head down passed out at the audio board. Feeling a little woozy myself, we agreed to go home carefully and that we'd reconvene at ten the next morning and get it done.

Chapter Twenty-Eight / Oh-Oh…Ouch!

I had about a twelve minute drive to the high rise I was living in. It was early, around 9:30pm. I drove very carefully as I knew I was out of it. About one minute from my garage I blacked out for a second on a two lane residential street. All I remember is hearing a tinkle. I woke up and discovered I'd hit something. All I could think was damn it, I never have wrecks. I got out to assess what had happened. I'd gone right of the lane about a foot and had clipped the rear end of a parked 1963 Thunderbird. There was negligible damage to the T-Bird as the rear corner was built like a tank. On my Mustang I had pushed the right front fender back some missing the hood altogether. I looked around and saw no one. I reached in my wallet and pulled out a personal business card and left it on the windshield under the windshield wiper. I figured the owner would call me, and my insurance would take care of the rest. I got back in my car and drove straight to my parking space in the garage. I took the elevator up to my floor got in the apartment and went to bed.

About two hours later Terry Donohue, with whom I was sharing the apartment came in my room and woke me up saying that two Policemen were on the way up to talk with me about a hit and run accident involving my car.

I scrambled to get dressed and make my self presentable for the police.

They wanted to know if I had hit another vehicle that night. I said that I had momentarily veered a little right and grazed the rear end of a parked car. Had gotten out and left my business card under the windshield wiper of the car to identify myself in order to be reached by the owner to get the auto repaired.

They wanted to know if I had been drinking. I told them no, but had spent months working eighty plus hours. They wanted to know the name of my employer and what I did. I gave them all the info, which was verified by Terry.

The officers said I would have to appear in court the following week and left.

I was too tired and too sick to get upset at that moment. There would be time with me in a better state of mind to deal with this unneeded mess. I thanked Terry and went to bed.

I woke up at six the next morning threw on some clothes and a coat and took the elevator down the ten stories to the garage to see my damaged car. It was less than I thought, but still unacceptable for me. I had a spotless driving record going back to when I got my first license when I was sixteen.

At a reasonable hour that morning I called the owner of the car I hit to give them my insurance information and where they could reach me. They were understandably curt on the phone, but thanked me for the information before we hung up.

After that fun phone call, I went in to work to edit the show.

Everyone looked haggard, but we got through it and were out of there by mid afternoon.

My mother's birthday was December 23rd and dad had invited me to join them for dinner weeks before. The birthday dinner was that Saturday night. Her birthday dinner was a big deal for it had been a family tradition since my parent's dating days. The year before I had missed the dinner because I was in Vietnam so this was even more special with all of us together again.

On Monday I took my car over to East Hill Garage where Duke the body man did his magic with the restoration to a like new condition of any vehicle that had had a crumple large or small. Over the years almost all of the family vehicles had made their way in and out of Duke's care for parking lot dings and worse. His ability to match colors and finish was second-to-none. He told me it would cost four hundred and fifty dollars and said he could start it in one week and have it done in two days. With my deductible at the time that meant my out-of-pocket for the repair would be two hundred dollars.

I then drove downtown to the unemployment bureau to file for the two weeks I was laid off from the show. Forms, forms and more forms. I felt like I was back in the Army. I had never been through that process before and could see that if one were out of work, it could be a challenge to keep your head up.

Two days later I had my court day on the car wreck. I put on my best three piece suit and went prepared to present my self as the responsible professional I was.

I went in to that court room with all the knowledge of a babe in the woods. Though I had covered the courts while doing news in Dayton just months before, I hadn't been the one before the judge trying to explain myself. In my mind going in I knew I had caused the wreck, had left my business card, had good insurance, saw to it that the injured party had already been contacted by my insurance company and was now ready to get this handled in court and get on with my life.

Once the police officer got through with his testimony which included reporting the technicality that I left the scene of an accident, Judge Thomas Nurre was ready to throw the book at me, but through due course he wanted to hear my side of the matter. I gave him the background on my months of long hours and that I was heading home from work when the accident occurred. I went on to describe how I had gotten out of my car in the middle of the residential street, saw no one and then left my business card under the wiper blade of the car I hit so they could contact me and then took my overly tired, sick self home for some sleep.

I continued to tell him that my insurance company had contacted the injured party to get their vehicle repaired. Once all the facts as I knew them were entered on the record, Judge Nurre looked at me with a pained expression. He told me that my actions after the crash had been both responsible and professional regarding my treatment of the other party.

He then read off the charges and asked me how I pled. Not understanding the letter of the law at this junction, I did not know that by pleading not guilty, I placed myself at the mercy of the court, basically giving the Judge the power to lay out justice under these circumstances as he saw fit to do. But, dumb ass dog, me, pled guilty. (*What had been stated had occurred, so, in my mind I was simply acknowledging and not denying the truth*).

When I uttered guilty you could have heard a pin drop as the room went silent for a good count of ten and then a rush of whispers. Judge Nurre looked at me in astonishment. He took a beat and then suspended my license for six months for technically leaving the scene, sentenced me to six months in the County Workhouse, which he immediately suspended, and fined me several hundred dollars. He then told me to meet his Bailiff, Henry Blake at his office immediately following to relinquish my license and with that he rapped his gavel making it all official.

I was confused. In my mind I'd done the right thing. I went to meet the Bailiff. Henry Blake was older than the judge by probably ten years and had been doing the bailiff thing for a long time. When he rounded the corner in the hall not far from the courtroom he was in a huff and after seeing me was in more of one. Holding many files in one hand and his brief case in another he fumbled to unlock his office door. He told me what a mess of things I had made with my guilty plea. We got inside and I explained my ignorance with a question asking what was wrong with acknowledging my responsibility. He then explained the difference it meant legally to plead guilty versus not guilty. Not knowing what to say, I reached for my wallet and pulled out my license and handed it to him.

He held it looking at it and then shaking it at me told me that the Judge essentially broke the law by suspending the six months in The Workhouse. He went on to explain that every attorney, policeman and bailiff in the courtroom had given the Judge hell for not following the letter of the law dictated by my guilty plea. He then told me to clear the building quickly and added that my license would be mailed to me in six months.

I walked out of the Hamilton County Court building feeling small and afraid. How would I get around? As I walked to my car I realized I would have to drive home without a license.

I got to my car, got in and started it. It was a cold December mid day as I sat waiting for the heater to warm me up. I had to come to grips with my reality. What the hell was I going to do? I kept looking around hoping there was no one from court around to see me sitting there behind the wheel of my Mustang, motor running with the right front fender crumpled. I got very quiet and asked for some direction from above. It was not the best decision of my life, but a somber, purposeful one. I decided that I would continue to drive being extremely careful to observe every traffic law, to never go over the speed limit, or run a red light. In effect, keep a law abiding very low profile when driving. I was taking a very big chance and I knew it. I also decided to tell no one that I'd lost my license or that I'd almost been sent to The Workhouse. This was heavy shit. If I got caught, it would cost me in many ways.

I took a few deep breaths and looked all the way around from where I sat behind the driver's wheel. Satisfied that no one was watching me in particular I pressed the brake pedal, released the parking brake and then consciously watched my hand move over to the floor shift, grip it and move it out of Park to Drive. My heart was pounding as I again looked around. I found traffic clear so I eased into the lane and held that nervous attitude all the way home.

I was so grateful to get back in the garage and into my space without incident. I wondered if I would be able to drive under those conditions for the next six months. I'd made the decision to drive despite the Suspension, was not happy about making it and was damned determined to sustain my vigilance throughout the term.

Had I known at that moment the number of miles I would traverse during that half a year, I may have made a different decision.

The holidays wound down to New Year's Eve. My Mustang had been restored to its pristine condition as I held my driving to only that which was necessary. I had been dating a woman my age whom I had met in the cleaners in the lobby of my hi-rise. I discovered by accident that one of the reasons we didn't go out very often was because she was boffing three other young professionals living in the building. We didn't have an exclusive understanding about our relationship, so it was easy at 1:00am to wish her a Happy New Year, get dressed, say good bye and return to my place eight stories above. Hey, it was a new year and I was ready for a fresh start alone.

Chapter Twenty-Nine / A New Year & More

The sixties were officially OVER.

New Year's Day was cold. I built a fire in the fire place, turned on The Rose Parade followed by The Rose Bowl Game and went to bed early to be ready for the return to work at the Wholey Show.

January ended with Taft Broadcasting canceling the Wholey Show immediately. We taped an end of the show segment timed to go on the end of an existing show in the can.

In it's just over half a year in production, over nine hundred national movie, television and recording artists along with political columnists and authors appeared with Dennis on the show.

I got some extra time in editing as a highlight reel needed to be edited for Dennis's use for future work.

I went to the unemployment bureau and reopened my file for benefits. This sucked, but it was the right thing to do.

I decided to return to my radio career and found an opening in Charlottesville, Virginia. After sending my resume and demo tape and a couple of phone calls I got an appointment for an in person interview.

I flew to Washington National Airport and then connected to a small commuter plane to Charlottesville. WCHV was looking for a personality for their nights from seven to midnight. It would be simulcast on both their AM & FM stations, which would give me reasonable coverage in central Virginia. We came to terms that day and agreed that I would debut in twelve days.

I caught the commuter back to Washington. With a couple hours to kill, I went for a walk through National Airport and was very surprised to see my brother sitting with his brief case and portfolio in the waiting area at my same gate back to Cincinnati. He too was surprised. He had been to Richmond, also on a successful job interview. We laughed at the coincidence of both changing jobs at the same time and landing in Virginia.

I was headed to Virginia within four days with a lot to do to get set up ready to work. I found a new, small furnished apartment rented on a month to month basis. It was not far from the station in a very nice area and met my needs giving me time to get to know the area before I put down more permanent roots.

When I first got to Charlottesville I called the station and was put through to Jack Creech the General Manager. He wanted to meet with me the next day at ten AM. We talked for maybe an hour. We seemed to be on the same page about what to do with programming WCHV during my show which I was finding out would run Mondays through Saturday nights rather than through Friday nights. I asked for more money than we had agreed upon from the week before, but he balked at that suggesting that I could get commissions off my direct sales of my show. Selling my show could have great potential so I went along with it. In the back of my head a flag went up. It did not sit well with me that the business situation was changing now that I was on site. But I decided to look on the positive side and give it a go.

One more thing came out of that meeting which gave me pause on another level. I was asked not to remain around the station after four thirty in the afternoons for the few days left in the prep week before hitting the air the following Monday night. They did not want me to cross paths with the man doing the evening radio show. Only four people knew I was hired and they were not telling anyone else on air or in the office until the following Tuesday. I was to say to those who asked that I was there to consult Jack Creech, the General Manager. That little tactic should have been my second clue.

Another day or two passed and Creech had me stop by his office. Closing his door he asked me, as he made his way back to his desk, what I would be calling myself on the air. I suggested Peter Bryan, which had been my on air name at WAVI-WDAO the previous summer. He said he had a better idea and handed me a three by five index card on which was written "Jerry Pace". Startled, but not showing it outwardly, I looked at it. I had never thought of myself as a "Jerry". I had always been Peter, to myself and on the air. Jerry Pace really sounded to me like a "radio name" right out of 1955. Then something clicked in my brain; perhaps I should not put any real identity to me on this radio show. All these little lights kept flashing inside my head. All those thoughts took a microsecond then, not missing a beat; I jumped up out of my chair and told him I thought Jerry Pace was perfect. (No, my pants were not on fire...but they should have been).

(It turned out a newspaper article/promotional piece on "Jerry Pace joins WCHV" had already been written, complete with my picture, for release the next Tuesday. I wouldn't know about it until that day).

I now resolved myself to the reality that Jerry Pace would debut on WCHV and I would give the venture an honest effort with my eyes open on a 360 degree angle. (*I thought I had left Vietnam!*)

I'd been home from Vietnam eight months and was beginning my fourth job. Statistically, this did not read well for a twenty-two year old guy. But I persevered because that's how you survive and I have never been a quitter.

1970 was a turning point for radio in the US. Top 40 was dying a fast death, the Drake-Chenault "Boss Radio" had run its course the last four years of the 60's. Free form "Progressive Rock", or "Album Oriented Rock" (AOR) had been turning up on small FM's but had not yet grabbed the ratings and the advertisers in the larger markets. Woodstock six months earlier had made a substantial impact on the record industry and was beginning to impact radio programming. Anybody under thirty who was breathing in February 1970 knew the change had happened, it was just a matter of time before it manifested itself in the market place coast to coast.

Charlottesville, Virginia was/is the home of Thomas Jefferson and his home, Monticello. It is also the home of his school, The University of Virginia. Consequently, I had a built in young adult audience to make happy at night.

I spent many hours those days and nights leading up to my debut Monday night listening to the competition and to WCHV as well. What I heard across the local dial was what not to do, WCHV included. The competition, WELK was a day timer Top 40-ish on AM. Which meant that they would be going off the air as my show got started.

All the dysfunction I was experiencing in the office at WCHV was more than apparent listening to it on air. I knew I had to stand out from the other day parts or die the terrible death of mediocrity I heard on air. The so-called Program Director was maybe two years older than me, but might as well have been twice his age and out of touch on just about every aspect of life in America, 1970. I knew guys in the business more than twice his age that were "with it". This guy, who I will not name, was an ass kisser, but more than that, did not have a clue about communicating, especially on radio. But he was the boss and reminded me of that in some way every day I worked there.

I would learn more about the others I worked with as time went on. The one thing that was very apparent. I had to go against every thought the so-called management team had because they were more than lost.

To be successful in the communications business whatever you do has to be real, and have a heartbeat. It must be alive, it must breath. It's an intrinsic thing. People just get it, if it's there. If it's not, then all the gimmicks in the world will, in time, fail.

Much as I was not "Jerry Pace" in my head, I knew I had to be real, that is to be me no matter what name I went by.

From Midnight to 6PM, WCHV at that time was a mish-mash of non descript so-called popular tunes from the fifties, sixties and a sprinkling of current Pop Tunes. The on air guys were mediocre to fair. The all night guy, Bill Avery was very funny and clever, but more so off air than on. He played the game of keeping his job and it was understandable considering he had a wife and family and needed the income. He knew what was what and was biding his time for a better condition. I came to like him a lot.

From 6PM to 7PM, the station ran ABC news, several of the networks information shorts and a local sports show with a well known, grumpy, local newspaper sports columnist. On the hour at 7PM ABC Information News and then the 7 to Midnight Show, which, before I began broadcasting my show, was more of the same boring mix as the rest of the day.

I resolved that I would be fighting "City Hall" from minute one if I truly wanted to make an impact in the market.

Although I was to be simulcast on AM and FM, they were so deep in the Dark Ages that the FM was not broadcasting in stereo. All the good music I was listening to had been stereo for nearly ten years. Every FM station was transmitting in stereo, but not WCHV. That would hurt the potential audience I wanted to build, but at least I would have fifty thousand watts of broadcast signal coming off Pantops Mountain, which would give me both high fidelity and signal reach way over the AM. The stereo issue would be a fight for another day. My immediate goal was to establish an on air identity, create an audience and build it.

The station was off the air from Sunday Midnight to 6am Monday. I wanted to get a good four to five hours on the main studio board to get a feeling for it before I hit air Monday night. So, while the engineering guys did their weekly maintenance on the transmitters, I rehearsed and got used to the audio board and where the controls for the on air equipment were. A tight, well run show relied on proper timing which is dependent upon having a solid feel for the equipment. Split second action and reaction supports the execution of the thinking processes. When done right, the communication carries over to the recipient without them thinking about anything except the content.

I left at 5:30 that morning knowing that I would be gone before the Program Director got there for his 6AM show. He could hear about me spending the night rehearsing from someone else. I wasn't going to let him see me or talk to me. I went home and to bed until the middle of the afternoon.

I got to the station at five and created a pile of the things I wanted for my first show on a large table in the studio immediately adjacent to the main on air studio. On top of my stack of things was my famous left ear only headphone. I always liked having my right ear open to the acoustics of the room where I was working while hearing what was on air in my left ear.

The afternoon DJ saw me through the glass and waved me into his studio. He said it looked to him like I was about to come in and go on air. I acknowledged that he was correct, that I was in fact starting as soon as he finished his show. He looked somewhat surprised, perhaps more confused than surprised.

He made note that just minutes before out in the hall he had seen the regular night guy getting ready like he had for the last several years. I thought to myself, great I get to tell this guy that he no longer has a job…yet another BIG Warning Light went off in my head…my thoughts progressed to: Were these so-called management types, the Program Director and the General Manager, so clueless that they would create one horrendous situation like this and not be on site to take care of it?

Not one to ever let the ball drop, I went back next door, got my things and brought them in the control room.

I remained quiet as the afternoon guy opened his microphone, said good night to his audience and started his last record which would lead into the station break and ABC News for five minutes.

He turned around looked at me and indicated he was getting the hell out of there. He guessed he would see me the next day and he left.

As he exited the one studio door, the other opened with the guy who thought he was going on the air. I was already reading the Broadcast Log preparing for what I needed to do to get through the station break and get ABC News on the air.

The night guy saw what I was doing, noted my pile of things and with anger wanted to know why I was there. I explained apologetically that he should have been told by management long before that moment that he was being replaced. Watching him was painful. I was not sure what he would do next. It was amateurish for the so-called "management duo" to have done this to him and to place me in this position. In retrospect, we both should have walked out of there never to return. I was twenty-two years old and needed the job. That was my limited perspective at the time. Writing about that awful experience I wish I knew the name of that man, he deserves recognition, but I never knew his name.

That "Opening Night" experience over shadowed the rest of my time at WCHV.

I was dedicated to my audience and poured my guts into reaching them over the air. I spent my days going around and getting to know as much about the community of Charlottesville as possible.

I quickly found one good alliance within the WCHV power structure in the person of Tom, the Sales Manager. As far as I remember, he had never sold broadcast time before, but he had the energy and the drive of a good sales person and had a reasonable grasp of promotion. There was no budget to buy other media to promote my show. No matter to me, I was happy to dream up ideas for things I did on my show that would draw attention to what I was doing, which would, if handled correctly, correlate to growing an audience and subsequently generate increased revenue.

In getting familiar with the station I started investigating unused offices and closets. In one of the closets in the sales office I found all this old WCHV promotion crap. Stuff like pins, T-shirts, small pennant banners, baseball caps all with the station call letters on them. Some of them were years old, but all I saw was shit to give-a-way!

I came up with what I called The Obscure Springtime Scavenger Hunt. The idea was to get people involved the minute they heard it announced, to get them out to find shit and be the first to bring it to me on air to claim their prize and get on air recognition.

I sat down and starting writing out things for listeners to go out and scavenge for. I didn't want it to be hard to find things. It gained immediate reaction from the audience. I was dreaming up truly wild stuff for them to find around town without trespassing on private property. After a week, Tom took the idea to the local Coca Cola Bottler who jumped right on it with cartons of Coke to giveaway as prizes. We had a pretty good wall of Coke in the studio all the time to award the scavengers.

On the show I was playing a lot of music unheard before in the Charlottesville radio market. The artists were already well known elsewhere, but I was the first to play on air in that market album tracks beyond the hits of Chicago, Crosby, Stills Nash & Young, The Moody Blues, It's A Beautiful Day, to name a few. As the clock got closer to midnight every evening, I would increase the number of album hits I was playing. I was getting positive feedback from the audience based on phone calls, letters and face to face chance meetings around town. Tom was getting good input as well and was looking for potential clients who would make for a symbiotic match to buy time on my show.

It was no surprise that the station did not have the albums I wanted to play on my show. Having great audio equipment at home, I transferred my LPs to reel to reel audio tape and used them on the show. It made for pristine audio quality and no wear and tear on my records. I catalogued my tapes and carried them to and from the station every day.

My demographics were sharply different from the rest of the day parts for WCHV. I was getting increasing reaction from the public in the 18-34 age range, whereas the audience for the other day parts was static to decreasing and for the most part was in a much older range of ages.

Doing a little digging and putting disconnected stories together I compiled this scenario about WCHV. The station had recently been acquired by Evans Communications. Evans, it turned out was the father of a young man who had been a student at Northwestern University. While attending Northwestern, he had taken broadcasting classes and among his professors was Jack Creech. One thing led to another and Evans junior got his wealthy father to get into the radio business and purchased WCHV. At the suggestion of his son, the older Evans then hired Jack Creech to run it.

Like any other business, broadcasting demands one hell of a lot more knowledge and experience out in the real world of commerce than what one will find in a pile of well written text books. Evans hired Creech to run a radio station when all he'd ever done was teach the subject of broadcasting. He had never earned a dollar working in a real station, much less run one. Learning this my second week added to my now growing list of warning lights about WCHV.

It was a strange mixture of thoughts that were going through my head. I had worked at four well run, highly motivated and very successful broadcast-production facilities prior to WCHV. Every action these guys took was counter to everything I had experienced. Communication is organic, not academic.

Approaching broadcasting with an academic organizational framework on which you hang creative, organic communication will spell success. But you must have both. WCHV only had the framework and that was not complete. There is no textbook for the creative part and these guys weren't smart enough to realize they didn't have a clue about how to do it, or even how to recognize it when it walked in the door and said "Hello".

At the time, and looking back on it, I never saw myself as some genius with the greatest ideas for a radio show. But I did have concepts formulated by my awareness of the times and had the fortitude to test the waters with them. I was willing to fail in my attempts, but was getting increasing external signs each day that I was on the right track and was succeeding at communicating with my audience.

Behind the scenes the Program Director (PD) started suggesting that I stick to the music he programmed and not add in my album cuts. I disagreed with him and presented the arguments that; a) after eight o'clock WELK signed off due to their "daylight only" license, b) therefore nothing was on air at night for young adults in the market. Those arguments muted him for a couple of weeks.

In sales, Tom was getting more enthused due to reactions to my show and was selling time bought for my show alone. It was not an immense amount, but a trend for listener habits was building with hard sales as concrete confirmation.

Interestingly enough, the Beatles THE LONG & WINDING ROAD was on the charts during this period. It was coincidental, but looking back, I think quite poignant for what I was going through.

Budweiser jumped on my show. It wasn't a large initial buy, but it was specific for my show and Anheiser-Busch's first time buy at WCHV in years.

I was only ten months out of Vietnam when, on April 30th, President Nixon announced he had sent US troops into Cambodia. On college campuses across the country already angry anti war activists seized this as a new yelling point. The anger boiled over five days later following the May 4th killing of four students by the Ohio National Guard at Kent State University in Ohio. (*I will discuss that tragedy in more depth later.*)

WCHV did not have a news department. The station did carry ABC News, but other than a United Press International (UPI) news teletype machine, there was nothing on site at the station to know what was happening locally, or anywhere for that matter. Primarily the UPI machine was on a circuit that provided weather reports and regional news briefs periodically throughout the day and night.

The night of Kent State, I started getting phone calls about things going on locally at The University of Virginia (UVA). Every hour, on-the-hour, I aired three and a half minutes of ABC News which was part of my nightly fare, but that night the stories were growing each hour of the unrest on campuses coast to coast. The students at UVA were reacting to the killings at Kent State too.

The newsman in me could not rest with all the events that were unfolding. The station had a battery powered portable audio tape recorder and microphone which I had located some weeks before. Early the night of May 4th, I had plugged the unit in to get the battery charged, thinking I might want it available to me.

When I got off the air at Midnight, I packed up the tape unit and drove to UVA. I did not know the campus map, but had an idea of a place off campus where I could park my car and walk on to the campus to witness and report anything going on.

There was not that much happening on that Monday night, but what I did discover was that the following night an event was to take place that had been scheduled for some time. Surprise, surprise, it had not gotten much promotion in the community-at-large. Chicago Seven defense attorney William Kuntsler was scheduled to speak on campus and with him would be Chicago Seven Defendant, Jerry Rubin.

I called the ABC News Desk in New York and let them know about the rally and that Kuntsler and Rubin were scheduled to appear. I offered to feed them what I could and they indicated they would appreciate any news I could report. Leaving it at that for the night, I packed it in around three AM and went home.

Kuntsler and Rubin arrived as scheduled Tuesday, May 5th. The rally took on an entirely different theme from what had been planned some weeks earlier. The ghastly shootings at Kent State the day before had left, in mere seconds, four shot dead, nine wounded and one paralyzed. All this had emanated from sixty-seven rounds of ammunition fired at unarmed students by "members" of the Ohio National Guard. Anger, fear and frustration were abounding from the Atlantic to the Pacific. It was a week of inappropriate actions that led to the shuttering of America's institutions of higher learning for the year and a shaking of the very core of our national spirit.

Among the things I witnessed that second night: an unnecessarily large number of Virginia State Police brought in to over power the few hundred student demonstrators; the students were not acting unlawfully, yet they were read the Riot Act, and given five minutes to disperse. Before the police completed reading it on their bull horns, they were charging the students with night sticks flying hitting whoever was within reach. Students trying to flee to avoid bashing from the police night sticks "looked" like they were rioting. The police were "handcuffing" everyone apprehended with plastic tie raps and herding them into tight groups.

After some ten to fifteen minutes of herding the students, a large, forty-foot moving van was rolled up and parked surrounded by police. They opened up the back doors of the trailer, attached a wooden walk up ramp to it and then starting herding the students into it.

The trailer was dark, empty with nothing inside to sit upon or hold on to. I could not believe what I was seeing. The police just kept pushing the students into it until no more would fit and then closed the doors on them. There were terrified screams from the female students and the men were yelling. I witnessed nothing on the part of the students that night that warranted this horrific treatment by the Virginia State Police.

They then drove this closed, moving van that was completely dark inside and full of students, packed in like cattle, downtown to process them.

Remember, nearly three years before in 1967, I had spent a week covering the racial unrest in Cincinnati. There were actions by groups of citizens then that required strong police action to end the insurrection. I had a very accurate picture in my head of what illegal rioting looked like. What happened that night in 1970 at UVA was far from anything one would label as rioting.

It took a few minutes to relocate downtown to follow the students in the moving van. I got to Police Headquarters to find the doors closed and locked. There were police and students everywhere. I could see through the single half glass front door that things were happening inside. I started banging on the door to gain entry. I had the audio tape machine slung over my shoulder with a microphone in one hand and my Press Credentials in the other which I held clearly visible up against the glass. A very angry Charlottesville Police Senior Officer came to the door and yelled at me without opening it. He ordered me to go away or he would arrest me.

I flashed on the idea to challenge him, but then thought that I could do more by reporting what I was seeing versus spending the night locked up and silenced. I yelled back at him that what he said would be part of my report. He started yelling even louder at me and I just walked away.

The UVA demonstrators gathered throughout the night inside various university buildings trying to work up a list of "demands" they wanted to present to the university administration. Despite their well intentioned rhetoric, not much was accomplished. I gave them some news airtime. Much of what they had to say expressed their frustrations with the government, the Vietnam War and rights overall. The complaints were common to their generational counterparts across the nation at the time.

At UVA the only destruction I witnessed at the hands of the students was a trash dumpster that got set afire and pushed down a hillside.

191

For many across the country, the events of that week were devastating. The generation gap truly reached a pinnacle. I wanted to put an appropriate melodic period at the end of my radio show for the week. I said goodnight at midnight, Saturday, May 9th with Crosby, Stills, Nash & Young's TEACH YOUR CHILDREN.

The week after Kent State was uneventful for the world of Jerry Pace and WCHV. The fact that nothing was said to me by the PD about my show suggested that something was up. I could feel it in the air.

The following Monday when I got to the station, the PD asked to speak with me. I didn't even get fully in the chair across from him in his postage stamp sized office when he told me that they wanted to retain me, but that beginning that night I would make my broadcast sound exactly like the rest of WCHV's day parts. I was not to play any of the album cuts I had made popular with my audience, nor run the Scavenger Hunt anymore.

I thought to stand up, tell him to go fuck himself and walk out. Just as quickly I realized how out of touch and stupid he was. I told him strongly that I disagreed with him, but he was the boss and I walked out.

My anger was gone. It was time for thought and then action. The first thing I did was walk into an empty studio where no one could hear me and get on the phone. I called my contact at Budweiser and told him that as of that night The Jerry Pace Show was dead and told him why. He was pissed and wanted to call and cancel his order. I told him that for the best impact to wait until the following day after hearing the change and to complain directly to Jack Creech, the General Manager and then cancel the order. I reminded him that he and I never had the conversation. He replied by saying, "what conversation?"

I did very sterile broadcasts on Monday, Tuesday and Wednesday showing up just in time to go on the air and departed right after. The studio phone rang and rang and rang each night. Unlike the months prior, I did not answer it and talk with my listeners.

Bill Avery, the guy who followed me with the all night show, and who I liked, asked me Wednesday before I left if I was pissed at him. I apologized and said it was nothing personal and left for the night.

Thursday I again arrived in time for air and did a sterile broadcast until nine o'clock. During the network news I ran out to my car and brought in my album music tapes. Right after ABC News, Jerry Pace returned for three hours in force. The phones lit up, I talked with everyone I could. I signed off at midnight the way I had for months, "Jerry Pace, Love and Peace, Good Night". (*I knew that neither the PD nor the GM would hear what I did after 9pm, especially after the previous three nights had been the way they wanted them*).

Avery came in the studio. I told him I would be around most of the night but couldn't really tell him what I was up to until later.

First, I took everything in the building that was mine out to my car and locked it up. All I had with me inside was my brief case.

I went out to the desk in Reception where the only IBM Selectric typewriter in the building was. Remember, this was 1970, there were no PC's.

I proceeded to draw up my Letter of Resignation addressed to Mr. Evans, the owner of the station. It was a tell-him-EVERYTHING letter. It was truth, raw truth about what I had gone through with both the GM and the PD. There would be no trying to put a different spin to these written words. I hung those two broadcast wizards out-to-dry and left them to twist-in-the-wind.

193

I was careful to keep it professional in content and appearance. The original was sent by messenger to Evans. Photo copies were put in manila envelops, sealed and slid under the office doors of Creech and the PD. I left personal notes to several staff members who I had come to like along with instructions as to where to send my final compensation and commission checks.

I went in the air studio and said good bye to Bill Avery and asked him to say nothing to the PD when he came in for his morning broadcast.

Around five with dawn rising in the East, I walked out of WCHV for the last time and went back to my apartment to pack.

I had mixed thoughts about the whole experience. As sole proprietor, Evans should never have been an absentee owner. That fact stood out to me as soon as I arrived. He was being led down the path by two guys who didn't have a clue about how to run a radio station. I don't think they were being intentionally devious. They truly believed they knew what they were doing. But the truth was they had no sense of the times, the trends in broadcasting, or, and most importantly, how to organically reach out to and communicate with an audience. You can't fake or package that.

As I packed my clothes and audio gear, my phone began to ring around ten that morning and did so every fifteen minutes until I walked out of my apartment around four thirty for the last time to leave Charlottesville.

I drove out of town with the radio off. I was heading towards Cincinnati. I had called my parents before I had my phone turned off to let them know I was headed their way and would be there by that Sunday. I had friends to call to connect for work, but decided to make those calls from my folks the first of the week.

I called my cousin Bobbie in Columbus to see if she was up for a one night visit. It was the only time in all of our years that we ever did anything together without other cousins or siblings around. She had been an education major at Ohio State and after graduation stayed in Columbus to teach.

We went out for an early supper and took in the movie M*A*S*H. I had surprising reactions to watching parts of it. I was out of Vietnam less than a year and some of the references to the preferential treatment of officers versus enlisted men as portrayed in the film pissed me off. Don't get me wrong, I know the medical corps had their hands full trying to keep up with the amount of carnage that was coming to them by the hour. They did the best they could under the conditions and frequently did truly amazing medical work. It was too close and personal at that time for me to find the humor in some of those scenes. I loved the film as a whole and laughed my ass off at most of it. My more recent viewings of M*A*S*H have been enjoyable from start to finish. That first time was too close to my raw, real experiences in war.

Chapter Thirty / Back to Square One

My parents welcomed me home but were concerned about my well being. I had been home from the war fifty weeks and had gone through four jobs in three cities. I had spent the long hours alone driving back from Charlottesville having the very same thoughts.

I had tapes from my better shows at WCHV and edited together new audition tapes to put with resumes as I went job hunting at stations in Cincinnati. One station, WEBN, had caught my musical ear since returning from the war. There were many terms to describe stations like it across the country at the time. Essentially they played Album Oriented Rock and Roll, were eclectic and usually had their own identity unique to the area they served. The audience was young and ranged in age from around fifteen to thirty.

WEBN had been started by Frank Wood, a second generation Harvard educated attorney whose own eclectic musical tastes ranged from classical to jazz. He got so involved in his love of both, that he became very knowledgeable in good audio recording techniques and made hard and fast friends throughout Cincinnati's wealth of professional musicians. He also had one large, amazing record collection.

One thing led to another and by 1966 Frank had found an untaken, open Class B FM radio license in Cincinnati on 102.7 MHz. He filed for the license and got it. One year later WEBN was on the air playing classical music by day and jazz all night.

Unfortunately it did not take long for him to realize that as great as the two music forms were, and as popular as WEBN was with the audience, it was not impacting the ratings logs. Without ratings quotients and a sales apparatus to sell the programming, WEBN was not financially sustainable.

Returning from the legal study books of Harvard came his son, Frank III full of piss, vinegar and a head full of newer music he had picked up during his time in Cambridge.

Long story short, Frank III's newer music at first got a few hours a week and over eighteen months had become two thirds of the stations on air music.

During my couple of weeks of job hunting before moving to Virginia, I had stopped by WEBN and had had a long talk with Frank Sr. At that time they were not in a position to hire anyone, but he was open to speaking with me at a later time and encouraged me to check in periodically.

It had been over four months since our last meeting, so I went by and talked with Frank. His answer was the same, but he said conditions were much better and that I should check in every few weeks.

I wasn't getting anywhere with possible work in Cincinnati, so I called a close friend from high school, Mark Ehrhardt, who was living in Chicago, to see if I could crash at his place for a few days while I job hunted. Mark graciously said OK.

It takes about seven hours to drive from Cincinnati to the north end of Chicago. As I got closer to the Windy City my mind wandered to the images of the Chicago Police and the Democratic Convention not even two years earlier. I then flashed on my lack of a driver's license. I was still a full month away from getting it back from Hamilton County Court. I rechecked my freeway speed, gripped the wheel a little tighter and again took a deep breath remembering my resolve to obey every traffic sign to the letter.

The beginning of summer of 1970 was a whirl wind of job chasing in Chicago. I got nothing but a Windy City run-a-round. Through my friend Terry Donohue, I landed a job in video tape production at National Teleproductions (NTP) in Indianapolis. We did all sorts of regional and national television commercials. It was a period of transition for many of the big Ad agencies as they were learning the value of video tape instead of film for shooting and editing high profile commercials. I, along with a highly talented group of production and technical types, all in our twenties, killed ourselves eighteen or more hours a day Monday through Friday shooting and editing commercials. The hours were long, but I loved the ever evolving and growing experiences. It was a great group of people with whom to work.

Within days of getting hired at NTP, Frank Wood called and wanted to know if I was interested in doing weekend radio shows at WEBN. I took the job immediately. I had that Friday off at NTP, so I drove to Cincinnati to meet with Frank and seal the deal.

As Frank was looking over the form I filled out for Employ Withholding, he looked at my last name and asked if I was going to go by Peter Breidenbach on the air. I told him of all the bad on air names I had used and said I was open for a suggestion. In his intelligent, twinkling eyes I could see the wheels turning. A smile crept over his face and he asked, "How about Peter Bright?" "Yes", I responded, "That's perfect!" Professionally and darn near every other way, I've been Peter Bright ever since.

(*Years later my three, wonderful Bright Kids, Rebecca Rose, Harrison Howard and Sydney Sarah would be born and legally named "Bright", as is their mother, Lynn, who hyphenatedly, goes by Rosen-Bright, combining her birth name with Bright*).

I poured myself into television production at NTP during the weekdays and whatever was left of me at the end of work on

Friday I'd get in my Mustang and drive the hundred miles to Cincinnati and do radio shows on Saturdays and Sundays at WEBN. Then either Sunday night, or Monday very early, I'd drive back to work the week at NTP.

I did that for six weeks until one Friday afternoon around five o'clock my wake up call was the bumpity-bump of the rocky, grassy median strip down the middle of Interstate 74 at 70 miles-per-hour. Talk about an instant cold sweat! My license had been back in my possession just over a month at that point. Lucky for me no one was around to witness my behind the wheel slumber. I eased my Pony Car back on the pavement, turned up WEBN to hear Frank sitting in for his son, Bo. I drove right to the station knowing that he would love to turn the on air doings over to me so he could take care of other matters. I walked in the studio; he turned around and said, "Boy, am I glad to see you".

Chapter Thirty-One / WEBN

WEBN offered me a fulltime radio show at the end of the summer. I quit NTP, but made certain that it was a happy break on both sides in order to secure my connection with them. They knew the high level of my work and we left the door open for freelance work in the future.

I settled into doing radio at WEBN. It felt right for my life and my career at that moment. As time passed I found myself in the middle of a power struggle between the two Frank Woods. The old man had pioneered and started the station. He had put his life, guts and money into it and here came his son with what was turning out to be music and a developing format that was more viable commercially.

Frank had hired me, his son, (known off air as "Bo"), saw me as one of his dad's boys hired to work on his, (Bo's), radio station. Stupid me…I had thought they were just one hard working family with a common goal. To be clear, they did share the goal of making WEBN a commercial success. But the way of getting to that, and who was in charge, the fall of 1970, was far from an agreed consensus.

At the time only Frank signed the checks. I did not know it when I started, but to make room on the payroll for me, Frank fired a guy who was very popular with the staff. It would be some weeks before I knew about it. I had a cloud hanging over my head and it was none of my doing.

Cincinnati has a wonderful community known as Mount Adams. It has narrow and very steep streets, with amazing hill top views of the Ohio River, Cincinnati's downtown plus within walking distance the immediate and beautiful Eden Park. People often refer to it as "Little San Francisco". It has also been compared to Greenwich Village. For years a middleclass Irish-Catholic neighborhood, it had drawn eclectic, creative types of various genres to pepper themselves throughout the community.

The large Cincinnati Art Museum and Art Academy centered itself there in the early 1900's. That physicality attracted artists who resided in and around Mount Adams for decades. Another creative force located in the middle of Mount Adams is the popular and well supported Equity Theater, Playhouse in the Park.

What had been local, neighborhood bars gave way to some featuring live jazz while others would on weekends have rock bands. It was the place to be Friday and Saturday nights if you were a young, upwardly mobile adult in Cincinnati.

There were then, and still are today, many great places in which to live with prices near nothing to many millions. Such price disparities can be literally across a street from one another.

I looked for and found an apartment in Mount Adams that was in a building known as The Barracks. It had been built for the Union Army as an officer's quarters during the Civil War. It was a two story building with four apartments across the top and four across the bottom. I had one of the units on the second floor with a comfortable bedroom, a large living room with a fireplace, a good sized kitchen and a bath. It had eleven foot ceilings and though far from fancy, was perfect for that time in my life. My décor was whatever I could scrounge that was clean.

Due to low income in the early years, the fertile minds around WEBN manufactured some fanciful, wonderful on air characters who created the on air ambiance that more people worked there than actually did. Among the suspects were: George Gregory,

Frank's on air alter ego; Michael Zanadu, son Bo's public voice; and the station Program Director, Miles Duffy who was known to sleep under the record racks to "get closer to the music". Duffy was also famous for escorting young females on "tours of the station" which inevitably always crescendo'd with a trip behind the Transmitter Shack. Duffy was seldom heard on air, that may have been because he was Frank's wonderfully animated and overly friendly Springer Spaniel, whom I surnamed "Shlop-Face". I met Duffy before I met Frank on my first visit to the station. He was at the front door playing Receptionist. He slobbered all over me and then having established us as friends, he took a nap with his head slung over my leg. Duffy was referred to and often spoken of, or about, in spontaneous vignettes by all of us on air. Sometimes we would get Memorandums from Miles Duffy; hey he *was* the Program Director.

Because of the lack of paid sponsors and commercials, Frank invented and promoted the entity Brute Force Cybernetics (BFC). It was a fictitious organization that was presented on air as real. BFC was forever introducing new items to the market place which were promoted through elaborate, well produced "commercials". The best example of these was when Brute Force introduced Negative Calorie Cookies. For months people around Cincinnati were going into stores trying to buy them. When strangers would figure out I was Peter Bright of WEBN, inevitably someone would ask where they could get Negative Calorie Cookies, or whatever BFC was pushing at the time.

As the staff got to know me both at work and socially away from the station, our relationships improved and the cloud over me evaporated.

During the time I was working weeks in Indianapolis and weekends on WEBN, I met a young lady named Samm on a video shot at NTP. It was part of a pilot for a possible TV series for syndication. A staff Director by the name of Eric Morrison and I had become good friends. We dreamed up this idea to take current hit tunes and shoot video to go with them. NTP fronted the studio, equipment, editing and paid for our time. Everything else was up to us. I picked a piece of music from the Moody Blues, a track called HIGHER and HIGHER from their To Our Children's' Children album. And "bursting forth with the power of ten billion butterfly sneezes" the video got made with Samm and a half dozen actor friends of hers looking like stoned out hippies frozen in space while sucking on the tubes of a fancy water pipe. At the end everyone slowly evaporated, disappeared while a large, lit candle, the water pipe and the furniture on which they had sat remained in frame. A summer 1970 music video, we were only ten years ahead of our time. (*I have still have copies in three tape formats*).

I was quite taken with Samm. We commenced a long distance relationship. She returned to Greenwich Village where she was living and I wound up at WEBN, but we telephoned late many a night after eleven, when the rates were low, all through the fall.

After the holidays we reached the point we wanted to give being together a try. I arranged to have one of the guys cover my weekend radio show so I could drive to New York to get her. I got off the air at three that Friday afternoon, got in my new Mustang and drove the twelve hours to NYC in non stop pouring rain.

Somewhere on the Pennsylvania Turnpike in the middle of a long straight stretch I was the only vehicle on the road. The east bound side at that point was on a different level and away from the west bound lanes. The rain was thick with the only illumination coming from my headlights. Suddenly an immaculate, large wild rabbit landed in the lane right in front of my right fender. Poised in a stately profile, eyes opened wide, ears straight up, facing right to left, he was frozen there lit perfectly for a fraction of a second. At seventy miles an hour, I had no time to react, only time to hit him. A microsecond in my life visually imprinted permanently. I felt no impact, nor heard one, but it is for certain that Peter Bright wiped out Peter Rabbit that night. There was no fault or blame about it and I felt sad that it happened. Sudden, unnecessary death was something I had had too much of in my life already.

The remainder of the drive was uneventful. I arrived at Samm's just as daybreak was coming to Manhattan. Her apartment was typical of so many in the Village at the time. A once truly classy building where they had taken a normal, large apartment and had literally cut it in two running a wall down the middle creating "two" apartments where one had been. Landlords would jack up the price and get two overpriced rents where before they had gotten only one. (*Sometimes capitalism goes too far.*)

We were too keyed up to get any rest so we got out and about in lower Manhattan for the day. After an evening with her sister, with whom she lived, and the New York friends she was leaving, we got some sleep and returned to Cincinnati the next day.

Samm and I were comfortable together. She was the first woman with whom I cohabitated. I was almost twenty-four and had a lot to learn about living with a woman. Our mutual levels of allowing and accepting of the other made it actually quite easy to settle in together. She mixed in well with the WEBN crowd and others. My parents invited us to dinner at the house. The evening was easy and fun. Samm's father was an artist and so she was right in there understanding and appreciating my mom. She and my dad hit it off right away too. I wanted that natural, unforced connection. You either get it, or you don't, from that first microsecond.

Samm had not been home to Indianapolis since the previous summer so I drove her there one evening. I met her parents and liked them immediately. I left her to spend some time with her folks. I was not clear on how long she was going to stay, but I left that up to her.

Samm liked having a lot of people around. She was easy to like right away. She had a comeliness about her that men liked. Women didn't seem to be threatened by her. She turned out to be a great cook. We had many an evenings' meal with guests and socializing. The WEBN crowd was over often.

A sudden series of changes came to WEBN. Bo Wood got an offer from ABC to go run WDAI, their FM station in Chicago. I thought at the time that it would be a great opportunity for him to learn more about how to run a radio station. He would have to live up to the expectations and discipline of big time American corporate executives. Further he would get to know organizational set ups and systems that support successful radio stations.

I never thought he would leave and not come back. I figured he was going to Chicago for a well paid on the job education and I was right. Having worked for well run large and small broadcasting companies, I saw WEBN's deficiencies from day one, but understood the milieu and knew that Bo's ego would prevent him from hearing about them from me.

We went through a period of many transitions in Bo's absence. Bo was very strong in the music, tone and direction of what was on the air. Those were his real strengths. While he was getting close to the hierarchy of ABC Radio, he connected his second in command at WEBN, one Denton Marr, to get a management position at KLOS, the ABC FM in Los Angeles. All the changes of personnel at WEBN would eventually affect me.

Early spring came and I was feeling amorous all the time. Samm was certainly amenable and responsive to my advances. Having never lived with a woman before I had no point for comparison, but to be somewhat discreet here I will write that her appetite was bigger than mine.

I was on air from ten to three during the week with my normal day being bracketed with writing and recording commercials before and after my air shift. I would get home around five thirty. I came home one evening to find WEBNs new weekend and partime guy, sleeping one off in my living room. Known to his radio audience as "Captain Nimmo", Geoffrey Nimmo was (and is) one of those characters you meet who you just can't help but love.

(I had worked with his father, Bill Nimmo, back at WLWT five years before who had been an on air fixture of early network television in the 50's & 60's. He worked with Jackie Gleason, Johnny Carson and had been the Pabst Blue Ribbon Beer man much the way Ed McMahan was later for Budweiser.)

Geoffrey eventually woke up, had some supper with us and then was on his Honda 250 motor bike and off for the night. I figured no big deal. He wasn't the only guy from the station who was hanging out at my place while I was at work.

It took a while to play out. Nimmo eventually stopped his daily siestas in my living room. But another one of our DJ's continued his daily visits and they were, shall I write, not innocent sleep-it-offs in the living room like Nimmo's.

I don't remember exactly how I found out, but it turned out that for some time, Chris Gray, who had been hired to replace Denton on air at night was following me into my bed after I left to go to work at the station. Samm's complicity in this was undeniable. They were spending their days amorously in my bed while listening to me on the radio.

I was hurt and angry. I confronted her and said she had to go. She packed and the next day I drove her to the airport. I walked her into the terminal and can still see her standing there a few feet away as we said a quiet, flat good bye. It would be a year before I tried cohabitating again.

Chapter Thirty-Two / A Station Break

I'll never know exactly why, but a few weeks after Samm left and went back to New York, I found myself out at WEBN and not by my choice.

I called Terry Donohue and got back into television production. We worked on a video taped syndicated TV music series, THE STAN GUNN SHOW. We taped complete shows with an audience for a couple of weeks at Six Flags over Georgia, and taped some production numbers on location in Atlanta's Underground. When then pulled up stakes and reconvened in The French Quarter in New Orleans. Gunn and his troupe of singers and musicians were quite talented and great to work with. He had a similarity to the style of Johnny Cash, but he was not Johnny and that is most likely why, though successful for many years performing live at venues around the country, he never made it into big time television.

The GUNN SHOW brought me together with an infamous television facility guru by the name of Howard "Such a Deal" Zuckerman. He became known as the "Golden Buddha", due to his ability to create many a business deal out of nothing. He could get monies to do things like the GUNN SHOW, hell he put together National Teleproductions (NTP), which wound up being a multi-million dollar video facility out of televising The Miss Indiana Pageant, (or something like that). His physical appearance added to the Buddha mystic as he was bald and somewhat round.

Not long after we finished the GUNN Show, Howard called me and wanted to know if I would help produce a News-Documentary Special for the Associated Press. It would mean working in New York City for a few weeks. I asked what it was about and characteristically he wanted to know first if I would do it. I said that I would, but would he please tell me about it. The next thing he wanted to know was how soon I could get on a plane to New York. Without a beat I said the following day. His response was to say he had to set it up, would call me later and he hung up. That was Howard. In those days he was a "right now guy", no fucking around, "just go". He did call back later with my airline information, the hotel I would be staying in and that he would meet me at Baggage Claim at LaGuardia as he would be getting in at about the same time.

You have to remember the year was 1971. The Associated Press was still primarily a news gathering organization providing news and wire photos to newspapers and radio-TV stations by wire on teletype machines in their news rooms. Television specials were not on their radar at that time. There was an occasional TV project like the one I was about to commence.

This turned out to be a fascinating project on China. Entitled: CHINA, AN OPEN DOOR.

The special was being written by John Roderick, of the Associated Press (AP), their main Far East correspondent since the end of World War II.

In 1943, in the middle of WW-II, Roderick had been drafted into the Office of Strategic Services, a precursor to the CIA. He was sent to China. During the war the Chinese Nationalists and the Chinese communists, led by Mao Zedong, shared a mutual enemy, the Japanese. Roderick got to know all the players personally. When the war ended, he rejoined the AP and stayed in China to cover the breakdown in relations between the two Chinese entities. During the four years of fighting between the Nationalists and Mao's Communists, Roderick lived with Mao Zedong and Zhou EnLai and other Chinese guerillas in a cave outside Yenan.

When Mao Zedong became Chairman of the Peoples Republic of China and Zhou EnLai became Premier, Roderick left the country for other assignments, but kept China at the top of his list of interests.

One of the few positive accomplishments of Richard Nixon's presidency was the opening of diplomatic, cultural and economic doors between The United States and The Peoples Republic of China for the first time since 1949.

Early in 1971, the US Ping Pong team went to China to compete and Roderick accompanied them. It became known as the famous "Ping-Pong Diplomacy". During that week, at a major dinner-reception, Zhou EnLai, Premier of The peoples Republic, stood up and raised a Toast to John Roderick in which he said, "Mr. Roderick, you opened the door".

Considering all he had done as a professional journalist, and having lived through the years in the caves outside Yenan with Mao and company, I was pleased to find John Roderick to be a very regular person. He was interesting and interested always in the people, places and things around him. He also possessed a great sense of humor around his core of concentrated determination. He was curious with an appetite for learning about people who were outside of his circle of knowledge. We met and liked each other immediately. We shared his quality of forever being curious about life. He told me he could not understand how anyone came to the conclusion that once they left the hallowed halls of a learning institution that "school was out". He said for him that was only the first chapter of an endless succession of chapters which would end eventually with death. I told him that on all of that he was "preaching to the choir".

I spent the better part of two weeks digging through the endless, amazing photo and film archives of the Associated Press finding one great historic piece after another to visually substantiate the script that Roderick was writing at a fever pitch. If what I needed was unattainable at the AP, we had access to anything we wanted at the United Nations archives. I made several runs over to the eastside to the bowels of the UN to get pieces to our ever growing photographic puzzle. I was excited to be able to go into the UN and be given carte blanche access to whatever we needed. They were exceedingly kind and helpful.

Gathering film and photos led to a monumental compilation of materials which would be traveling with us to Atlanta to bring it all together on video tape. Why Atlanta you ask? We were on a very small budget compared to what CBS or NBC would have spent on a similar project. The AP provided Roderick's services as host and writer plus all the materials I had been gathering. The producing, compiling and getting it all on video tape and edited for air was on me and Zuckerman. This is where Mr. "Such-a-Deal" Howard made a home run. Remember, this is 1971. Howard knew that a fully equipped UHF television station in Atlanta had gone off the air due to a lack of sales. The facilities were available for use at a fraction of the cost for the same in New York, LA or Chicago.

We shot Roderick in the studio to do his on camera pieces. I put a camera with moves on all the stills I had gathered, we transferred all the film we had to video tape and then sat and edited the entire hour together for little more than the cost of the airfare, hotel, rent-a-car and out-of-pocket expenses. The program was remarkable and that was due mostly to John Roderick. He was as fascinating on camera as he was face to face. It was a lot of leg work for me and I enjoyed every moment of it. I wore five, maybe six hats and that's how I work best.

My life long working philosophy: What ever needs to be done, get it done…NOW.

Roderick flew back to Tokyo right after we finished. The AP had him based there for years and for him that was home. I never connected with him again after that. I wish I had, but we were in two different worlds except for several weeks the summer of '71.

That Atlanta UHF television station facility we rented to put the program together would eventually be bought by Ted Turner. It became WTBS, the Super Station of the 70's and 80's with the separate creation of CNN in 1980. The rest, as they say is history.

I free lanced my way around after the China special and connected to a start up production company in Chicago. They hired me and I moved to Chicago and got a place over looking Belmont Harbor. The company had nice second floor offices on Ohio Street. By my third day at the office things did not seem right. I had set up my office and was ready to get on the phone and do what one does prepping for a production, but there was nothing for which to prepare. The President of the company who had hired me was always behind closed doors and was avoiding me. Talking with other employees, I knew there was trouble in the air and it was not about me. I saw an opening and walked into his office. I looked into his nervous eyes and asked if the company was dead before it started. Like letting the air out of a balloon, he deflated into his chair and said that all the financial backers had taken advantage of an escape clause written in to their contract and had bailed.

He had tried to get other investors but to no avail. My contract was worthless. Stupidly I had spent good money to move, get a nice apartment and poof, no job. Shit.

I wasted no time getting my things out of that office. Before I left I made three phone calls. One was to Bo Wood down the street at ABC Radio, WDAI. He said to come over and talk.

He shut the door when I came in and then told me that his dad had some health issues and that he would be returning to run WEBN. I said that I would like to return also. He agreed that would be a good idea as he didn't understand why I had been let go several months before.

I left Bo to go back to my place on Belmont Harbor to break my lease and pack.

Chicago was now history and I was in a rented van returning to Cincinnati and WEBN after a summer of work and travel from coast to coast and points in between. I'd flown to San Francisco, worked in New York, Atlanta two times and New Orleans, taken a seven day jeep trip to Virginia, moved to Chicago and moved back to Cincinnati all in one hundred and nine days.

Chapter Thirty-Three / WEBN Take 2

Back at WEBN, things were different. Bo's nine months with ABC Radio-WDAI-WLS were, (as I had thought they would be), a great education to a fast learner. Behind the scenes WEBN was in a constant state of reorganization for programming and administration.

We were beginning to change on air as well. Before we had been more free form with the DJs controlling their shows choosing what they played and when. The new era brought program formatting such that we could choose a piece of music from a given list in a rotation of lists, with each list being a type of music. The intended purpose was to provide the listener a broader variety of music and feelings within a given space of time. There was certain reasonableness to the plan. Unfortunately, once a control freak like Bo starts to micro-manage one aspect of something, it doesn't take long before every other incremental piece is dissected to the same degree.

It took me almost a minute to get back into the groove of being on the air at WEBN. It was reassuring and fun to get "glad you're back" phone calls, letters from listeners and personal greetings when out and about. I took Chris Gray aside and we talked out the "Samm Issue" putting her and that mess behind us.

I took a week break during the non rating period at the end of the holidays in December to go televise The Peach Bowl football classic in Atlanta. It was good money, a needed break in the routine, kept up my television production contacts and put a period on 1971. Whew!

Early in the next year I was walking through New Dilly's Pub in Mount Adams one night after my radio show. I ran into an acquaintance from my high school days. I had known her as Betty Hyman, a striking natural blonde who was highly intelligent, quirky, funny, intense on her interests and very nice. I had always found her attractive, but she was tied up with a guy named Barry with whom I had worked at Aglamesis' Ice cream & Candy Store when I was seventeen.

I had not seen her in over seven years, but recognized her immediately. I walked up and said hello. We talked for maybe an hour during which time I found out that she had gone back to her birth name of Elizabeth versus Betty. She and Barry had been married for several years and had just recently divorced. She had become a legal secretary after some years of political activism.

Involved with the 1968 Democratic Party Presidential campaign she had worked in campaign headquarters at the infamous Convention in Chicago. Among her many great stories about that week in the Windy City was when, late one night, the Chicago Police stormed into the Party Headquarters hotel suite and busted all the heads of the staff and volunteers, then dragged them outside where they were immediately arrested and charged each with whatever was convenient. She too would have been beaten and arrested had she not answered Nature's Call and gone into one of the bathrooms just before they stormed in. Behind the locked bathroom door she got to sit there relieving herself while hearing her coworkers being beaten and dragged away, not by muggers, but by the Chicago PD.

I won't go further into all of that, I was not there. If you are lacking in knowledge of that unfortunate week in our country's history, then look it up. Many mistakes were made by individuals all over the issue. It was a very definitive period and out of it there was, eventually, some growth and understanding...I think.

I felt immediately moved to ask Elizabeth out. From that evening forward we were inseparable and were quick to live together. She was a voracious reader on many subjects. Her mind accurately stored everything she read. She was exceptional on so many levels.

I could write volumes about Elizabeth. We had some very good times together. She was a loving, good partner and wife. I loved her and yet I hurt her deeply and ended our marriage after only two years. She moved to the high California desert north of Palm Springs and I moved to Barrington Hills, Illinois, north and west of Chicago to work with Howard Zuckerman at the newly formed Mobile Television Services.

Chapter Thirty-Four / On the Road (by Plane)

Cat Stevens wrote the song: ON THE ROAD TO FIND OUT. Thinking on parts of my life, it would be a fitting title for some of it.

After splitting up with Elizabeth I was a wondering soul for the next year and a half. We had a Separation Agreement with part of the terms being that I would send her monthly support payments to restart her life. I wanted to help her and agreed to it lovingly.

Elizabeth and I remained close and in contact periodically until her untimely death in 2011.

Mobile Television Services (MTS) was, in 1974, the "Cadillac" of large mobile remote video facilities for doing both live television shows and the recording of shows for editing and later broadcast. The four and a half million dollar rig looked from the outside like a low riding forty foot moving van. (*The fifty-three foot trailers common today were not allowed at the time. I wish they had been, we could have made good use of the extra thirteen feet*).

I was hired with the title of Production Coordinator. My responsibilities: Do whatever it took to successfully accomplish the many increments that went in to getting productions completed. I'll give you the laughs of some those shenanigans later.

Initially the company was formed with the commitment to facilitate and produce THE WORLD FOOTBALL LEAGUE Game-of-the-Week.

From July to December, 1974 every Thursday night at 9PM, Eastern Time, the World Football Game-of-the-Week hit the air from coast to coast on the TVS Television Network. With me were roughly twenty five men involved in the on air production and facilities.

A little history: TV sports watchers from the 1960's and 70's will remember the TVS Network. Started by Eddie Einhorn, it was a network that for years existed on paper and lived out of Eddie's brief case. Back when nobody was interested, Eddie went around to dozens of universities and athletic groups, like the Missouri Valley Conference and signed them up for the TV rights to broadcast their basketball games.

In time as television sports grew, so did TVS. By 1973 Eddie was approached by the multi-station corporation, Corinthian Broadcasting, who wanted to buy TVS. After considerable negotiations Eddie agreed to sell it for an undisclosed mountain of money and stay on as Chairman of the Board to continue TVS on its successful path.

World Football was an attempt to start a whole new professional football league. Eddie jumped on it right away knowing it would either succeed or fail. If it caught on, there were endless millions to be made for many years. He understood that in order to make an impact in the national market place, there would have to be a weekly national game-of-the-week on television. Because of his years of successful sports television, Eddie was able to broker enough national sponsors who signed on for the entire run of the season, no matter what happened. Eddie and TVS were covered and into profit long before there was a kick off.

Based on that Eddie called his good buddy, Howard Zuckerman and the deal to televise the five and half months of games was sealed. With that commitment, Howard got the backing to form

Mobile Television Services from an investor who put up over four million dollars to build the truck.

The truck would not be ready for air for several months, so we leased other trucks for the early weeks of games. We televised games originating in California, Alabama, Florida, Tennessee, Illinois, Oregon, and many others.

We had two on air broadcasters. Play by play was handled beautifully by Merle Harmon, who also did baseball broadcasting for the Milwaukee Brewers. His color commentator, side kick was an ex-NFL player, Alex "The Hawk" Hawkins, who had been a Running Back for the Baltimore Colts and the Atlanta Falcons. Alex was colorful both on air and off. He knew the game and the people in, and around it, both forwards and backwards. There's a line there, but I'll pass.

We featured a guest commentator each week. Among those who joined us during those twenty-four Thursday night broadcasts: Alex Karras, McClean Stevenson, and Burt Reynolds to name three.

I was the Associate Director, Associate Producer, Stage Manager and Production Coordinator. All of us at MTS were forever shuffling our hats of responsibility from one conversation to the next and frequently within a conversation. It was the only way to run the company successfully. We were competing with the three networks who, at that time, still maintained their own rolling remote facilities with dozens of personnel across many disciplines. Their remote trucks and crews were essentially an amount which was part of the direct costs on a production therefore a convenient cost-of-business write off for the corporations.

We at MTS would not have existed nor competed successfully if we had carried the amount of employee overhead they had.

I saw MTS as an opportunity to learn more about production techniques, technical facilities, the finances, and the costs while working my ass off seven days a week. Additionally I made contacts while creating a name for myself across the industry. I dedicated myself to living my life out of my suitcase in order to do all that.

Though based in suburban Chicago I was there a fraction of the time. It was 1974…no cell phones, no internet, no phones in planes, just pay phones everywhere. Many a time I would board a plane early get to my seat, leave my locked brief case in it, establish myself with the cabin crew and then run off to the nearest pay phone and conduct business on the phone until I saw them closing the gate for take off.

At Chicago's O'Hare airport I would park my car convenient to the airline on which I was departing to return days to weeks later, late at night, after exhaustive, long days not remembering where the hell I parked my car. I devised a system for knowing where I left it. I would put my keys in an envelope in my brief case with the garage, floor etc… written on it. In my work I had many things put to memory every day which were available to quick mental recall, but for some reason, where the hell I left my car, was not one of them.

In Chicago, especially during the many months of snow, garaging was the ONLY way to survive one's arrival back in The Windy City. I learned to do that the hard way. I had been parking my car in an economy lot for several months and then arrived back following the first big Chicago snow for the year. Standing outside my hardly recognizable car under twelve inches of snow, suitcase in one hand, brief case in another in a blinding snow storm at two in the morning convinced me to garage my car from that point forward.

Getting an eighteen wheeler around the country in a timely manner for live network television broadcasts every Thursday night required a coordinated team effort. Part of my job was to see to it that our drivers had everything they needed to get from point A to point B each week on time. This meant phone calls in from them as to their location and progress as they traveled. On the wall across from my desk I maintained a large AAA map of the United States on which were all the interstate highways. At my desk I kept an up to date detailed AAA road atlas of all the states. When the guys called in I wanted to be able to grasp exactly where they were.

Since the broadcasts were Thursday nights, after a good night's rest, they would hit the road Friday towards the next city. They had instructions to call the office 24/7 immediately if they had a problem, but were to routinely call at the end of each driving day and leave word of where they were with the answering service. Regardless of where I was in the country I would check in with the answering service before going to bed every night for my messages and to know the location of the truck. The basic rule: "go-the-distance first"; if, after the destination had been reached and some time remains, then the driver(s) had time to goof off a little.

That's the way we set things up. So, about half way into the season of broadcasts we had a game on the home field of The Southern California Sun at Anaheim Stadium. That broadcast suffered from a vandal who cut our primary and back up audio lines just as we hit the air coast to coast. It took eighteen minutes to find the point where they severed the lines. It was out over a marquee where one would have to have gone intentionally to jeopardize the broadcast. We never found out if the outage was NFL-WFL related, or possibly because our technical crew was non union.

Following Anaheim, the next weeks broadcast was to originate from Houston. That would have been about a two and a half days of travel time for the guys in the truck. It was an easy trip, no need to hurry.

I noticed over the weekend that the drivers had not checked in with the answering service. I was not happy about being in the dark on their location, but had become accustomed to their being where they belonged at the right time.

In the office on Monday I continued to put together the crew and all the supportive elements for Houston. I was scheduled to fly there that night for I had many on the ground coordination's to make being our first trip there.

Middle of that afternoon the drivers had not yet called in and I was getting concerned. The phone rang and it was Eddie Einhorn at TVS calling to let me know that the location for the week's game had been changed from Houston to Orlando. Holy shit! Instead of 1400 miles, they had to go 2400 miles.

Everything had to be changed and worst of all; I had no idea where the damn truck was! I called the highway patrols in California, Arizona, New Mexico and Texas and asked them to help us locate the truck and to have the drivers call me ASAP. Additionally I called into some truck stops along the way to be watching for them.

Our boys called in after a Texas Ranger stopped them and let them know they needed to call us.

My first question; "Where in hell are you?" Answer: "On Interstate 10 just west of San Antonio. We'll easily make Houston during the day tomorrow". I then told them that the location had been changed to ORLANDO I said loudly. Dead silence on the other end.

I won't go into the inflammatory comments made during the minutes that followed. I arranged to fly a driver to New Orleans to help them make an around the clock drive across to the Sunshine

State. They literally rolled the semi up to the airport front door and picked him up within an hour of his arrival from Chicago, and kept rolling.

I put a competitor's truck on stand by for two days just in case the guys did not make it.

In Orlando, I hired extra crew to be waiting at the stadium to set up the truck for the broadcast. It was so tight that we went on the air with one working camera, freshly plugged in and one microphone while the crew finished the installation by the end of the first quarter of the game. Fortunately, we were able to get additional facility dollars out of TVS for the week due to the change of cities.

The World Football League season did go through to completion, but barely. In early December at the World Bowl, their version of Super Bowl, sheriff deputies were there to literally repossess the uniforms of one of the teams for lack of payment. I don't remember what was done to hold off the Court Order until the end of the game, but I can assure you it was not According to Hoyle.

After the WFL season ended, we picked up a potpourri of video facility jobs. One that went down in history was the Muhammad Ali and Chuck Wepner fight on March 24, 1975 at the Richfield Coliseum south of Cleveland.

In this instance we were strictly providing facilities and crew. I had a mountain of preparatory coordination work to do before and after the broadcast, but during the actual fight, for the first and only time in my life, I was given an eighth row ticket to sit and watch it. I knew nothing about the on site "pageantry" of such a spectacle so I decided to expose myself to it from the perspective of a spectator. Expose is the proper description of the events that transpired in front of me that day.

First off I was amazed at the adrenaline that was obviously pumping in the veins of those around me. I had never been amongst the men and women who were into boxing at a boxing match, or in this case, miss-match. Ali was being paid one point five million and Wepner, one hundred thousand dollars. That was a lot of money in the day for Wepner.

I walked in and took my seat just before the two made their entrances. There was electricity in the air. I could feel it. As I wrote earlier, I was in the eighth row so the high rollers were well within ear and eyeshot. Men in five thousand dollar suits and thousand dollar shoes were everywhere, (and not necessarily in good taste). Women were likewise wearing tens of thousands in outfits, carrying handbags with matching price tags and way too much make up. Even before the competitors made their appearances, there were cash bets being made row to row. This was an expensive carnival.

Once the actual boxing started the cash bets increased as some of them were over which opponent bettered the other within a round.

After the second round I was glad I was no closer as Ali's hits on Wepner were causing blood spray on the first rows. This was one of the realities of being in a boxing match crowd that had never occurred to me watching at home on television. Additionally, when Ali landed a strong punch, the sound of Wepner's flesh and bones absorbing it was stunning to me. I kept wondering how anyone could take such a hit and still be standing.

The fever of the crowd around me kept rising. It was truly amazing to me to sense the blood thirsty-ness of the men and the women. The betting became more abhorrent as Wepner's beating increased. By round number twelve most of the bets were whether he would fall to Ali by minute one, two, or three in a round. Wepner's nose was obviously broken and re-smashed and his eyes were swelling along with most of what had been his face. The crescendo to my experience came when Wepner fell on the ropes, was given a count of nine and it was over nineteen seconds before the end of round fifteen. People around me were in a salivating frenzy like lions around a downed zebra. Wepner was down, and I was out of there! I had witnessed a carnivorous side of "man" that I never saw in the midst of battle in Vietnam. I was truly sickened at heart. I went back by the truck and circled it a few times pacing off my feelings.

After a few minutes of calming down I came around the front of the truck to be passed within two feet of Wepner being led back to his dressing room. I froze in my tracks not believing close up the amount of demolition that had been done to that man's face. It was truly astonishing.

Three weeks after our MTS cameras sent images of Ali pulverizing Wepner in Cleveland all over the world, I was on my way to Washington DC to facilitate a CBS News Special out of The US Capitol Building. The special followed President Gerald Ford's State-of-the-World Message to a joint session of the House and the Senate. CBS had us set up in a senate conference room down at street level.

We rolled up to the Capitol the morning of Wednesday, April 9 to set up for the live broadcast which was scheduled to immediately follow the President's Address on Thursday night.

Being a CBS News broadcast inside Washington, they would be providing a full crew comprised of their IBEW technical staff. Our three technical guys were there simply to show them where everything was on the truck and to answer any questions that came up. My job was to make sure that everything went smoothly and represent MTS in any and all negotiations with CBS and or officials with the Capitol Building. For me it was a coat and tie event both days, requiring me to have a presence, yet stay out of the way and be immediately available if needed.

First thing I learned about being an outsider coming into the Capitol is that there are Sergeant-of-Arms for every square foot of that building. If what you are doing crosses lines of demarcation, then you are dealing with multiple Sergeants-of-Arms. As long as you meet ahead of time, discuss fully what you are trying to do, and you get their OK, then you will be able to do what it is you want to do. If not, then you're in deep doodoo. I should point out that this was in 1975. Security was at a much lower level then than it is today.

I was given an all access Pass for the entire Capitol Building. I still have it.

The CBS News team was made up of Roger Mudd and Bruce Morton with political guests comprised of sitting Senators and Congressmen of the day. The preparation and the broadcast went off perfectly. Once all the good nights were said to the CBS News people, the technicians had several hours of work to put all the equipment away.

During the two days I had been on the Capitol grounds I had taken many walks around the wonderfully historical building during my breaks. Following my usual practice on location, I had made myself familiar to the guards so that they would already know me on first sight if anything unforeseen occurred and expedience was needed for assistance.

I now had nothing to do for at least an hour and a half, so I took a walk up stairs to the main room under the Capitol Dome. Except for the occasional guard walking around at a distance, I had the building to myself. I first walked around the floor of the Rotunda taking in the paintings and the statues of the Presidents. I thought of the impression made on me and the rest of the country during the funeral of President Kennedy with his flag covered casket Lying-in-State in that room and the tens of thousands who walked through in silence to pay their respects all through that unforgettable night.

I walked down the hall and stuck my head in the Senate Chamber and at the other end of the building likewise stuck my head in the House Chamber. As midnight hit I was back in The Rotunda. The main interior lights were turned off. The flood lights that bathe the exterior of the Dome all night were casting a wonderful indirect light every where inside coming in the narrow arched windows that circle the Dome half way up. I was sensing a lot of energy in that room that night.

I have always revered our nation's history and considering where I was with absolutely no one to disturb my experience; I was compelled to walk to the middle of the room. Standing on the white marble circle in the very center of the Rotunda floor, I looked straight up. Though in suit and tie, I sat down and then laid down placing the white marble circle directly under the middle of my back.

Laying my hands on my chest I meditated for about twenty minutes. It was singularly the most surreal experience of my life either before that night, or in the forty years since. If I ever levitated during meditation it may have been then. I completely relaxed into it and though I never left the room visually, I went somewhere else and it was truly sublime.

Relating the experience to a close friend back in Chicago a few days later, her reaction was to say she now knew someone who had lain-in-state in the US Capitol and walked away from it. I hadn't thought of it that way, but I guess she had a point.

A month after the CBS News Special out of the Capitol I found myself at Le Club International in Fort Lauderdale, Florida for a week of celebrity tennis, golf and evening entertainment. We were there to tape all the day and night festivities and then I would take all the tapes to Los Angeles and edit a TV special together from all the parts.

Here is a partial list I can recall of the on site and on camera celebrities taking part. Bill Cosby, Burt Bacharach, Oleg Cassini, Pat Boone, Edgar Bergen & Charlie McCarthy, Burt Parks, Phyllis Diller and George Peppard. I get the sense there were more, but frankly I do not remember. Shooting the tennis was pretty straight forward and considering Cassini, Cosby, Bacharach and Boone; we had some reasonable to very good players. Several nights we shot in the Club Room and got some great entertainment pieces. Comedy from Phyllis Diller, music from Pat Boone and an amazing medley with Burt Bacharach at the piano playing many of his well known hits ending with him singing, What's It All About Alfie right into my lens at the end of the keyboard.

The third day Burt Parks arrives at the Clubs wharf aboard a friend's one hundred fifty-foot yacht and offers it for a night yachting party for us to video tape. We shot maybe sixty minutes on tape of which perhaps forty-five seconds was worth putting in the finished show. How long can you look at people you don't know drinking and eating?

We were not prepared to shoot golf, but one of the days we did shoot some putting and then found that we could either shoot a routine with Edgar Bergen within minutes that afternoon, or we would lose him entirely. So, against my wishes, we shot the dear old fellow where we were outside in the heat. I feared we'd lose him, that he would expire on camera before he finished his act. He was elderly, somewhat feeble, but the old trouper wanted to do it. He and Charlie McCarthy were funny as hell as he sweated profusely. I feared he would pass away while I recorded it.

There were entirely too many tanned, amazing looking women in their twenties all over Le Club International unofficially, yet truly teamed with many, (not all), of the celebrities and others around who were obviously of great financial means. One of the women tagged on to me for two days until she found out I was a working stiff and then she was gone, funniest thing.

By the end of the week we had shot enough for two one hour specials. I shipped the tapes to the edit house in LA and jumped a plane for the City of Angels.

Editing went well for the first three and a half days and the Executive Producers, a pair of brothers I won't name, arrived to take a look at the unfinished edit. It was coming together very well and they were pleased with what they saw and then they completely blew my mind.

They wanted to know right then what they owed us for the shoot in Fort Lauderdale, the travel, the video tape and the editing to date. I said it would take a few hours at least to compile all the information and give them an honest and fair estimate. They almost got huffy with me as they wanted a number immediately. I did know in my head what Florida had cost and was aware of the hours and rates I was running up in the edit, so I started adding gross numbers and travel costs in my head. I came to an amount and I doubled it.

Meanwhile one of the brothers had pulled out a large company style check book. He looked at me matter-of-factly and said, "I need a number now so I can pay you". With certainty I took my doubled number, added twenty percent to it and gave it to them.

He wrote out a check for that amount made out to Mobile Television Services. They both signed it and handed it to me. They then announced they wanted all the original masters, the edit masters, and said that the job was finished. I was thanked for my great work and they had the edit house tape room guys take all the tapes outside to their waiting limo. Once all the tapes were loaded they left never to be seen again.

228

It was one of those times when you don't ask questions, take the money, smile, say "thank you" and move on to your next project.

There were some great moments captured on those tapes. Bacharach singing Alfie was probably THE moment of that week. Unfortunately, it is gone forever.

The next project of note with MTS turned out to be an extended series for ABC. Part one was shot as a summer series. First entitled Anything Goes it soon became renamed Almost Anything Goes after some legal beagles got involved over the rights of the Anything Goes title.

Television, film and publishing share the same legal arguments over who owns what when it comes to rights and control of the cash flow around those rights.

Almost Anything Goes was this crazy show featuring what I called "sort-of-sports" competition events between three neighboring towns in a given area. For the chosen city it was like having the circus come to town for a week. It was shot at night on a high school football field wherever we were for that weekend. In the middle of the field was a large, above ground swimming pool which often was utilized in an event that either went over it, or in it, or both. Women and men would be dressed up in wacky costumes, example: As chickens, to do truly odd ball, funny feats within sixty seconds. There would be a number of events within the hour and the town that won the most events then would be advanced to the regionals. The regional winning town would be advanced weeks later to compete in the national finals.

Along with my MTS coordination responsibilities, I put myself on the show as the hand held camera operator. I had a ball running around chasing the competitors getting close up shots that would put the viewer at home up close and "in it". I frequently would have a forklift standing by to run me quickly all the way up thirty to forty feet to get a great high reverse cover shot from above to then be brought down equally fast to get the up close winning interview.

The summer series did well on ABC and aired through the summer long after we had finished taping them. There was a lull in MTS projects and I got antsy.

The mobile video technical facility business relies on suppliers and artisans from coast to coast. Paying them on a timely basis means the next time you call them they're right there ready and eager to work with you. Howard and I put the bids together for the projects we went after at a profit with contractual times for payment. We demanded it from our clients for MTS. In order to be successful at what we did, we likewise paid for services in a timely manner. It was the good and right way to do business.

In late Spring MTS was sold by the original owner and the new regime in New York was counting pennies everywhere. It got to the point that although I had approved payments for suppliers, they were being made to wait for payment. A big warning bell went off inside me. I was out there making arrangements and committing to expenditures for our jobs and suddenly I'm getting calls from good reliable companies and individuals wanting to know why they were waiting for payments that were overdue. We were selling profitable projects and being paid on time for them. All I could think of was what's going on in New York? It was no secret; I'd seen it before at other times in my career. The tens of thousands we were collecting were being diverted to investments of an individual, or two at the top.

In the middle of my initial discoveries that our suppliers were not getting paid on time I'm on a flight to Los Angeles. I picked up Time magazine and read it cover to cover like I always did in those days. I got to the Business page and was dumbstruck as I read the headline: *Is Eddie Gilbert at it again?* I just stared at it. Eddie Gilbert was the millionaire who had bought MTS. The flight was passing Palm Springs which meant I had to read quickly before our final approach into LA. More than that I wanted the whole story in my head before I hit the ground running to bust my ass on the project we were in route to perform.

It was all there in black and white. He was a convicted felon who had filched millions, and spent time in prison for it. Wall Streeters and others in the financial world in New York were seeing him back in action and were looking to see what he was up to and how he was doing it.

MTS was a small operation within the larger company, but we were being ripped continuously to add dollars into the bigger pot.

My reputation was hurt. I heard about it for some time from some guys who waited way too long to be compensated for the good work they had done. I was pissed, but not at anyone in our group in Chicago. We were all pawns in Gilbert's dirty business dealings.

During my run with MTS, I frequently spent ten days to several weeks on the road. I would wake up in one city, fly to another for a meeting on an up coming project and then jump another plane to sleep in another city in order to wake up for a production in that city that day.

In my hotel rooms I would always get two double beds. One to sleep in and the other to spread out the file folders for all the projects I was working on. I would systematically go through each file update it and make notes each night before sleep. I would fill a page or two on a legal pad of things to do the next day. Remember there were no PC's or MAC's then. It was a lot of paper files to lug around, but it was my system and it worked well.

After sixteen months of little sleep and unbelievable miles in the sky I woke up one morning at my usual 5am, looked around my hotel room and said, literally aloud to myself, "you can get out of bed when you can tell yourself what hotel you're in, what city you're in and what project you're on today". I sat there for about five minutes and could not fill in any of the blanks. I gave in and looked at the hotel phone. I was in the New York Sheraton and then it came to me I had to catch a morning plane to Los Angeles. After those five minutes of blankness, I went through my appointment calendar and figured out what date I could leave MTS after completing all the projects I had in the pipeline. From JFK before boarding for LA, I called the office in Chicago and gave Howard two months notice. He was not happy with what I had said, but not angry either.

Almost Anything Goes (AAG) did well on ABC the summer of 1975. It did so well that the network ordered a second run of it. In the meantime I had left MTS and moved to Los Angeles. I was on their list for doing hand held camera on a freelance basis if anything came up.

Chapter Thirty-Five / Free Lance

They called me a month after I left the company and asked if I wanted to do handheld camera on the next run of AAG. Additionally I was asked if I would do the same on a CBS Sports Spectacular five day shoot in Costa Mesa, south of LA. I said that I would be interested in both. I then found out that there were two catches. The first part of AAG would be shot on the east coast and that I would have to be based east of the Mississippi during those four months. They would fly me out of where I was to the production city-of-the-week and return. The second half of the AAG production run I could be based back in LA. Having a friend in Cincinnati with whom I could stay four nights a week for four months, my east coast city of origin was covered.

There was one small hiccup in the schedule. The Shoot in Costa Mesa would end on a Sunday. I had to board a plane in Cincinnati five days later to go to the first weekend of AAG in Virginia. I drove to Costa Mesa with my car packed to then drive east for the four months of winter weather and weekends of AAG production. In between Costa Mesa and Cincinnati would be a driving marathon. Fortunately it was that in between summer – fall season when it's neither hot, nor cold. I got a good nights sleep in Costa Mesa and hit the road east Monday morning. Working with a map I took Interstate 15 north and east out of Costa Mesa to scenic Barstow and got on Interstate 40 to drive straight through to Amarillo, Texas. Stopping only for gas, water, bathroom breaks and food, I arrived alive, strung out and on schedule. I got a hotel room there Tuesday night and woke up Wednesday driving then non stop to Cincinnati getting there sometime late Thursday afternoon.

It was roughly eleven hundred miles to Amarillo from Costa Mesa and roughly the same from Amarillo to Cincinnati. By my plan, I had about sixteen hours more than needed on the clock for any weather or car problems. Fortunately I had no problems on the trip. I knew to push myself all the time, that is to always "go the distance" until I reached The Queen City. Whew! I made it!

AAG was a trip to work on. There we were in small towns across the country from October to May every week on the week end. It was, for the local towns people, like having the circus come to town.

Besides the local team that competed on the show, many area residents were hired to help with various aspects of the production. We needed help with building and taking down scaffold towers, rigging and wiring for lighting. The wardrobe department always needed help with all the costumes that had to be created, sewn on, (literally), and removed. I always had a minimum of two cable pullers to follow me and keep up with my movement as I needed to cover the action in any direction without warning over roughly sixty yards at anytime. I got teased a lot by everyone as my cable pullers were often teenage girls who were fast on their feet to keep up with me as I raced around the field in order to stay up close and personal with the competitive action and the winning moment followed with the interview of the winning squad.

The interviews of the winners were conducted by Regis Philbin. He would come running in with me right behind him on a wide angle lens covering the winning moment. He was a hoot to work with. He was no different then than he is now. He was and is Regis. What you see is what you get. I liked working with him and he with me. It got crazy at times especially when the event ended with the contestants in the above ground pool. Regis would be right there hanging on the outside wall of the pool interviewing the winners in the water with me literally two, maybe three feet way. In those instances we usually got splashed by the winners in their exuberance. I was wearing over one hundred thousand dollars of a plugged in, high voltage television camera. But hey, it was show biz!

Calling the action of the Almost Anything Goes competition was sportscaster, Charlie Jones. You no doubt heard Charlie broadcast many an NBC NFL Football telecast over the years. Charlie called the AAG play-by-play with many a laugh making him a perfect match in the broadcast booth to Regis's wacky-ness on the field with the contestants.

We shot the shows on Sunday nights. Many of us had flights home to catch on Monday
Morning. During AAG Regis was hosting AM LOS ANGELES on KABC-TV. He was very popular in the City of the Angels and KABC's Vice President and General Manager, one John C. Sevarino, was not happy about him missing the Monday show every week because of AAG and apparently said so often. But, since AAG was an ABC Television Network show, the boys in New York basically told Sevarino to shut up about it.

Regis's best act was portrayed those Monday mornings near the gate for the plane back to LA. There were maybe a dozen of us who were on that flight. We were usually pretty beat up from all the physical running around we did rehearsing and shooting the show for several days, plus the set up and tear down of the cameras, cables and audio gear. Sunday night's sleep time was usually abbreviated due to a late wrap up, followed often with an early get up for a long ride to the nearest airport Monday morning to catch the first flight out.

There we would be lumped on chairs near the gate waiting to leave and then we'd hear him way down the airport hallway, "I didn't know they could land a jet in a rinky-dink place like this!" Always funny, always making an "entrance" that was our Regis on those Monday mornings.

AAG's run on ABC finished in the late spring of 1976. It would resurrect as Junior Almost Anything Goes some months later for Saturday morning kids programming on ABC with Soupy Sales as the host. We shot that on a large sound stage in Los Angeles. Many of the staff and crew came back for the kids' version which was fun to shoot.

While we were shooting Junior AAG on the weekends, on other days of the week we simultaneously were shooting a similar Saturday morning kids sporting competition show for CBS called WAY OUT GAMES (WOG). This one we shot north of Los Angeles at Magic Mountain amusement park. It was in direct competition to Junior AAG but was produced by a completely different production company.

The host of WOG was Sonny Fox, a long time often seen TV host especially on shows out of New York in the fifties and sixties. He was very adept at dealing quickly with live contestants and especially kids. The irony of his hosting WOG on CBS is that he was named Vice President of Children's Programming for NBC while we were in production.

WOG ran on CBS during the first six months of his tenure at NBC. That's part of the business of television. If you're good at what you do, you will frequently find yourself playing in many sand boxes at once. That certainly has been true for me.

I didn't finish the run of WOG tapings as I got a call out of the blue from Norman Lear's company to be the Associate Director of MARY HARTMAN-MARY HARTMAN (MH).

I jumped at the opportunity and actually took a substantial pay cut to go with MH. The show was burning out writers and sending them off to the funny farm. I do not want to come off insensitive to the plight of the writers, but, in some cases it was damn near reality.

Lear was some years into his monstrous hits ALL IN THE FAMILY and MAUDE. His reputation was on the line with MH. The audience and the programming executives expected MH to live up to the edgy, driving, dialogue and story lines for which the other two shows had become so successful.

There was a big difference with MH. The other shows were running in primetime on CBS and producing one episode a week, whereas MH was a syndicated, strip show meaning it aired five days a week like a daytime soap opera. In fact, we were producing six episodes a week so we could take a week's break every six weeks!

The CBS shows had very large budgets. They could buy the best writers and anybody else they wanted in front of the camera, or behind it.

I was offered Directors Guild scale for a forty hour week as an Associate Director. If I didn't accept it, they'd get someone else, pure and simple. The answer was an easy one for me as I saw this as a career move to get in with the Lear organization in a high profile position even if, for the immediate period, the pay was comparatively crap.

What I could not see was the snake pit that awaited me. (Talk about a babe in the woods!)

My first day at MH I was introduced to Nessa Hyams, the Director. I had never heard of her in the business, (but that happens frequently in Hollywood). What I did notice immediately was that everything she wore was in good taste, very good taste, like New York City good taste and extremely expensive. Secondly, everything she talked about were of dealings involving high executives and, or well known celebrities in film and television.

I have to interject here that we were on the first day of six, straight, five day work weeks of production. The basic set up was to rehearse in the mornings from nine to noon. Take an hour break during which I was to prep the camera operators on their shots for all the scenes for the day in order to be ready to begin shooting on tape at one o'clock so that we would be done by five.

Nessa's chatter continued. It out weighed the rehearsing and the directorial preparation. I was mentally dancing as fast as I could knowing that the framing and the angles to best shoot each scene were not happening. During a fast five minute break, I pulled a newly met associate aside to ask who Nessa was referring to as "David" in all her chatter. I was told that Nessa was married to David Picker, the head of Paramount Pictures at the time.

Her background was nothing close to directing. She had been a well known talent coordinator who had been involved in connecting many of the big names in film and television at the time to their jobs. Being married to the head of Paramount Pictures had put her where she was that Monday morning and I had to deal with the obvious lack of knowledge and experience with regards to directing.

I knew my job and how to do it, but was quickly coming to realize that this "playing field" was far different than any I had worked on before. The snake pit was on quick sand, but it was shrouded with the familiarity of a studio, cameras, lights, actors, stage hands, etc....

Directors, Associate Directors and Stage Managers are a team who succeed by working closely together to make the director's vision become reality. I have been privileged over my career to have worked with many of the best in all three of those categories. I have performed each of those capacities applying what I learned while working with so many talented professionals.

So, there I was on my first day at MH trying to learn who all the people were, how the different departments collaborated, or not, therefore to understand on that show on that stage how long it took to get X, Y, and Z done. I needed to have a strong connection with the people among the diverse disciplines of; production, writing, audio, video, wardrobe, lighting, staging, props, make up and hair, particularly the ones who got things done.

At the same time I was quickly coming to recognize that there were high stakes and intense politics going on around the work that needed to be accomplished. I made up my mind to give this first six week cycle my best efforts while I danced as fast as I could through all the political bullshit that was going on in a hush-hush fashion every minute of every day.

On a personal level, I liked Nessa Hyams. The fact that she was not a Director in any way shape, or form did grind on me. I was used to working with Directors who rolled up their sleeves, left all the "Biz" bullshit out of the day's workings and collaborated with all of us in the trenches of production to get the best possible rendering on tape. About that she was clueless. She was above all that and considering how smart she was, in retrospect, I'll cut her some slack, but only due to her ignorance. However, at the time it was more than frustrating for me to do all that needed to be done to get the scenes in the can, keep her placated and not threaten her insecurities.

On Monday of the fourth week of this six week cycle, without prior knowledge, I walked in to be told that Nessa was gone and I was introduced to yet another first time television Director.

Kim Friedman was a lady about my age. She had absolutely no knowledge of how to shoot a sitcom on television and told me so as we met. To the positive, she had directed a fair number of stage plays and had a good background in theater. She understood staging and had a good grasp on how to direct actors. And, unlike Nessa, Kim was a player with the production team in the trenches. I got to immediately open the "Peter Bright University of Advanced Television Directing". At least Kim started right out saying she knew nothing about it, whereas Nessa's ego would not allow her to make such an admission.

While there was with Kim a sense of collaboration, it began to eat at me that here we were in Big Time television and I was continuing to be the instructor for two people who should have arrived fully experienced to perform their high profile, well paid jobs. At that level school is out, or should be. Of course every production is an on-going set of circumstances that afford opportunities to learn and grow. But this wasn't right and I was most definitely on the short end of the stick.

The real problem was, oddly enough, Norma Lear. He liked rewarding people with opportunities. In addition to having two inexperienced Directors for me to work with, the Producer of MH had been a high end secretary prior to becoming the show Producer for this run of the production. Viva Knight was as nervous and insecure as any one I had ever worked with before, or since. She was given a golden opportunity, but she did not have the experience to be where she was and it showed every minute of every day.

There were some wonderful people throughout the ranks on MH. Some were in the office, many worked behind the scenes in wardrobe, make up, scenic design and props.

We shot the show on Stage 5 at KTLA. Right across the driveway from where Donnie and Marie Osmond were shooting there ABC show on Stage 6.

Our technical crew comprised of camera operators, audio boom operators, lighting and stage manager were second-to-none. Their contributions were substantial and consistent.

From the kibitzing during morning rehearsals and the breaks between tapings in the afternoon, some of the cast members and I hit it off. At nearly a dozen total, I will hit a few personal stand outs.

I have fond memories of chatting with Victor Killian, who played Gran Pa. The oldest actor on the show, he was kind, friendly, very funny and had wonderful anecdotes on Hollywood from the 1930's when, as a film actor, he had cut quite a profile. Dodie Goodman was another favorite of mine for great chit-chat. I had watched her many a time with Jack Paar on the Tonight Show and later his prime time show. She was funny, interesting, very real and nice as hell. It takes someone very bright to carry off "ditsy" on screen. Dodie had that down to a "T". Mary Kay Place was forever coming up with and working on a new song. Never far from her guitar, her music was definitely her voice to the world. Greg Mullavey, who played Tom Hartman, was a constant source for the sharing of off-the-record guy-to-guy talk about all the BS going on around us. (*He and I would work on another series together later in our careers*).

And, of course there was Louise Lasser, Mary Hartman. She usually came to morning rehearsals with an idea or two about the scene at hand. Her instincts about how Mary would perceive things were good and often better than what had been written into the script. Quick changes would be made to be ready for the taping in the afternoon.

Over lunch I would meet with the camera operators giving them their shots for the scenes and pass on any notes to audio and lighting pertinent for the days taping that were not scripted. The actors would get made up and into their wardrobe as lighting, audio, staging and props readied for putting the scenes to tape.

During this important hour Louise would sequester herself in her dressing room suite. Hair, make up and wardrobe would work on her as they could around her telephone conversations. The hour in her suite was often a mystery to all of us. I can not write of her hour as I was only in there once for maybe two minutes, along with other key people, trying to solve a momentary question. What I can write about is the striking difference we would experience in Louise from her lively, involved persona in the morning and her zoney, "what's my motivation?" and stare we experienced frequently during the afternoon tapings. It was like working with two different people. She wasn't just in the Hartman character, something else was going on.

The media at the time had many reported "this's and that's" about Louise's personal life. Rumor Central in Hollywood only exists to perpetuate itself. Some of the reported things about Louise were far from for what I experienced first hand five days a week for six weeks.

I will add that the tapings were often elongated as she was obviously distracted. What the origin of her distraction was I do not know. Frankly, for me, at times, I don't think she knew.

After repeated, sporadic delays over some weeks, nerves were unraveling across the actors and staff. One late afternoon with lights and cameras rolling Louise looked up into the lens of Camera 3, which had her close up, and said, after a pregnant pause and wiping her hand across her teeth, "what's my motivation?" I said on my headset to everyone on the line, "Hold in place, this won't take long". I took off my headset and ran out of the Control Room truck and sprinted down the alley and on to the stage. I got right in Louise's face and said, "your motivation is to shoot this and every scene when we're ready and to stop making everybody else wait for you…Now, you got it?' She nodded a yes. "Good" said I. With that I ran back into the Control Room truck and we rolled tape and shot the scene.

That action is normally one of a producer and in my opinion is a last resort. I believe in kindness and supportive reinforcement for everyone involved in a production. Unfortunately in this instance there had been no positive reinforcement for Louise over the entire production cycle.

Everyone occasionally may need a reassuring coddle to help them through a rough moment. I am the first to offer the helping hand to my fellow worker at such a time.

All too often some celebrities are indulged and coddled all day, every day by some of the people around them. That is a big mistake at any time with any one in any circumstance.

Louise was a victim of over coddling from day one. What she deserved was positive reinforcement. She was not afforded that. There are many pieces to what I call positive reinforcement. For this instance I will point to two that were missing: 1) encouragement to do well; 2) the delineation of the lines of acceptable behavior in the work place. When someone does not practice number two on their own, then you afford them a private conversation to spell out those lines and what is expected of them.

The week following my confrontation with Louise was our scheduled break between the six week production cycles. I had a couple of one day jobs that week with Friday off. Sometime in the afternoon on Friday, I got a call from the show's Associate Producer telling me that I was being replaced and not to come in Monday to start the next production cycle. I told him I was not happy to hear that and asked if we could meet and discuss the matter. He told me no, that the decision was final. I then reminded him that under the rules of the Directors Guild that they would have to pay me for the following week due to the last minute notice of my release. He argued that was not the case. I told him that he could deal with the Guild. I hung up and immediately called the Guild who backed me up.

I had mixed emotions about being let go. In one sense, given the conditions under which I had to work in that swirl of politics, insecure personalities and teaching on the job, I was glad to be out. On the other hand, I'd lost my place in the Lear organization and career wise that did not feel good.

A week or so later, I wound up working on an episode of MAUDE. The show was shot on what used to be the Metro Media Lot, immediately across the street from KTLA, where I had been shooting Mary Hartman. Lear's other big show, ALL In The FAMILY, was shot there too.

The *Read Through* is a very important step in the process of producing a successful situation comedy. On a primetime show like MAUDE each production week started with one. This was held either on the stage, or in a rehearsal hall with the actors, producers, directing team, writers, assistants, wardrobe and props all sitting around a large table. Everyone would have a copy of the script as written. The point was to have the actors read the script aloud, so that everyone could get a feeling for it. Out of this would often come immediate small rewrites of certain words, or lines that worked better. Once in a great, great while the consensus would be that an entire rewrite of a script was called for. As any playwright can tell you, what works well on paper, does not always play well when put on its feet.

In this particular episode Bea's character, Maude, had a line to be given to Bill Massey's character, Maude's husband. The line was to be delivered ala Bela Lugosi, it was, "I'm going to suck your blood!" It was a highlight in the whole script and Bea had her delivery down to a "T". The line had been in every draft of the script from day one.

Allow me to backtrack for one moment. The year was 1976. CBS (and the other two networks) had a department known as "Practices and Standards". The purpose was to safeguard against improper words, language and visual images judged to be in poor taste and unacceptable within the rules set down in writing. Maude being a show that often delved into subjects of controversy was highly scrutinized by this department. They would be issued the script and all the rewrites thereof throughout the week of production. A "P & S" person would be seated in the audience during the taping of the dress rehearsal and the final taping. If anything was deemed unacceptable, they could order a retake of the scene in question overriding the producers. It was often a matter of artistic differences that could come to, shall I say, major confrontations.

We shot the Dress Rehearsal and the Final with Bea's excellent delivery of her line as written. With the audience released we were in a holding pattern on the stage awaiting any notes from the producers. Bea and I are standing in the set talking about how good the tapings had gone and that we were glad to soon be going home for the night and a weekend of needed sleep. Suddenly I hear my name being called. I looked at Bea and whispered, "Uh-oh, I'm being summoned". She whispered back, "Go get the bad news Peter." We exchanged an all knowing look. I crossed the stage to the producers who had moved to an empty area in the audience seats. In the back of my head I was thinking: This is not good. If it were a simple matter the note would have been given aloud across the twenty feet to us, but instead they wanted to give the note to me privately so that I would carry it back to Bea alone. Whatever.

I got over to the producers who told me the Bela Lugosi line had to be changed to, "I'm going to <u>drink</u> your blood." I asked why and was told P & S says you can't say "suck" on CBS. I broke out laughing. "That's ridiculous", I blurted out loud. In response they shrugged. I then said, "The line has been in every draft of the script, and they wait until now to change it?" I looked at them and said, "You know Bea will NOT like this." "We know", was their quiet reply.

Suddenly I was pissed. The original line was the right one. P & S had had five days to flag it and had not mentioned a problem to any one. My guess was they hadn't bothered to read the script at all, plus, though they were there during the taping of the Dress Rehearsal, they missed it then as well.

When I got back to Bea she asked, "Well, Peter, what the hell was that all about?" "Practice and Standards say you can't say "suck" on CBS and they want the line changed to "Drink". Bea's anger was not at me; rather she looked right to where the P & S person was sitting in the audience seen only in profile due to the stage lights and said, "That is the dumbest thing I ever heard. It takes the power out of the line and ruins it. It's been in the script all week and you wait until now to say it has to be changed?" There was no response. "You better roll tape now because I will only give you one take on this." We did and she did.

I would see her at events every once in a while and worked with her a few more times over the years following that and every time we saw each other the first thing out of our mouths before hello was, "You can't say SUCK on CBS!", and then we'd laugh.

Following my week with MAUDE, a pair of phone calls let me know I was up for two distinctly different television jobs. One was with Norman Lear's company and the other was with The Jacksons, (Michael, his bothers *and* his sisters). I went into what turned out to be a four day waiting period not hearing from either concern after their initial inquiry as to my interest in the jobs.

My mind was swimming with a potpourri of thoughts of what each potential job would be like and what each might do for my career. It was during these couple of days that I adopted one great pussy cat.

Through a lady I was dating at the time, I was introduced by phone to a friend of hers in Chicago who was about to marry a widower with children and pets. She had a great big black pussy cat named Maxwell with whom she had lived for five years. He was special to her, but he would not mix in well with her new extended family. She literally interviewed me for over an hour on the phone to determine if she would be comfortable with me adopting her "boy". My love for animals shown through in the conversation and at the end she asked if I could pick up Maxwell the following night at LAX. Yes was my reply and the following night I drove out to American Airlines at LAX and picked up one gorgeous, big, black, furry, long haired and scared Maxwell.

We got along from minute one. I asked my girl friend to come along for the pick up so that I could hold him as she drove us back to my place. Picking him out of the cat carrier on the counter at American, Max was immediately very vocal. I talked right back to him as I held and comforted him all the way home. I had bought food, a dish for that and one for water as well as the mandatory "cat box" and sand and had them ready for him when we walked in. Still holding him I walked around to give him a quick visual of his new home ending at the cat box where I put him down so he could satisfy his own curiosity. He immediately emptied his bladder and then went on his first excursion of his new home. He concluded at his water and food bowls where he got his fill of both. We had eleven great years together and there will be bits on him from time to time as I continue.

The waiting for a deal was driving me nuts so I went to an art store and bought a large three by four foot poster board, a thin chrome metal frame to put it in, a bottle of flat finish, clear polymer and a brush to spread it over whatever I was going to create once completed.

When I got home I started rummaging through every magazine I had from Rolling Stone, to Time, Newsweek, and some photos in my own collection. All the visual images were not connected to one another. Having created a substantial pile of pages from diverse sources, I then went through pulling images that I found interesting with no particular context in mind. From the smaller pile of images, I would pick one and then cut out precisely the face or image on it that intrigued me. Once cut, I placed the image loosely on the big, white board. I continued cutting out pieces large and small for about twelve hours pausing every so often to move pieces about the board letting my eye guide me. There was no one statement, rather many statements covering politics of the time, influences in the media that were current from Charlie's Angels to Bob Dylan to Harry Reasoner, Barbara Walters to Linda Ronstadt and more. By five o'clock, day two it was finished, framed and hanging on the wall by my breakfast nook. I do have a picture of it; unfortunately the piece itself got away from me during a move in 1994.

Exhausted from my creative marathon, Maxwell and I crashed until the next day when we were awakened by my phone ringing. It was Producer Bonnie Burns to seal my deal to work on The Jacksons, a weekly half hour music-variety show on CBS. Preproduction was to begin the following week.

Again, for your reference, it was fall, 1976, the period between the days of The Jackson Five and Michael Jackson's solo act. Their record sales had fallen for many reasons, but mostly because they could no longer ride on the musical little boy songs they made popular on Ed Sullivan around 1970 with the preteen image of Michael and his older brothers, as the Jackson Five. They needed new music and a new image. Motown for whom they had made many millions for over five years didn't drop them, they just never bothered to extend their deal or offer a new one.

Another factor came into play as brother Jermaine Jackson had married Motown boss, Barry Gordy's daughter. The Jacksons needed a record deal and along came CBS to offer them not only a record deal, but a summer series television deal and a lot of cash up front. Joe Jackson, who at that time still made the deals for the group jumped at the CBS offer.

The story is that Joe asked each of them one at a time into his bedroom/office to sign their new contract. Jermaine too was asked, but, as the rumor goes, he refused as he had been signed to a new Motown deal by his father-in-law, Barry Gordy. Joe, reportedly, got angry, Jermaine left the house, and was out of the CBS deal.

The CBS summer television series got reasonable ratings and it was because of them the network programmers decided to bring the series back for late fall into winter 1976-77.

Joe Jackson had nine talented children. The following week I got to meet eight of them. They were all involved in the show. Along with Michael were Jackie, Tito, Marlon, Randy, Latoya, Rebe and Janet. Janet and Randy were still kids, Michael was eighteen with Marlon, some what older as was Jackie and Latoya. Rebe and Tito had spouses, but were very much part of the group and the show. On a personal note I found each of them likeable, fun to both be and work with. They were disciplined, professional and all different, but united and committed every day to making a great show.

I worked on this show the way I have always liked to work, meaning I was totally immersed in all the aspects from planning, rehearsing, shooting and editing. It was a group effort and we all worked well together.

I first met Michael and his siblings at Sunwest Recording Studios in Hollywood to record the tracks that would be performed on the show. We began in their largest studio in order to accommodate the ensemble that had been put together consisting of great session players known across the LA recording business. Michael and his brothers had plenty of input over the production of the music as it had to meet their performance values to a "T". They would be singing and dancing to it so the tempo and the mix had to be perfect. Tito was part of the ensemble playing which ever one of his many guitars fit the written score.

Those days at the studio were a great way to get to know everyone. The control rooms were built for maybe ten to twelve people. With all the Jacksons, audio engineer-mixer second-to-none, Ed Greene, the studio crew, the rest of the production team and me, there were over twenty people in very close quarters and we were having a ball while working our asses off.

There was always an urgency to get the ensemble recorded each day within straight time due to the high cost of union musicians. The mixing and final production of the tracks we did after the musicians went home.

At the same time all the music was being recorded and mixed, preparation was well underway a few miles away on the sound stage where the performances would be video taped. Our offices were located there as well which made it easier to keep track of the set construction while we would meet and plan before taping commenced.

The lot we were on had been a film lot going back to the twenties and thirties. Parts of it had been remodeled, but not for producing television, or film. Instead some of the stages were turned into high end indoor tennis courts. In the early 1970s quite a few Hollywood studios had made similar conversions to create revenue from facilities that had been inactive for years. In order to attract high profile players, adjacent facilities on the lots were expensively outfitted spas featuring, steam, sauna rooms with all the luxury bath accents and dressing rooms imaginable. This lot on North Cahuenga a block and a half north of Melrose in Hollywood, was one such lot.

There were no video facilities on the lot. A truck with video facilities was contracted to provide cameras, audio and video tape capabilities to record the shows. The practice of rolling a video track on to a lot to record a show is a common in LA. This truck was from out of town and though it had relatively new equipment in it, our hand picked top notch LA free lance video tech crew found themselves in a constant state of repairing, more like rebuilding the unit every freek'in day. As one who had been in the facility business I knew first hand that these trucks demand constant maintenance. It was obvious from hour one that this facility was in piss poor shape. I had not been involved in the selection of the truck, but I can say without reservation that it was anything but carefree.

We recorded three very nice production numbers; One each with Carroll O'Conner, Linda Carter and Tim Conway.

Carter's singing was great and for me at the time a surprise. Like most of the country I only knew of her as WONDER WOMAN. She was very personable with me and, I will admit, we distracted each other a bit, but left that bit where it belonged, within the studio walls.

O'Conner displayed his "Broadway Joe" song and dance side. I had heard about it but when he showed it off in rehearsal any doubts I may have had of his ability were doused.

Tim Conway was just plain hilarious. I tried to have several conversations with him and he would find that split second where he could insert a "Conway-ism" and I'd be in yet another convulsion of laughter. I got him a few times too. Throughout he proved to be very real, and very funny.

David Letterman came in and did his very funny bit of delivering a newscast in the style of a sportscaster; "Looks like Jerry Parsons won't be going out to the old ball game anymore…he was gunned down this morning", a perfect Letterman goof ball routine.

We prepared a big musical production number on the Eric Clapton hit, I SHOT THE SHERIFF. The setting was an old western bar. We'd rehearsed the hell out of it and choreographer Anita Mann had designed the movement to accentuate every musical nuance in the great score that had been produced for it. The Jacksons were happy with the preparation and we all went home late one night leaving the stage and lighting crew to build the western bar over night in order to have it ready for final rehearsal and taping the following day.

I got to the set early, as was my practice, to work with all the departments so that production would be ready for on time commencement of the day's production. The set was a mixture of a real western movie style long, wooden bar on the left, framed peripherally with very large, clear acetate frames on which were painted abstract impressions of the walls for such a bar. Round wood tables and chairs were spotted around. With the lighting, there was no doubting that it was an old western bar. But it was a "stylized" setting suggesting what it was versus being "literal".

Everything was ready for the taping. The Jacksons were arriving one by one and each came on the stage to see the western bar set before going to wardrobe and make up. The large stage door was open when the family's vintage white Rolls Silver Cloud drove up. Michael, Randy and Janet got out and walked on stage. I was with Marlon, Jackie and Tito standing in front of the set. I had learned to watch Michael's facial expressions for visual clues to his state of mind. He was very open around me and instantly I read growing distress on his face as he got closer to us. His eyes were all over the set glancing left and right, up and down.

Whispering as he got closer I could make out the words, "…isn't right, it isn't right". I walked up to him and said, "Talk to me, what isn't right?" Pointing at the set, he said, "That is not the set I asked for". He was tearing up. The brothers circled us. I stayed with him as his state of upset grew. The circle of the six of us moved as a unit across the stage behind a curtain out of sight from everyone else.

"Talk to me, Michael", I said, "how can I help make this right for you?"

"It's not real. It was supposed to be real", he whispered through tears. "I did not know that", I said. Marlon, Jackie, Tito and I talked with him for about a minute. They were nervous about complaining about the set. I stopped them and said, "This is your show. It has your name on it. If you did not get what you want, what you had asked for, then don't accept it". I don't remember which brother said it, but one said, "Peter's right. Let's go". We all looked at each other and I said, "You fellows go ahead, I'll deal with the producers".

Still in our circle, we moved out from behind the curtain. The boys continued towards the open stage door and I split off walking towards the producers who were huddled across the stage looking at me with frowns on their faces.

As I got closer, Bill Davis asked me, "What the hell was that all about?" I told him and the others that Michael was very upset about the set and that he and his brothers were leaving. I was ordered to go stop them and get them ready for the taping. I said flatly, "No. It's not possible. Their minds are made up; they're gone for the day".

Production was suspended for over a week. There were many meetings between the producers and Joe Jackson. The outcome was positive. We moved our offices and the production to CBS Television City. A solid, great facility with a rich history in the production of television shows.

The move to TV City created a milestone involving me. Up to that point, in 1976, all Associate Directors (AD) and Stage Managers (SM) working in the building were CBS staff and had been since it opened in 1953. The Jack Benny Program, the Smothers Brothers, Sonny & Cher, Carole Burnett, Red Skelton and many others had all been produced there. In bringing in our show, it was written into the contract that I would be the Associate Director and not be on CBS's staff. From that day forward, free lance AD's and SM's were allowed to work on productions at TV City. I returned many times over the next twenty plus years.

As I mentioned before I was involved in all aspects of the show. This meant recording the show at TV-City in Hollywood, editing the show at Compact Video in Burbank and doing the post audio at Sunwest Recording back in Hollywood. A lot of shuffling of reels of two inch video tape to and from each of the three was required. Due to the long hours and the days for each step of the process, I found that it was often more practical for me to lug the tapes myself from place to place rather than rely on assistants.

Since I was transporting the original masters and back ups for a primetime network television show, I never left any of the reels in my car over night, or in a parking lot while shopping, or whatever. I frequently got home from any of the three work locations at midnight, or later, followed with an early get up and go the next day, it took some deep down dedication in the wee hours not to just leave the reels in the car. Understand that ninety minutes of two inch video tape on a big metal reel in a substantial plastic case built to ship is not light. Times four or more per show and the trips to and from the car for my production book and papers gave me some good late night, early morning exercise up and down the several flights of stairs to my Silverlake apartment at the time.

I refused to focus on the reality that on the floor of my living room were Master reels of CBS primetime television shows worth millions of dollars in various steps of the post production process. I kept it to myself and told no one. My long hours and the need to keep the processes moving along for timely delivery of the finished shows presented few options. The tapes and I needed to be in the same place at the same time.

At home Maxwell was not a happy camper. His "Dad" was gone twenty hours day and night. Getting the tape reels in and out the front door was often an act in futility as he would make every attempt to escape past me. I think he wanted to know what was out there that kept me away for so long every day. He didn't run away, but did play an intense game of "catch me", just what I wanted to play at one in the morning. Not.

The lined up reels in the middle of the living room provided Max a great narrow cat run. I would often find him sitting on them as he cleaned himself.

Production on The Jacksons at CBS went very well, but the show never reached the ratings levels needed to sustain it and just before spring in 1977, it was canceled.

Damn. Out of work. I knew I would connect with another production, but that feeling
in my gut was gnawing at me.

Again I would be faced with deciding between two opportunities. One was historic in nature for the nation and one was historic for me personally.

The first was to Associate Direct on the David Frost interviews with former President, Richard Nixon in San Clemente not even three years after his disgraced resignation. I knew that I would experience history in the making and that I would hear things that would never get on the air. I had followed the whole Watergate fiasco and the subsequent actions that followed it closely. I really wanted to fill in some of the blanks of that part of our history.

At the same time, I was offered a five and a half week job to Direct location video all over Australia. I was torn. The Nixon job afforded the historical experience, but would only be several days income, but a once in a lifetime opportunity. Australia afforded the trip there and all over the country for over a month, good money, working with good people I knew from LA. What to do?

I chose the Australian trip.

The company, Rex Humbard Ministries, was a religious television ministry with his CATHEDRAL of TOMORROW seen literally around the world every week. It originated out of Akron, Ohio. At the head of the ministry was Rex, the preacher, who had grown an immense following which had begun after World War II. As his children grew they turned out to have great musical abilities which, as they developed, were worked into service for the ministry. Their popularity grew over the years and by the time I was called they were a multi-million dollar religious enterprise with there own mega church, a full blown television production facility, with hundreds of affiliate TV stations in the US and more around the world.

There had been standing pressure on the ministry from the thousands of followers in Australia to come there and tape several weeks of their weekly world wide ministry broadcasts. The Australians had the dollars to cover the expense for the trip, so, despite some major hurtles, the decision was made to go and record five services.

256

The first hurtle was that the technical standard for television in Australia was totally different from the American standard. In simple words the ministry could not record their services using the equipment in Australia. They would have to take all the television equipment with them from the states.

Once configured for the five weeks in Australia, the equipment, consisting of a computerized lighting package, six television cameras with a control room and video tape recorders, a multi-channel audio booth and multi-track recorder along with a complete audio package of microphones, cables, stands, and staging sets, plus an american electrical generator big enough to power everything because the voltage standard in Australia would destroy it all. Whew! All this stuff, (don't you love technical talk?), was packed into containers that fit in five semi-truck container trailers.

Problem: All this "stuff" had to get to Sydney, Australia on time ready to roll by a certain date in early May. Everything was shipped to California and was then loaded onto a container ship for a thirty day voyage at sea. No, I'm not kidding.

Everything made it to California and sailed on time.

I took the seventeen hour flight out of LA on Pan AM, (remember them?) We were on a 747, and although coach, the flight was far from loaded providing great space for sleep. It was 1977. The coach passenger space and service was still human. We landed in Honolulu for fuel and a convenient repair of the vertical tail rudder. It seems that as we flew over the Pacific at thirty-eight thousand feet, the boys on the flight deck lost control of it. No problem for a multi-engine aircraft as they could steer left or right with the individual thrust of each of the four engines and flaps on the wings. It only took a few hours and we were back on our way.

We stopped to refuel at Pago Pago. Other than the mountains, I think that 747 was the biggest thing on the island. I have a great picture I took out the door of the plane looking back over the left wing. All you could see were palm trees and the ocean beyond. The "Terminal" was a thatched roof hut with lots of tourist trap "souvenirs". The locals came out and played music at our early morning arrival. They were extremely nice. I thought I was in a scene from South Pacific and remain convinced Bloody Mary tried to sell me something unsavory while smiling so wide her bright teeth nearly blinded me.

We then bunny hopped our way to Auckland, New Zealand. There was no time to deplane as we grabbed some fuel, a few passenger exchanges and were off for Sydney.

We were in Sydney to get everything ready to commence the five weeks of production. My old friend Terry Donohue was the Production Manager who had his hands full as soon as we got to the Sydney Hilton. He got a ship to shore radio phone message from the captain of the container ship still in route on the Pacific. His message: "Very high seas for days-*Stop*-Too rough to go out on deck-*Stop*-Can see from the bridge some containers broke loose and are lost overboard-*Stop*-Don't know if any are yours or not-*End*."

We spent over a day wondering if we had much needed equipment locked up "below" in Davey Jones' Locker.

The good news finally came that all of our containers had stayed aboard. The bad news came when the containers were opened for Customs Inspection. From a month of pitching and rolling on rough seas, everything in the containers had come loose. Many rack mounted pieces of video and audio equipment had literally come loose and fallen on the floor of the container, or were hanging semi loose presenting a nightmare for the technicians who had to rebuild them. Round-the-clock hard work by some very dedicated men got everything put back together and working.

We flew to Adelaide, where the first program was scheduled to be taped. I don't know how the back roads are in Australia today, but in 1977, between cities, they were two lanes, one in each direction and were not paved. We did not have to drive over them, but our trucks with the equipment did. The drivers would have to hit a truck wash once they got to our next city to remove the coating of mud before arriving at our working locations.

The Rex Humbard family and organization impressed me over that five weeks. They were very professional, kind and considerate of the dozen, or so of us LA based "TV Folk" who hired on to work their Australian tour.

I was hired as a Director to shoot all the location color shots particular to the various locations we went to. For instance, I took a crew out to an animal reserve outside Adelaide to capture video of Kangaroos and Koala Bears. We shot many of what we TV Folk call establishing shots showing the cities we were in. We returned to Sydney for the Humbard's scheduled program in the Sydney Opera House. That wonderful, architecturally unique building presented many angles and therefore opportunities to see it from various beautiful points of view both up close and from afar.

The Opera House sits on a peninsula jetting out into the water of Sydney Harbor. I grabbed my crew and went out on the end of the peninsula just east of it in order to record the Sunset which occurred behind it in the shot. The proper framing of the shot I wanted required video photographer, Ted Ashton, to put the feet of the camera's pedestal literally in the water. It was worth it. The shot was amazing. Too bad HD-TV wasn't around at that time.

When I wasn't Directing, I was working with Terry Donohue on all the coordination duties required throughout those very busy five weeks. In addition to Adelaide and Sydney, we went to Melbourne, all the way to the west coast to Perth and south to Hobart, Tasmania, (no, we did NOT find the Tasmanian Devil…but we looked for him).

As I relate this short story, I want to remind you that the year was 1977. At the time there were two airlines operating inside the country; Trans Australian Airlines (TAA) and Ansette Airlines (A). We came to discover that the two flew every major route in tandem with one another and on the same departure-arrival schedule. They both had nearly new wings of Boeing 727s. It was a running joke between them as to who would pull away from the departing gate first. TAA was owned by the Australian government and Ansette was a commercial company.

I discovered that on a flight of any length on Ansette, I could ask the flight attendants to ask the Captain if he would allow me to join him in the cockpit. The commercial air traffic in Australia was very low in number. Nine times out of ten the only aircraft near our plane at thirty-five thousand feet, was the TAA plane flying the same route either two minutes ahead of us, or behind us.

Surprisingly, and happily for me, the frustrated pilot, the answer to my question to join the boys-in-the-cockpit was always "yes". I would only make the request when I knew they had over an hour before getting anywhere near a point of destination. In my brief hands on piloting of little Cessna 150 two seater training planes back near Cincinnati a decade prior, many of the flyer's rules-of-the-air had stuck with me. I knew when there was heavy traffic in the air around us, the answer would be a capital NO.

The best of all of my experiences in the cockpit "jump seat" was while flying out to Perth.

Perth is to Australia, what San Diego is to America and just about the same distance to cross, implying several hours in-the-air to get there from the east coast.

In the early model years the flight deck of Boeing 727-100's had three man crews consisting of the Captain, the First Officer, (or Co-Pilot), and an engineer. The engineer sat behind the first officer in front of a control panel monitoring fuel consumption, the performance of each of the three jet engines and other on board systems.

There I was in the cockpit, not too long after Midnight. The sky was totally clear all around and below us. We were over the Outback meaning there were no cities, towns or lit villages below us. Zero man made artificial light. The only illumination outside of the cockpit windows was coming from the stars and planets overhead.

After about twenty minutes of conversation the Captain said, "Let me show you something we enjoy for a few minutes every trip out here, if conditions allow it". He checked all instruments on the control panel and then dimmed them out completely. It was like being in outer space. Everything was dark except the stars and planets which, at thirty-five thousand feet were at eye level and below due to the curvature of the Earth. For five memorable minutes there was not one sound out of the four of us.

Chapter Thirty-Six / Many Changes

When I left LA for Sydney, I knew I would not return for seven and a half weeks as I had been booked to shoot ABC's Allstar Anything Goes (AAG) at Six Flags over Georgia near Atlanta right after the Humbard Tour. A neighbor was kind enough to take care of Maxwell and my place for the duration.

The timing was perfect. I left the late Fall, chilly weather in Sydney, returning to LAX where I went right from Customs in the International Terminal around the bend to Delta to catch the red eye to Atlanta where I arrived in time to get a shower, shave and go shoot outside all day in the June, ninety degree, humid, Atlanta weather with twenty pounds of camera on my shoulder. At the end of that day I was toast. I had been directing in Australia's cool, Fall for over five weeks and suddenly there I was running around in Atlanta's hot humidity with a camera hanging on me. I was fine from day two and beyond, but I learned a lesson about my physical limitations.

Following my week of AAG, I flew to Cincinnati to see my dad and mom and go to a family reunion. My father's health had taken a turn for the worse as his fifty plus years of cigarette smoking had him terminally ill with lung cancer. I arrived having not seen him for ten months. His appearance was noticeably changed. I loved my father and it was difficult to see him looking so ill. I reminded myself that it was much tougher for him.

My job was to be loving and supportive. He had injured his left ankle some months before and the cancer throughout his body had quickly metastasized into a growth on his left ankle which had rendered this life long active man to moving about on crutches.

Doctors had already determined that to remove the growth would have hastened the cancer and shortened what time he had left.

I wanted to cry the second I saw him and looked into his sad eyes. I made every effort to stiff upper lip the moment and not let him see my shock. All I wanted to convey was my love for him.

I spent as much time as possible with dad and mom, though I did not stay with them. To be honest, and I am sorry to report, that I wasn't strong enough at the time to tough it out for the 24 hour thing at home. I stayed with an on again, off again girlfriend.

My relationships with women during this time were overlapping, confusing and in retrospect, exhausting. I hurt, or frustrated all of them and predictably, ultimately myself.
A perfect example of how one can become one's worst enemy. It took passage of time after the fact to see my mistakes, own up to them, learn from them and grow as a person.

As I write this I'm digging back over three decades to relive a period of my life during which time my career was rising, but as a man, I was ultimately failing at every attempt to have any kind of healthy relationship with a woman. I had pieces here and there of sane time with respect to the relations I was having, but to be fair to each of the ladies, at that time, not one of them got all of me. Knowing that reality now, is profound in one sense for me and devastating in another.

My father's failing health preoccupied my mind through what was a very heavy working period. I flew back several times to be with him and mom in those final months of 1977.

Precipitating my trip in December, he had been hospitalized for some complications. Once they were cleared up it was then rationalized that, with hospice care, he would be better off at home for his final weeks. A hospital bed had been rented and placed in the dining room as he could no longer negotiate the stairs. It was bitterly cold and a lot of snow had fallen, but an ambulance was ordered and we took him home.

With his cancer in its final stages the poor man was having indescribable pain. Hospice had the refrigerator well stocked with morphine, but my dad preferred scotch. He felt disoriented on the morphine; the sensations were not familiar to him, but scotch he wanted so I bought a case for him. Mom argued with me about his consuming so much of it and I argued back, let him drink it like water if he wants. She backed off about it.

Like anyone who has lived some years, I have my fair share of regrets. Among the greatest over all my years was my decision to leave my dad and return to LA in the middle of the holidays.

Bed ridden, my dad cried as we hugged and kissed when I was about to leave. I was a mess inside for I knew I did not have to leave that day for any reason other than I was squirming inside not able to deal with my building grief. I was forcing the timing of our final good bye before it had to be and I knew it.

My dad loved classical and jazz music, but over years through radio listening in the car had become fond of the sound of Karen Carpenter. Just before my December trip to see him I had spent a week with Karen and her brother Richard shooting their ABC-TV Special, A CARPENTER'S CHRISTMAS. It broadcast a few days after I left him and he called me to say how much he enjoyed it. That was the last piece of my work he ever saw. When we hung up the phone, I cried my eyes out.

The beginning of 1978 brought about a new working venture on The Jim Nabors Show. It was a five day a week talk-variety hour syndicated nationally. I called my dad and mom regularly while I buried myself in my work to ease my emotions as I knew my dad's days were down to a precious few.

Each time we talked on the phone, his voice was noticeably weaker and his thoughts were more and more disconnected. It was difficult to hear him deteriorating so. He died on February fifth. I took time off from the Nabors Show and with everyone's blessing flew off to Cincinnati to be with my mom and pay tribute to my dad.

My cousin, Jim Steiger, was there when I got home. His mother Edith and my dad had been close siblings. Though a first cousin, Jim was a full generation older than me. An Air Force Colonel at retirement, he had piloted B-17's and B-24's over Germany during World War II. In the absence of his own father during the 1930's, my dad had been a close, fatherly influence during his High School years before his enlistment into the Army Air Corps at the start of the war. He flew in from his home in Virginia and was wonderfully supportive to my mom in those days after my dad passed.

My dad beat the lawyers out of their usual piece of the pie by signing everything over to my mom long before he died.

The only matters left to deal with were our emotions. The most positive thing that came up immediately for me was the knowledge that my dad was no longer suffering. The rest was painful on many levels, some surprisingly so as time went by. I could have wished that the reoccurring experience of someone in my life dieing, which had become routine in Vietnam, were not so. My father passing away was far different to be sure, but that inner track of emotions had a road I had walked all too often and it was uncomfortably familiar and surprisingly numbing. In war you have to immediately get up from the side of your fallen comrade in order to survive. Doing it dozens of times cements a habit engraved somewhere in your subconscious. The feelings and emotions go on hold only to emote at some later time.

There was an overflow gathering at the memorial service. Dad had many long term friends who validated their relationships that day not out of duty, rather out of love. It warmed my grieving heart to feel it.

During mom's senior year in High School in 1930, at the height of the Great Depression, she was the student and dad was the teacher. At that point they did not date, but, in their mutual reminiscent words, there was no doubting they shared an attraction.

Mom was an Olt, dad was a Breidenbach. The Olts had a very successful brewery for years in Dayton prior to Prohibition. The Breidenbachs had a very successful bakery, which closed suddenly when my grandfather succumbed to a routine illness.

Dad was the youngest of six and was only twelve when his father died in 1920. He had three older brothers who were adults and could have taken over the business, but none of them aspired to be bread makers. Each had gone off to college to pursue their interests.

As was common in those days, the Breidenbachs lived in a residence above the main building of the bakery. The living quarters were built within a five thousand square foot area and have been described as "very nice".

I mentioned the main building for across a private court yard there was a separate garage for the three polished, delivery wagons, and two family carriages, along with stables for the horses that pulled them. Imagine that, one hundred years ago your freshly baked bread was delivered daily right to your door.

With my grandfather's death, the bakery was quickly liquidated, and the property sold. My grandmother bought a very nice new house for her, my dad, his sister, Luella and their brother Carl to live in.

Unfortunately, the remaining monies from the sale of the business did not carry them very far. For my dad, and his family, the financial depression hit years before the 1929 crash on Wall Street.

(Returning to my progression as a person following my dad's passing), I flew back to LA and the Jim Nabors Show which was cancelled not too many months later.

Despite the abrupt end to the Nabors Show, the rest of that year was filled with work, a lot of work. I was working constantly and thankful for the incredible income. The six and seven day work weeks created an all too easy diversion from long thought and personal introspection.

1978 was the year I met and worked with Frank Sinatra for the first of many times. It was a unique and wonderful production. A prime time television special saluting dancer, actor and singer, Gene Kelly featuring all his co-stars with whom he had worked over his years in film and television.

As a Stage Manager, I was assigned to get Frank and Gene where ever they had to be throughout the production. Gene was given a wonderful dressing room suite consisting of a large living room, with a make up room, wardrobe and bath. After two days of rehearsing it was the afternoon of the live, on stage performances to video tape for the show in front of an invitation only audience of VIPs. Sinatra was not able to make it until the on stage performances due to prior engagements, but definitely wanted to be there for his old friend.

With all the performing personalities in attendance, in the middle of the afternoon, we ran out of dressing rooms. Sinatra was due within the hour and there was no place to put him. Having had two days to get to know Gene, I went to him to ask if I could bring Frank in to share his large suite. "Absolutely" was his response.

Whew! All I had to do now was meet Frank Sinatra for the first time, in a matter of minutes, and let him know he had to share a dressing room. This would either go well, or not, and my ass was on the line.

I went outside to wait for Sinatra's Limo to arrive. I didn't have to wait long. The car rolled up, I reached out, grabbed the door handle, opened the door, saw that famous face and said, "Good afternoon, Mr. Sinatra, I'm Peter Bright, welcome!" He looked at me and without missing a beat said, "Call me Frank, Peter".

Taking his garment bag from him as he stepped out of the car I said, "We have one problem, Frank". "What's that, Peter", said he. "We've run out of dressing rooms. Would you mind sharing a suite with Gene?" "Are you kidding, Peter, that would be great. Lead the way".

When we got to the dressing room I knocked and Gene opened the door. Those two guys who had worked together thirty-three years before on the film, ANCHORS AWEIGH, had a homecoming before Frank even got in the door. It was the first of many nice, warm, personal moments I got to share with the two of them that late afternoon.

There was about two hours before the star studded evening of performances would begin on stage so Frank and Gene first talked down what they would do on stage. It came together beautifully. *I believe that show, GENE KELLY, AN AMERICAN IN PASADENA is available on DVD.*

Chapter Thirty-Seven / Managing Others...Dumb

The fact is introspection was what I needed most as I began 1979. The year would mark a decade of my life since returning from Vietnam.

Behind all the activity of the heavy overlapping work in 1978, at some point I went to Colorado to shoot something. I've been to Colorado many times over the years, but every trip was for work. In this particular instance, I don't remember what it was we were there to shoot, but, one night in Boulder some of the crew and I went into a music-bar joint after dinner.

We were in the main recorded music-pick-up-bar area which was loaded with attractive tourists sucking up Coors and hooking up. In my ear during short seconds between the spinning musical discs I could hear something melodic that was different. Very different.

My musical curiosity got the better of me and I ventured away in search of the source of what I was hearing. In an adjacent room in this large, multi-faceted bar I found a six piece rock and roll band on stage in the middle of a set of what had to be original tunes as each one was different from the one prior and totally unfamiliar to me. The crowd was sitting around at tables *listening* to the music as they sucked up their intoxicants.

It was obvious to me that the crowd was made up of locals who knew and liked the band's music. There was a myriad of melodic influences emanating from the stage. Hints of jazz, new age, rock and country were all wrapped in Steely Dan-ish, Crosby, Stills, Nash and Young-ish arrangements. The vocals were strong, musicianship was good and the tunes were very melodic and positive representatives of all the genre and influences.

They were known as REDTAIL, named for the Hawk of the same name common to Colorado.

I saw them as a talented group that needed polishing; a diamond in the rough.

In retrospect, I was somewhat delusional, as I immediately convinced myself that I could manage them, oversee and direct their polishing plus help connect them to a recording career.

I won't go into all the momentary ups, downs, ins and outs of the next nine months REDTAIL and I spent together. That tale is a book in and of itself. It is prophetic, or should I write pathetic, that we parted ways after nine months and were born into the rest of our lives. I learned a valuable lesson which was: Do not invest more of yourself into a group than the members of the group invest in themselves, (*and I'm not referring to dollars*).

A rare opportunity came my way. In the world of popular music the biggest name at the time was The Bee Gees. Their album, SPIRITS HAVING FLOWN was in the million plus selling zone.

An NBC primetime special was to be shot to air during the main ratings period that fall. This would be a blockbuster event.

We were going to shoot them in concert on 35 millimeter film with 48 Tracks of digital audio at the Oakland Coliseum across the Bay from San Francisco. Those two production facts were unheard of and stand outs technically for the time. But it didn't stop there. The live concert would be shot by thirty-three, 35 millimeter Panavision movie cameras.

But before we even got to the concert it was decided that to open the television special we would shoot their SPIRITS HAVING FLOWN TOUR Boeing 720 aircraft both in the air at thirty thousand feet and on the ground as it rolled up and parked to be met by a waiting twenty motorcycle police escort as they deplaned.

The band had completed their Los Angeles concerts. A corporate sized jet built for aerial photography was hired to chase the tour plane for the forty-five minute flight from LA to Oakland. Set against the background of the Sierra Madre Mountains and the Pacific Ocean on a charted flight plan, the movie clips were spectacular and mixed well with the Bee Gee track TRAGEDY as the produced broadcast began.

For the concert, Director and friend, Lou Horvitz designed a shooting pattern whereas at 15 locations would be two 35 millimeter film camera systems in place. There would be one cinema photographer at each location lensing their way through the concert moving back and forth from camera A to camera B. While the one camera was shooting, a crew would be unloading exposed film and loading in fresh film in the other. As a camera shooting got to the end of a roll, (roughly twelve to fifteen minutes), the other camera would roll and the operator would move to the fresh camera and continue to shoot. In addition to the fifteen double systems, from France was brought a first of its kind Louma Crane. This put a camera at the end of a very long metal arm with the operator at the other end panning, tilting and zooming. While these camera arms known today as Jibs are rather common in video and film now, in late summer 1979, this Louma crane was the only such design in existence. It was huge and mounted on rails where as not only could the thirty plus foot long arm raise and lower the camera, the base could be rolled on whatever length of dolly track was required.

The Louma was a Directors dream for smooth moving, sweeping, high and wide visual experiences. The business had had camera cranes for years, but they were heavy, cumbersome platforms that had to support not only the camera, but an operator, and assistant and frequently a Director as well. This new design with only the camera to lift immediately changed how impactful moving visuals could be obtained.

The next new thing about this concert shoot was truly a first. All the camera operators and their crews were put on headsets so that Lou could direct their moves. It was very disconcerting at first for the film operators as they were used to having their Director in person right next to them and discussing and rehearsing each shot. Now, much like live television, they were shooting live action with no possibility of reshooting. They stepped up to the challenge and met it.

Today we would shoot in an advanced form of High Definition, but that was not possible then. Lou, the Bee Gees and Robert Stigwood, who headed their overall management company (of the same name), wanted the highest quality picture possible to document this concert moment in their career. Unfortunately all this gorgeous 35MM film footage was expensively transferred to Standard Definition video tape for editing. It was all we had at the time. Considering Barry is the only Gibb still around, it would be even more valuable esthetically if it were HD. (*I assume the 35MM is safely stored and could be transferred to HD and reedited for a re-release, but the cost to do so would be extremely high.*)

I was taken aback the night the special aired on NBC as I sat there watching the credits to find that my name was missing. At first I was stunned and then truly pissed off. I could have gone to The Directors Guild and complained, but it would have made a mess in many of my personal and professional relationships so I didn't having decided it wasn't worth it. I have never brought up the issue with any of the dozen or so individuals involved, one of whom, as of this writing in May, 2014, sadly, just passed away.

Following the Bee Gees shoot, I got a call out of the blue to work for CBS News in their Los Angeles Bureau. They were beginning a new overall west coast experience for the news division. For the western states, The Walter Cronkite Evening News would now be known as The Western Edition of The CBS Evening News. There would be an on-going group responsible for providing a daily, up-to-the-minute broadcast exclusively for the Pacific states. It was the first time any network had committed to a Western Edition.

CNN was not around at the time and the internet was hardly a mental concept. Ted Turner was making noise that CNN was coming together in Atlanta, but the leaders of the established news organizations were watching him out of the corner of their eyes and not so sure he would get going, or prevail if he did start.

I was in seventh heaven. I had loved being a radio newsman and was excited with opportunity to be working with the best in the broadcast news business.

If I had any frustration out of working at CBS News it was that I was not successful at jumping the moat between the production of the broadcasts and getting into the actual news reporting, writing and broadcasting. That moat was wide and very deep. The news people liked that we production-TV people could completely understand a story to take it and combine pictures with narrative and foretell the essence accurately into a concise piece for broadcast and incorporate it with many other stories into a very intricate half hour production everyday, yet they did not accept us as news people, meaning ones who could research, source, write and report a story. They were the journalists, we were not. They had degrees in journalism and we didn't. A degree doesn't make someone a journalist. Walter Cronkite and Peter Jennings are perfect examples of newsmen who did not have degrees in journalism, or, for that matter, degrees at all.

Looking back thirty-four years as I write I should have taken the cut in pay and taken the jump, swim and climb out of that moat. I was then and will always remain a news junky. I love digging into a story and relating it for broadcast consumption.

I was making good money between CBS News and all my free lance production work plus new offers kept coming. We production people in LA share a motto: "You're only as good as your last job". Although there were hundreds of us, word traveled fast…if you fucked up it could get you "benched" and out-of-the-game faster than a lightening bolt. Sometimes a benching was earned, but all too often rumor of a fuck up, real or not, would haunt one's career. That was never my problem, thank God.

I chose not to give up my ever increasing income, along with the many interesting and challenging work experiences I was having. Breaking out of my pattern and jumping head first into that moat would have made for a totally different set of experiences.

I could go on here, but I'm only half way through my life up to this point as I sit here writing.

Still to come are: marriages; deaths; changes of addresses along with good, and not so good, personal experiences plus many interactions and relationships with dozens of the biggest names in film, television, music and more.

You will not be bored with the continuance of my torrid tales in:

MY OVERDUE BOOK - Volume Two

To be continued…

Made in the USA
Las Vegas, NV
24 July 2022

52101354R00154